Mutiny in Force X

Mutiny in Force X

Bill Glenton

Hodder & Stoughton
LONDON SYDNEY AUCKLAND TORONTO

British Library Cataloguing in Publication Data
Glenton, Bill
    Mutiny in Force X
      1. Lothian (*Ship*)   2. World War, 1939-1945 —— Naval operations, British   3.
      World War, 1939-1945 —— Personal narratives, British   4. Mutiny —— Great
    Britain —— History —— 20th century
    I. Title
    940.54'5941   D772.L6

    ISBN 0-340-38015-2

Mutiny in Force X

Contents

Illustrations

Bill Glenton in Glasgow[1]
Lothian in Pacific[1]
Clan Lamont[2]
Glenearn[2]
Empire Arquebus[2]
Empire Mace[2]
Empire Battleaxe[2]
Empire Spearhead[2]
Admiral King[2]
Rear-Admiral Talbot[2]
Rear-Admiral Talbot with Commander Nevill Porter and
    Lieutenant Ian Forbes Watson[3]
Talbot in khaki[1]
Bill Glenton in Sydney[1]

1. Author's collection
2. The Imperial War Museum
3. By courtesy of Commander Nevill Porter

PART I

1

Out of the Blue

The War Room of the First Lord of the Admiralty had been the scene of many top-level Naval decisions in nearly five years of war, no more so than in the recent months leading up to and following the Normandy Invasion. This fourth day of July it was once again filled with senior officers, mainly heads of operational departments, plus a number of top civil servants from the Ministry of War Transport and supply services brought together to make a vital decision. Yet their serious intent turned to an air of puzzlement as the reason for the sudden meeting was revealed.

For all of them the endless days and nights had been concentrated on the massive planning and carrying through of the invasion of Europe. There had been no time to consider anything or anywhere else. Now, out of the blue, they were being asked to come to an immediate decision about Royal Navy action in a war zone that was as far geographically as it was possible to go and about which they knew barely more than that learnt briefly from communiqués.

Whatever doubts they held, however, they kept to themselves as the nineteen officers and civilians heard their chairman, Rear-Admiral R. M. Servaes, insist on decisions being made for a deadline only three weeks away. Even by urgent wartime reckoning it seemed impossibly short. There had to be some special reason why an assault force, even a moderately small one, had to be created from scratch when most suitable ships were fully occupied elsewhere, and sent on a voyage of over 12,000 miles in only twenty-one days of preparation.

The one they had just been given only perplexed them further – not only because of its unusual contents but because of the person whose *name was attached to it. The top secret, urgent signal read out to them had, apparently, come from none less than Fleet Admiral Ernest King, Chief of Naval Operations. Communications between this augustly stern personage and the Admiralty were rare enough, which surprised no one. Around Whitehall he was understood to be antagonistic towards the Royal Navy, for some personal reason.* His co-operation extended only as far as the demands of war and as far as his overall C-in-C, President Roosevelt, made him do so. Yet, it appeared, he was now making a complete about-face and actually asking the Admiralty for help.*

What was equally surprising was the war zone in which the aid was sought, the Pacific. As the senior officers present knew well King had made it quite clear that he wanted to keep this vast area of operations as exclusively American as possible. Exploratory talks between the Admiralty, through the British Naval Mission, Washington, and King with a view to the Royal Navy assisting in the Pacific when warships could be spared from Europe had met with reluctance on the latter's part and his firm view that the U.S. Navy was capable of handling everything on its own.**

It was causing added friction between him and the First Sea Lord, Admiral of the Fleet Sir Andrew B. Cunningham, G.C.B., D.S.O. (later Viscount), who was very keen to see a British fleet and assault forces involved in the war against Japan. Could determined insistence from the latter, perhaps with help from his close supporter Winston Churchill, have forced a change of heart? The thought may well have crossed the minds of those present seeking an explanation for the mystery and the excessive speed with which they were being told to deal with the appeal.

If it did it was quickly replaced by the pressures created by the American request. As used as they were to dealing with wartime emergencies this one imposed some impossible looking demands. Demands, some present could have suspected, that King as a very

---

* According to some Naval officers the reason for King's antagonism dated back to an incident in World War I when he was an official U.S. Navy observer to the Royal Navy. He had, it is believed, suffered some supposed serious insult during a visit to the fleet in Scapa Flow, although exactly what is clouded in mystery.

** According to Sir Andrew Cunningham, in his autobiography, *A Sailor's Odyssey*, King emphasised his demand to keep the Pacific campaign to the U.S. Navy at the Quebec conference of war leaders in September 1944.

experienced commander must have known would be extremely difficult to carry out by a Navy stretched to its limits. But whoever had drawn up the signal, if not the U.S. Chief himself, had felt it necessary to start it with some acceptable explanation for the urgency.

The message began: 'An urgent requirement has arisen in 7th Fleet for APAs [landing ships] in which to train divisions for CCS approved amphibious operations in November and for subsequent use in these operations [the Philippines invasion]. I cannot now divert shipping from intervening Central Pacific operations to accomplish this training. Even if new schedules are fully realised I will be pressed to provide total ship to shore lift for the operation itself.'

In view of King's earlier insistence on his having the capability of ships and a general belief that the U.S. Navy was adequately stocked with assault and troop ships with dozens more being mass produced all the time the explanation may have struck some as strange. The next sentence also seemed odd.

'In view of COSMED 137 and related despatches [reference to signals about release of ships after Normandy] would you consider immediate transfer of 6 L.S.I.(L)s [Landing Ships Infantry Large] released by SCAEF and not essential to SACMED [European commands] to SOWESPAC [S.W. Pacific command] for duty in 7th Fleet.'

As the War Room gathering was aware the release of landing ships was dependent on the still strong demands of Normandy and the landings in the South of France still to take place and that the signals referred to gave no immediate sign of these vessels being available. But it was the next part of the signal that disturbed the meeting most.

'Arrival by August 15 is necessary if training is to be completed in time.'

That was only six weeks away. It did not need the navigational expertise present to appreciate that it would take comparatively slow-moving landing ships with a cruising speed of no more than fifteen knots on average all of that time just to steam from Britain to the South-West Pacific regardless of the concentrated time taken to pick and assemble such a force. The request looked even more dubious – almost as if King had set out to make it impossible to fulfil. If so he had reckoned without the determination that someone outside the War Room and higher up the scale was applying to take advantage of the request that could let the Royal Navy get a toehold in the Pacific campaign. Rear-Admiral

Servaes seemed clearly to have got his orders to ensure a force was created and despatched as quickly as humanly possible.

The three week time limit he set underlined the pressures on him. Even if ships had been readily available it was an indecently short time to assemble and prepare them for such a long voyage, mostly through the tropics for which they would need special stores and other equipment . . . a great deal extra of all types since they would be operating far from established naval bases. Extra men, too, for a voyage of such a great distance with the prospect of action at the end of it and the risk of heavy casualties. There would be no handy replacements anywhere near the Philippines or South-West Pacific islands. Even if all this was achieved, and much else besides, it would not permit the working-up period that was normally thought essential for a newly created assault force.

Yet even these problems began to look insignificant as the meeting got down to thrashing out the details. As it discussed which ships might be chosen for the six strong force it became clear that there was barely any of the type required available. Not that the Royal Navy, even at the height of its assault ship strength, ever had many suitable for long-distance operation. The great majority were fitted out for landings in or around Europe.

There were only twenty deemed appropriate for ocean-going operations and all but a couple of these were either heavily engaged with Normandy, chosen for the landings along the Côte d'Azur or out of action for one reason or another. And one of the two was currently without a proper complement and landing craft. With little other choice this pair was selected to form the nucleus. Half strength was achieved by a decision to withdraw one of the landing ships from its currently busy duties off the French beachheads. But where to get the other half from? Heads were scratched and lists of ships minutely examined again. Still no solution.

It was Captain Charles Hughes Hallett, the Director of Planning (Q), who suggested the answer. There were a number of newly arrived American Liberty type, mass produced, ships which could be used as they already had troop decks and were similar to the kind of assault vessels in common use with the U.S. 7th Fleet for landings. There was only one difficulty – they were under the Red Ensign and manned by T124 (merchant seamen employed in R.N. service) hands. For the kind of naval operation planned it was essential they should be replaced by Naval ratings and the ships put under the White Ensign.

16

The civil servants responsible for dockyard work quickly pointed out that past experience had shown that it took much longer than the three weeks allowed them for ships to be converted to naval use proper, particularly as extra accommodation had to be added for the greater number of ratings and officers that formed White Ensign complements. But Admiral Servaes was not going to be thwarted now. The added crew could use part of the troop decks although it was far from a perfect solution since these decks were intended for temporary occupancy of days rather than the months the ratings would have to suffer them. Realising this he added that the three ships to have colours switched should undergo proper conversion in Australia after their release by the Americans. In proposing this he confirmed the impression among several present that the Admiralty was intent on making use of the force for its own Pacific intentions.

That, and more besides, became clear when Captain Hughes Hallett, with Admiral Servaes' approval, proposed a surprise addition to the force that went beyond the request in the signal signed by Admiral King. As well as the six landing ships there should also be a headquarters ship with a senior flag officer, he suggested. In a memo he wrote immediately after the meeting he stated: 'If the Force is to play a full part in the South-West Pacific and not just be submerged in a mass of U.S. ships it is considered that it should be commanded by an officer of adequate status and experience in an assault force.'

In other words he, or perhaps someone of still higher authority at the Admiralty, was calling for a full-blown Admiral to command the force.

Bushy naval eyebrows might well have been raised at such a suggestion. Many a far bigger, far more imposing squadron of warships were commonly commanded at the time by officers more junior, say four-ring Captains. One of the assault vessels chosen, the Glenearn, *had a highly experienced, very capable Captain admirably suited for overall command of such a small unit. What was more there was a serious shortage of Admirals with proven assault force know-how. There had to be some hidden reason for wanting to impose one on the tiny force. If so it was not divulged at the War Room meeting but those who guessed could have come up with a couple.*

The Admiralty had always been sensitive to loss of face or authority when having to attach any of its ships to a foreign Navy even if it was a wartime ally. The situation was less feared when the ships concerned operated within reasonably close proximity but in this case they would be very far beyond any watchful Whitehall eyes. That was one possible reason but another might have been due more to the determination of the First Sea Lord and other top seadogs to establish as strong a Royal Navy presence in the South-West Pacific as circumstances allowed. An experienced Admiral in charge could not only assert more authority but might even be able to impose some British influence on the conduct of the Japanese campaign.

However admirable these advantages might have looked they created another big headache for the War Room gathering. Choosing the landing ships had been difficult enough but finding a headquarters ship was worse. In the whole assault fleet there were only four properly adapted for such a role. There were others but used only on a temporary basis as needs demanded and not suitable for long ocean crossings with a full command staff. Not that the four were that appropriate since flag officers and their big entourage were only expected to remain aboard for days – not longer. In any event one had to be discounted since she had been badly damaged at Normandy and was out of action. Two others were still fully occupied in a back-up role off the French beaches and the fourth had been allocated for Operation ANVIL *(the South of France landings).*

Yet it was the latter that the meeting eventually decided upon. Although it would impose considerable strain she would have to be replaced for her Mediterranean duty by one of the two other, still operational, L.S.H.(L)s (Landing Ship Headquarters Large). The fact that she was the only one that had never ever been in an invasion, had virtually seen no action at all having only entered service a few weeks earlier counted less than the fact that she formed the only way the meeting could get out of its predicament.

There were many other aspects of this ship that made her a dubious selection for such a demanding task ahead but the over-pressurised manner of her choosing was typical of how the whole force was put together, at least of how the Admiralty hoped it had now been assembled. Even the choice of title for the squadron underlined the fact it was an exceedingly unknown quantity – 'Force X'.

Any similarity between the high-level conference that took place in the First Lord's War Room and the discussion held some days later in one of the prison-like stone buildings of Devonport Barracks, euphemistically called 'Jago's Mansions' by the Lower Deck, was totally coincidental. Both, so to speak, did involve 'heads' and were in secret behind closed doors but that was as far as it could be stretched. Nothing, in fact, could have so literally underlined the vast gap between the top brass and the bottom rung of the Royal Navy than the contrast between the War Room planning and the rumours being discussed in the barrack lavatories or, in Naval terminology, the 'heads'.

From behind the cubicle doors, deliberately foreshortened to expose legs and any perversions, rose wisps of fag smoke and the idle gossip of half a dozen examples of Ordinary Seamen (O.D.s), like myself. In spite of the baggy bell-bottoms tumbled around our ankles we were relieving only our natural loathing for the pointless chores of barrack life while awaiting draft. The task thought up for us that morning had been even more pointless than usual. Issued with hoes and trowels, we had been detailed by the duty Petty Officer to weed the flower bed fronting the Commodore's residence. As endless working parties before us had been ordered to do exactly the same, it wasn't surprising that weeds there were as rare as dahlias in the desert.

No sooner had the P.O. departed to find pleasanter company in his mess than we rapidly took flight to the one place of sanctuary that seemed to us to be safest from authority – the heads. The more experienced among the 'barrack stanchions', who successfully avoided both detection and drafts, might have advised securer hiding places but we eighteen-year-olds fresh from training establishments still had a lot to learn about Naval tactics.

There wasn't much we needed teaching, however, about that Naval art form called the 'buzz', or rumour. It was an essential mental and morale mainstay for men kept in a constant state of uncertainty by an authority extremely reluctant to take any junior ratings into its confidence. This was more marked than ever in barracks where men could be kept guessing about their future movements for weeks. Every tiny crumb of information from any source, likely or ridiculous, was passed on with ever added embellishments. Several of these buzzes were being airily tossed from one cubicle to another as we sat in semi-anonymity killing time and boredom.

'You 'ear abaht the draft that's going to the 'owe?' That was Cockie, whose brash air earned him the nickname as much as his Cockney background.

'Yeah,' retorted Mick, the Ulsterman, 'but you can stuff them effing big ships – too much effing bullshit.'

'I don't give a shit where I goes as long as it's out of this effing prison, like,' bemoaned Yorkie, whose fresh, open face and a perpetual homesickness for his Yorkshire Dales made his conscription into the Navy seem a particularly sadistic act.

It was our fellow O.D. who lived just across the Tamar in the birthplace of that local delicacy, the Cornish Pastie, or Tiddy Oggie and, therefore, earned the latter part of that name, who raised a buzz that made us pay more serious attention. Oggie, had, as Naval parlance put it, been born between 'pusser's blankets', or come from a long line of Royal Navymen, and was credited with an intimate knowledge we total strangers to the Service did not possess.

'My oppo 'oos a chef in the pigs' [officers'] galley says the chat around there is all about a big draft going to the Far East or somewhere in them parts. 'E says now the Jerries look as though they've 'ad it we got to take on the Japs.'

We pondered this revelation in silence for a while. It raised serious issues beyond the immediate anxiety of getting our first active service draft. None of us objected to saying goodbye to 'Guz' (the nickname for Devonport), which we loathed for its cramped, grim, Victorian accommodation and atrocious food, or even to getting a first taste of warship life, which might not be any better, yet having been lucky enough to miss most of the war in Europe, including the Normandy Landings, we were hoping we might also be spared any remaining hostilities. The prospect of being sent to fight the Japs and having our war and Naval service stretched by several more years was bad news indeed.

It was Scouse, the wiry little Liverpudlian, who put the feelings of some of us into emphatic words. 'They can stuff the Far East right up the Drafting Jaunty's [Master at Arms'] arse. Buggered if I wants to be stuck up some jungle creek. Leave it to the effing Yanks – they was in no bloody 'urry to 'elp us.'

Yorkie didn't think it was that simple. 'Ay, it's all right you griping but just you try an' get out of it when they 'and you that draft chitty.'

Finally, Scouse sneered: 'There's nothing what a bar of soap won't get rid of. If them dodgers around 'ere can get away with it I don't see why I can't. Unfit for draft – that's me.'

He was referring to an old trick commonly reputed to be used by barrack stanchions for avoiding an unsavoury draft. They would carve, we had been told, the letters 'UN' in a bar of Navy issue soap, almost as hard as a block of wood. Inked over it would then be imprinted in front of the words 'FIT FOR DRAFT' stamped on chitties.

More determined dodgers, so the old hands said, would go so far as to eat some of the poisonously carbolic soap to make absolutely sure of being '*UN*FIT FOR DRAFT'.

To do either was probably beyond our immature years. Nor could we attempt what was more commonly resorted to by determined draft avoiders – outright bribery and corruption. There was, we had learned, an unwritten but almost standardised rate for paying out to the Drafting Office staff or the influential go-betweens, a race of barrack barons, who could kill an unwanted draft or arrange an exceptionally pleasant one. The back-handers ranged from handing over daily tots of rum to hard cash or its value in kind in the shape of 'rabbits' (stolen goods). Since we, as O.D.s, were not entitled to a 'bubbly' (rum) issue and our pay barely sustained us in necessities our chances of taking advantage of this system were virtually nil. In any event someone had to be drafted and by the time the expert dodgers had got omitted there were mainly just the young innocents like us left.

We were still indulging in our favourite pastime of bemoaning our unhappy lot when a bellow from the Captain of the Heads (lavatory cleaner), who had been keeping a weather eye open for trouble from outside, brought our chat to an abrupt ending. 'Douse them fags,' he yelled as he hurriedly began sprinkling disinfectant around to try and smother the smell of tobacco. A moment later we heard the heavy tread of a pair of distinctly authoritarian boots.

For a few seconds they came to a halt in front of our closed doors and then began pacing slowly up and down before us. It was like rolling claps of thunder before lightning strikes. Then we nervously heard the unmistakable boom of crusher (Naval policeman) wrath working up into full-blooded fury.

'So this is where you bunch of skivers 'ave got to – the call of nature proved too strong, did it?' The mocking tone in his voice sounded even more menacing.

'All got your trousers down, 'ave we? I bet your arses are right sore. But one thing's for sure it ain't due to 'aving a shit.'

There was an ominous pause before the crusher really let rip.

21

'Now get out of them wanking boxes double quick before I really give your bums something to be sore about.'

Trying to do up bell-bottoms with their big buttoned flap for a fly at any time called for time and sure fingers. Trying to do it in extreme hurry under the threat of punishment was almost impossible. The six of us made a sorry sight as we emerged from the cubicles with flaps half done and white 'fronts' sticking out where they should be tucked in.

The crusher, for such was the Petty Officer standing before us eyeing us with total scorn, couldn't resist one more verbal lashing. 'Bloody H.O.s [Hostilities Only] – no effing wonder this effing war's taken so effing long. Get yourselves smartened up – you . . . you look like you been dragged through an 'awsepipe an' if I 'ad my effing way you bloody well would be.'

In my six months' Naval career I had never been a defaulter and I doubted if most of the others had been but that now looked a distinct possibility. But only Cockie had the bravado to ask if it was to be our fate.

The crusher, regarding him like a gardener views a bad attack of greenfly, made an almost Mephistophelean retort: 'Taking you lot before the Officer of the Day is a waste of good Navy time. What I've got lined up for you skivers will make you wish you'd got a year's No 11's (extra duties and stoppage of leave). No, I've been searching the barracks to 'and you a nice juicy draft chit. Where you're going should really make you buggers sweat.'

As we marched ahead of the crusher towards the Drafting Office we exchanged nervous glances. Scouse, in an effort to bolster our fears, whispered: ' 'E's only trying to scare us.' Maybe he was but he was definitely succeeding.

The approach to the Drafting Office was packed with reluctant conscripts. As each rating emerged from receiving his chitty he faced a barrage of questions about which ship he was being sent to. In most cases the answer was *Lothian*. Always it was accompanied by a similar blank reaction. No one had ever heard the name and it didn't signify any known type of warship. The only clue was that she must be a fair size to need the barracks to be scraped dry. Where she lay and where she would be bound also remained mysteries. Wartime secrecy demanded such information be kept under wraps as long as possible but it could usually be winkled out. Not so this time.

We were still guessing two days later when, laden down with kitbags and hammocks, we were piled into the back of a Naval lorry and driven to Plymouth railway station. All our draft chits clearly bore the stamp 'FIT FOR DRAFT'. The bars of soap in our kitbags remained uncut. We had toyed with trying the old dodge as rumours grew that we had been chosen for a particularly unpleasant mission, but in our teenage nervousness had agreed it was too risky. It proved only days for us to rue our cowardice.

2

Make (Do) and Mend

The Clyde had seen many types of ships in its long history but rarely such a varied or large collection as were assembled along its mighty length this day in early July 1944. Almost every kind of merchant vessel and many sorts of warships lay at anchor or alongside from Glasgow all the way down past Gourock and on beyond Rothesay. Most of them had some active connection with the invasion of Europe: the big troopers bringing reserves from America; freighters loading or unloading supplies for the Normandy beaches and ships of all types waiting for or undergoing urgent war damage repairs. Few among this huge armada, however, looked quite as unusual or so detached from the war effort as the peculiar shaped, seagoing mongrel lying near the tail of the Bank.

In broad outline H.M.S. Lothian was a cargo ship, a role for which she had been built in 1938. But while she retained her chubby hull and cargo welldecks this 8,036 gross ton mutation had a superstructure that looked more like the afterthought of an absent-minded naval architect. Deckhouses sprouted where they had originally never been intended and a large steel carbuncle had been stuck on both her bow and stern in the shape of twin 4-inch gun turrets. From her several masts aerials of all shapes and sizes sprayed out. To complete the mix-up her sides were overhung with landing craft. Yet these only helped to mislead since she was not, as some might have guessed, an L.S.I.(L) (Landing Ship Infantry Large) but an L.S.I.(H) (Headquarters Ship).

About her only fitting aspect was her new name. Originally City of Edinburgh *the Navy had decided to substitute the county in which the Scottish capital stands* – Lothian. *It would have been far more* *appropriate, however, if a different ship altogether had been chosen for her very special new role.* Within a short time of commandeering her and putting the ship into a Liverpool yard for conversion it became obvious that she was basically unsuitable. Instead of the three to four months planned for her transformation it took all of seven and even then she was incomplete and in urgent need of a mechanical overhaul.*

Matters had not been helped by the attitude of her civilian dockyard maties who seemed to have regarded her as a lost cause from the start. Although there were as many as 1,100 of them working aboard, tasks that should have taken days took weeks with supervision lax and card schools common. In the midst of it all two senior yard officials were arrested for various illegalities including the employment of a 'ghost' force of workers. The situation had become so desperate that the first Royal Navy officer sent to supervise her completion swiftly returned to the Admiralty to announce she could not possibly be ready in time.

But Lieutenant-Commander Kenneth Buckel, R.N., was told in no uncertain manner that H.M.S. Lothian had to be ready by her scheduled completion date only eight weeks away. She was, it was confidentially revealed to him, to be one of the three vital Headquarters Ships for the British sector of the anticipated invasion of Europe – just four weeks on from her expected completion.

If anyone could help achieve the seemingly impossible it was this determined young Lieutenant-Commander, one of those rare officers to have actually worked himself up from the Lower Deck, having joined as a boy in an old 'wooden wall' training ship. His enthusiasm was enhanced by the fact that he had only just been raised to his rank and this was his first full executive appointment.

Yet the Admiralty were clearly expecting too much of him. Whether they were short of officers or, in the heat of planning D-Day, simply overlooked the fact, but he was left without help, the only other 'officer' being a civilian in Lieutenant's clothing, recruited to help design the important and complicated communication/operations set-up on board. He was not, however, a Naval Architect but someone trained to design offices and houses. A smart young Warrant Telegraphist, Mr. Pattison undertook the complex radio installation. The structural problems in

---

* A report to the Admiralty from the Director of Combined Operations (M) on August 28 stated: If the D. of S.T. (Director of Sea Transport) offers as unsuitable a ship as *Lothian* the time will be about seven months. A more suitable ship with accommodation already available in superstructure would be a month or so less – a reference to converting other vessels for a similar role.

trying to squeeze so much into her unyielding hull were immense. Although she was installed with the most advanced communications system by which she would be in constant touch with all sea, air and land forces plus direct links with Chiefs of Staff ashore and even Churchill himself, the ratings' accommodation had barely any ventilation and just a coat of paint for what were her former cargo holds.

April 1944 arrived with much still to be done and, once again, Lieutenant-Commander Buckel returned to the Admiralty to report that in spite of every human effort on his part the ship could definitely not be made ready on time. By now even the deskbound superiors saw the futility of persisting. H.M.S. Lothian, they decided, would not be one of the three main HQ ships for D-Day but would be given an alternative, back-up role. Exactly what this was to be was not revealed but as she would still be needed on the appointed day of invasion whatever her condition, Lieutenant-Commander Buckel went back to Liverpool still facing a seemingly impossible task.

Three weeks later on May 15, her scheduled completion date, hundreds of items remained unfinished. When the transport arrived bearing the majority of men to make up her complement of around 300 only one messdeck and one galley were properly fitted out. The next day as they stood to attention during the commissioning ceremony and the White Ensign was hoisted for the first time they were well outnumbered by the dockyard maties still trying to get her ready.

The newly appointed Captain, a Royal Naval Reserve Commander, and Lieutenant-Commander Buckel decided they would have to take the ship to sea and get the work finished as best they could at some Naval dockyard under the guise of 'Alterations and Additions'. This was fine in theory, but with working up trials and an urgent need to sail South to link up with the invasion forces impossible in practice. It was the end of May before the far-from-complete H.M.S. Lothian left Liverpool to sail North around Scotland for Rosyth to load some essential equipment before heading towards the Channel.

So secret had the invasion plans been kept, however, that no one on board knew exactly when they should have to go into action, whatever form that was to take. As they lay in the Firth of Forth an urgent message of a different kind reached the ship. It was from a Manchester manufacturing company. Could someone collect a pressing machine ordered for the officers' laundry? Lacking any more serious demand than this the Warrant Telegraphist, Mr. Pattison, was despatched to secure this vital piece of equipment. He had barely reached the factory when he was ordered back to the ship at all speed only to find on reaching Edinburgh the next day that she had sailed! It was June 6 – D-Day.

Mr. Pattison had every reason to be alarmed. He was directly responsible for the all-important radio communications system. Worse than that he had the key to the safe that contained the secret orders for the transmissions that were to be made from Lothian *during the invasion. Already tired and hungry from his earlier rail journey he leapt aboard a southbound train for a tedious cross-country trip to Harwich, where the ship was heading. Worn out and totally dishevelled he at last boarded a launch in the port and set out in search of his ship. By great good fortune he found her just as she was coming to anchor. Scrambling up a hastily thrown-over rope ladder he tore up to the safe and extracted the vital orders only minutes away from the deadline.*

But if he or anyone aboard had thought the transmissions were directly connected with the massive assault already launched against the Normandy beaches they were rudely taken aback. For sixteen days, at Harwich and later at Sheerness in the Thames Estuary, the ship's sole duty was sending out 'phoney' signals intended to mislead the Germans into believing another landing was to take place in the Calais area. Throughout each twenty-four hours her large staff of 'sparkers' (radio operators) constantly sent out easily decoded messages to dozens of receivers being driven up and down the nearby British coast in scores of lorries! The intention was to fool the enemy into believing they were all part of a second big invasion force.

As important and as useful as this odd operation may have been it was not the exciting, all-involved action the officers and men had been expecting. Gradually the majority felt like useless bystanders unfairly robbed of any glory and no one more so than the seamen gunners. They felt doubly grieved. During most of the time they lay at anchor a steady succession of German pilotless 'Buzz Bombs' crossed overhead directed towards London. Most were in range of the ship's 4-inch anti-aircraft guns but not once was the order given to open fire. Perhaps it was felt wiser not to reveal the Lothian's *presence, and, possibly, her secret role but it made the seamen both angry and frustrated.*

What made them feel really dissatisfied was that they still had to go to Action Stations every time one of the 'Bombs' passed over. To show their disgust they began to react to the call more and more tardily – until it brought down the wrath of Lieutenant-Commander Buckel, as 'Jimmy the One' (First Lieutenant). With his Lower Deck background

27

he spoke to them in their own down-to-earth language making no bones about what he thought of their reluctant attitude. It did the trick but won him no friends. It was they, the seamen, they told themselves, who had been the more determined to open fire and it was the officers who had always stopped them. What was more the seamen, who had a basic dislike of officers who had 'come-up-through-the-hawsepipe', felt aggrieved at being dressed down in their own terms. Although the incident itself passed over the men were quick to recall it when, later, more alarming events took place.

Although only a month since commissioning, it did not take much to cause friction in what had already become an unhappy ship. The squalid accommodation lay partly at the root of it but there was also an uneasy relationship between the rest of the ship's company and the Captain. Ever since leaving the Mersey his erratic and unpredictable behaviour had created tension. His war record was as fine as most, but it was obvious that the strain had created a serious drink problem. It also added to the difficulties of Lieutenant-Commander Buckel as second-in-command. To all intents and purposes he had to take over control of the ship with the real captain often incapable of doing so.

Suddenly, in the midst of all this, there arrived a totally unexpected order. H.M.S. Lothian was to be put into 'Care and Maintenance' (temporarily laid-up). No one in authority could offer a reason why a newly commissioned ship with such sophisticated equipment and, apparently, deemed vital to the war effort was now to be shoved into idleness. It remained a puzzle ever after. But on July 1 she sailed from Sheerness for the Clyde, seemingly to go to anchor with her complement run down for weeks if not months to come.

Three days after anchoring in the Clyde, with work well under way to put her into temporary cold storage, any thought of that longed for leave was abruptly taken from the ratings' grasp by a signal from the Admiralty for the ship to be made ready for an undisclosed operation. July 6 was a date that many Navymen, not least those responsible for organising Force X, would wish to forget.

On the day the Lothian *received her change of plans the L.S.I.(L) Empire Halberd, a converted American war-built cargo ship, also received a sudden command – to sail at once for the Clyde from the Normandy beaches where she had been ferrying troops from Britain ever since D-Day. It was 1714 as she steamed at her full 15 knots in sight of the Longships lightvessel off the Isles of Scilly, heading from the*

28

Channel towards the Irish Sea when a loud explosion brought her to a shuddering halt. She had become yet another victim of a German mine.

With Allied ships being sunk or damaged by enemy action daily the report of the Halberd's *mining would normally have caused little reaction at the Admiralty. This time it caused nearly as much upset as news of a capital ship in trouble. She was one of the only two ships chosen for Force X with a complement experienced in landings and already properly fitted out for them. To replace her meant appropriating yet another of the recently arrived freighters from the United States. There was no other choice.*

As the Halberd *crawled into Falmouth with a destroyer protection a party of oil-stained engineers were crawling through the bowels of the S.S.* Pampas *lying off Southend. She, too, had been part of the invasion transport, but age, overwork and out-dated machinery – not enemy action – had made her a casualty. Previously used by the Navy as an assault ship, it would now be weeks if not months before she would be fit for any kind of seagoing duty decided her surveyors. Their depressing report for the Admiralty sent ulcers aching once again. She was yet another of the tiny number of L.S.I.(L)s thought available for Force X.*

Finding a replacement of almost any kind would be difficult enough – finding one in good fighting order would be well-nigh impossible. Long lists of vessels were closely studied; names proposed and quickly dropped. Some ships were suitable but too far away. Others were more conveniently positioned but suffered mechanical or other delaying problems. After hours of searching and discussion only one candidate seemed remotely likely and there were serious misgivings about her.

Lying alongside a repair berth at Swansea, H.M.S. Lamont *was fresh from the Normandy beaches but distinctly tired from that ordeal and her two long years as an L.S.I.(L), including the North African and Italian invasions. Although only five years old the machinery of this 7,250 gross ton cargo ship (ex-*Clan Lamont*) converted to carry 800 troops and their landing craft had been stretched way beyond the economic, carefully nurtured limits for which it had been designed. As with the* Pampas *engineers were surveying her multitude of mechanical problems and planning their extensive repairs. As far as her complement was concerned the* Lamont's *war was temporarily over. The sudden order to raise steam and head at once for the Clyde to form part of a new assault force being urgently commissioned was received with incredulity. The 'nuthouse' was really living up to its nickname agreed*

*both officers and ratings but there was no choice but to obey. Carrying
out the best patch up job they could her engineers coaxed her reluctant
engines and auxiliaries into life and set sail.*

*On the opposite side of the Welsh peninsula, at Milford Haven, the
9,784 gross ton L.S.I.(L) H.M.S.* Glenearn, *was getting a much
needed brief respite from intensive action at Normandy. Having visited
the beaches thirty times and taken part in every Allied landing from
Sicily onwards had left her in need of repairs and her ship's company
wanting rest and relaxation. Yet now she too received orders promptly
to turn about and head for the Clyde.*

*Of the six vessels originally chosen for Force X she was, however, the
only one under the White Ensign that could be deemed suitable for a
long ocean voyage through the tropics and with a complement well
trained for a major assault. Built six years earlier for the Far Eastern
service of the Glen Line, she was a fine example of a modern cargo liner.
Although built in Scotland her twin diesels were, ironically, designed in
Germany. They gave her a speed of 18 knots, fast for a cargo ship, and
her accommodation was more comfortable and spacious than many.*

*The war had not long begun when the Navy converted her to carry
over 1,000 troops. Many more than that had packed into her when she
played a heroic part in the evacuation of British troops from Greece.
Later she had been transformed into an L.S.I. with twenty-seven
landing craft and three sets of twin 4-inch guns.*

*In selecting her for Force X the Admiralty had no hesitation in
choosing her to be the command of the Senior Officer of the L.S.I.s as
such. Had she not lacked the sophisticated Operations and Communications system of the* Lothian *she would undoubtedly have made a
finer flagship for the entire force, being larger, faster and better manned.
As it was her presence was always to emphasise the makeshift disadvantages suffered by the other warships including* Lothian.*

*Yet the flagship looked no more ungainly than the four remaining
Force X ships, which also found their way to the Clyde. Typical
mass-produced 'Liberty' type vessels turned out in weeks rather than
months, their hulls and utilitarian box-shaped superstructures were as*

---

* Captain Hughes Hallett, Director of Planning (Q), having reflected on the
difficulties, suggested in a memo to the Board of Admiralty that the Force might
sail without a Headquarters Ship and an Admiral and that the Captain of
Glenearn be given overall command plus a temporary HQ vessel such as an
Australian frigate for any assaults when reaching the South-West Pacific.
Although a way out of the various difficulties the idea was rejected.

simplistic as a six-year-old's drawing of a cargo ship. No more simple than the troop and messdecks, which were newly converted cargo holds. Without the cargo they were designed to carry, however, they had become topheavy – a problem made worse by the tiers of landing craft now suspended from their boat decks. Even at anchor they rolled sickeningly. Such instability was soon to prove an obstacle.

But as July rapidly disappeared no one aboard any of the ships in the Force could believe they were being marshalled to go any distance or with any great urgency. Even in war it took weeks to prepare for a serious mission, yet these ships were being left to swing idly at anchor. The problem was, however, that with so many other ships needing berths to meet the Navy's continuing demands following the Normandy invasion there were none available for Force X. With hundreds of tons of stores, some urgent repairs and other vital work needed for such a long, taxing voyage and assault mission the scheduled date of July 25 was clearly over-optimistic. Had the Admiralty stuck by the U.S. Navy Chief of Operations' request just for the six L.S.I.s the situation might not have been so bad but adding the Lothian, *which required a great deal more doing to her to turn her into a flagship for a lengthy period, made the position far worse.**

It did not help when, at last finding a berth in the James Watt Dock, Greenock, she struck the entrance and badly dented her bows. At least no one could blame her first Captain – he had been removed from the ship on reaching the Clyde. Now there was another R.N.R. Commander, a bluff, no-nonsense mariner who spoke his mind no matter who was at the receiving end. But the ship's company were never given a chance to discover his other qualities. An equally outspoken and certainly outranking Naval officer intervened.

---

* A signal sent on July 16, 1944, from the Secretary to the Vice-Chief of Naval Staff at the Admiralty to Admiral King, stated: '. . . if you have no objection these ships will be placed under the Command of a Flag Officer, in which case H.M.S. *Lothian* (L.S.H.) will be added to the Force as his flagship. From an administration point of view this is most desirable.'
The signal diplomatically omitted any reference to the reasons given at the Royal Navy meeting held in the First Lord's War Room on July 4, when the decision to add a flagship was actually taken. Whether Admiral King concurred is not known but what seems to have been his apparent silence on the subject might indicate his disapproval as later believed likely. He was also thought to have seen through the ploy.

3

Tar and Brylcreem

It was the 'low road' to Scotland in the worst possible sense. For thirty-six hours we ratings had been squashed together in rickety, old third-class compartments stinking worse than well worn seaboot stockings, or forced to stand for hours in packed corridors. And our tortoise-paced journey with constant halts and shuntings into sidings to let vital troop and ammunition trains through was only threequarters way over. It was about norm for wartime rail travel but none the more acceptable.

A more painful agony was our desperate hunger. All we O.D.s had been issued with for food at 'Guz' was one 'Tiddy Oggie' and one slice of stale fruit cake – supposed to satisfy us until we reached Crewe. It had taken nearly thirty hours to get there and desperate for food we had made a dash for the Services' canteen only to be told that our connecting train for Glasgow was due to depart. Several of the *Lothian* draft had sneaked away, preferring to face a charge of absenteeism than starvation. We innocents lacked such strength of will and by now, as we ground to yet another halt somewhere near Carlisle as best we could judge in the blackout, our plight was desperate.

'They'll 'ave to carry me orf this effing train when we gets to 'aggis land,' moaned Cockie.

'Buggered if I'll get that far,' added Oggie, whose only passion in life was eating.

The six of us indulged in the only feast we could enjoy – an outburst of self-pity and righteous indignation – when the mateloe who had been sleeping off the effects of the bottled tots of rum he

32

had earlier been demolishing to our envy suddenly awoke and told us bluntly, 'You effing O.D.s are all the bloody same – all griping and no effing action. Get off yer arses and do something about it.'

We eyed him in hostile surprise but he was clearly a tougher, older hand than any of us.

'So what?' retorted Scouse. 'You want us to 'old up the train and rob the passengers?'

Ignoring him pointedly the hard-case looking A.B. rose, stretched his arms and then barged his way past us to the corridor. Turning he announced, 'I don't know about you effers but I ain't going without my scoff.'

With that he departed out of sight. It was the last we saw of him for half an hour and as we heard the engine raising steam to continue our reluctant journey we wondered if it was to be the last we would see of him.

'I bet you 'e's nipped off train – 'e looks looney enough,' commented Yorkie. 'Serve 'im right if 'e misses it.'

But just as our carriage shuddered into motion there was a frantic flinging open of the door near our compartment and we watched as two 'pongos' heaved the A.B. aboard. Dishevelled and puffing hard but distinctly jubilant he sank back into his corner seat. He, mysteriously, looked fatter than when he had left us.

'You left it fine,' I said.

''Ad to 'ide behind an effing 'edge until the train began to move, didn't I? Couldn't risk the bloody guard seeing me, not with what I got.'

Instinctively our mouths started watering. Our eyes bulged, too, as the A.B. at last slowly began extracting the cause of the bulge inside his blue jumper. We hardly dare believe it. First he brought out a plump, cold chicken. Next half a loaf of bread. Then a sticky wodge of butter and, finally, a whole Madeira-like cake.

'Christ! You're an effing marvel,' burst out Scouse. Oggie looked as though about to jump on the A.B. and seize all he could but like the rest of us remained on the edge of his seat praying this unlikely miracle worker would be generous enough to share his spoil. For a few moments he remained apparently indifferent but then, to our overwhelming joy, he began breaking pieces off and sharing them around. It took only minutes for us to wolf the food down and for the world to become a rosier place. But not for long.

Cockie should never have asked the obvious question in all our thoughts but he could never resist talking. 'Cor, mate, you must 'ave robbed a bloody caff or something to get that lot.'

The A.B. smiled phlegmatically. 'You ought to keep yer effing gob shut,' he replied but not aggressively.

'Go on tell us – we won't talk,' persisted Cockie.

The older mateloe was clearly feeling proud of his achievement. 'O.K. but I'll smash the face in of the bloke what says anything. When I nipped off the train I found this row of cottages. Dead quiet they was like everyone had crashed their swede for the night. So I 'unts around and finds a back window that's 'andy. One tap on the glass with a stone and that's me inside. That's where I find the cake in the larder. At the next 'ouse I gets the chicken and the bread and butter. I ain't 'ad an easier break-in. You'd think they'd take more effing care – grub being that 'ard to come by these days.'

As he spoke our faces fell lower and lower and while we suffered no indigestion from our stolen feast our consciences stabbed us painfully. I thought of the poor cottagers finding their precious food stolen and wished my own craving for it had not been so desperate. What was worse – our 'saviour' was obviously an experienced thief.

Mick, the Northern Irelander, whom we suspected of strong religious views, put it into words: 'You . . . you mean you done this sort of . . . of thieving before?'

The A.B. studied our reaction scornfully. 'Look you effing buggers it's every man for 'imself in this effing war. Yer don't think the effing Andrew's going to give two effs for yer? Sure I've been on the 'oist before otherwise I wouldn't 'ave just done me 180 days in the Glass'ouse.'

He was, as far as I was concerned, the first real criminal I had come across and probably was for most of us. For that, at least, he carried an aura of importance but what he told us next turned our worries back to the greater evil we had been facing since we had been given our draft of dubious virtue. He had been let out of the military prison only the day before we left Guz. No sooner had his feet touched its stony ground than he was hauled into the drafting office and ordered to join the *Lothian*. What was more foreboding in our minds was that, according to him, he wasn't the only ex-Glasshouse rating to be similarly sent to the ship.

'You can be effing sure she's some kind of shithouse if they're drafting all the old cons to 'er,' he said, relishing our dismay.

34

By the time we tottered off the train with our kitbags and hammocks after forty-eight hours en route, however, any ship would have been welcome. We would gladly have gone to sleep stretched out on a bench at the Glasgow station. What awaited us three hours later after a lorry ride to Greenock and then being taken by launch to the *Lothian* at anchor was hardly any better.

As we found to our cost as we tried lugging our heavy luggage the seamen's messdeck was approached by a steep, fairly narrow steel ladder via the 'flat' containing the 'heads'. It was more like descending into darkened wine cellars except that the smell that arose was distinctly less invigorating. As our eyes adjusted slowly to the gloom, relieved only by small deckhead lights encased in thick glass, we could barely credit the congestion. Every inch seemed packed with mess tables, tiers of steel lockers and a press of ratings elbow to elbow.

What our instinct also told us was that we and the crush of other newly arrived ratings were about as welcome as a press-gang in an eighteenth-century ale-house. The obvious overcrowding was going to be made far worse. A messdeck designed for some seventy or so seamen now had to take nearly double that number. But no sympathy was wasted on us as we struggled through the narrow gaps between messes and the lockers that separated them to find what only a drug-crazed optimist would have described as our 'home' to be. We jaded six had been detailed to No 8 Mess where ten ratings were already filling almost all the benches on either side of the long table. As we stood waiting in a forlorn little group they eyed us with icy distaste while from the end of the table a bearded figure bearing a 'hook' (anchor) on his arm and clearly the leading hand of the mess bellowed: 'Don't just stand there. Get them effing bags and 'ammicks stowed. This ain't the bloody *Queen Mary*.'

If the messdeck was tiny for the number of men the lockers were minuscule for the amount of gear that had to be squeezed into them. Even after forcibly ramming essentials inside we still had a pile of our more personal possessions in our kitbags. Just as we were contemplating what could be done with them the burly figure of a Petty Officer, who we later learnt was the Messdeck P.O., appeared, took one look at our problem and snapped: 'Ditch them – over the side if you must. There ain't room for you miserable lot let alone any fancy doodahs to remind you of your effing loved ones.'

All this time our hunger had been mounting once again and we were acutely conscious that we had arrived in the middle of dinner. But by the time we had ended our drawnout labours the messdeck was rapidly clearing and the mess fannies (food containers) being hauled away for cleaning.

'Ain't there no grub?' almost sobbed Oggie.

'Not 'til supper there ain't an' when you bin aboard 'ere long enough you'll be effing glad of that.'

What we wanted was food – any kind of it – not a culinary critique. Oggie grabbed the mess fanny still on the table and, picking up a scrap of bread, desperately began scraping the remains of what could have been stew. In a flash we had all joined in fighting for every tiny scrap left over.

The sweeper looked on in amazement before saying: 'I seen some 'ungry bastards in my time but you're a right bunch of Oliver Twists.'

He couldn't have put it better. Dickens would have been inspired by the messdeck's workhouse atmosphere. It would also have been a good model for Fagin's Den, as we found out later. One thing was for sure – even the most lax of public health inspectors would have condemned it out of hand. That it lacked any comfort was blatantly clear. That it was also deficient in certain vital essentials became even more alarming. All it was, in fact, was a steel box with barely any trimmings. The shipyard had simply welded on a steel deckhead and a steel deck under foot and slapped on a coat of paint for the sides of what had been a cargo hold. Since it was on the waterline no portholes were provided and the only ventilation was a simple one-way duct that fed a trickle of air in, but did not extract the thick, foul air that accumulated from so many bodies.

An equally distressing problem was the condensation caused by the presence of so much steel and even in the temperate climate of the Clyde the bulkheads ran with water. Later, in the tropics, this turned into a steamy, jungle-like cloud that attacked our lungs. But the most irritating example of sheer dockyard idiocy from the beginning of our fresh commission was the way that the deck had been laid with a coating of concrete as a cheap, quick alternative to something more practical.

36

Constant wear from the crush of occupants had turned the surface into a dust heap so that the slightest movement sent the fine particles rising over everyone and everything. Clothes, tables lockers and even food received a coating of grey cement which constant sweeping could not prevent and watering down the deck simply added to the condensation. One awoke in the mornings coughing from the dust that had settled on hammocks during the night. Yet for several of us new arrivals that was the least of our sleeping hazards.

Scouse was the first of us to discover what those were to be. With a sharp eye for the main chance he had, that first evening aboard, begun slinging his hammock early from one of the rows of bars welded to the deckhead above the mess. He had barely got one end lashed when a bellow from one of the original occupants of No 8 stopped him dead in his tracks. 'Get that 'ammick down before I strings you up in its place – that's my billet.'

Scouse tried again further along the bar. Once again an angry yell halted him. 'Ain't there any spare 'ooks?' he begged at last.

There definitely were not, he was told bluntly. The six of us fellow O.D.'s exchanged worried looks. 'O.K., then,' said Scouse, 'if no one 'asn't got any objections I'll grab the table.'

This time the answer was louder, angrier and more authoritative. 'You effing well won't – that's reserved for me,' shouted the leading hand.

And before Scouse or any of us got ideas above our stations the sweeper and another member of the mess told us emphatically they laid claim to the benches on either side of the table. That night, and for many weeks after, we spread our hammocks out flat on that dirty, dusty deck although Scouse at least booked the safest place – under the table. The rest of us unfortunates ran the perpetual risk of being trodden on by men going on or coming off watch let alone the boozed-up lurchings of ratings returning on the last liberty boat.

Our own runs ashore were more taken up with bemoaning our bad luck in being drafted to what we were already calling a 'hell ship'. More than once we wished we were back in the comparative purity and luxury of our training establishments, forgetting what a mortifying experience they had been for all of us leaving home for the first time. Yet all these 'stone frigates' (shore bases) had done was to give us a totally misleading notion of what shipboard life could be like. If we suspected that we were being wrongly treated in the *Lothian* according to K.R.s and A.I.s (King's Regulations and Admiralty Instructions), even by wartime standards, none of us felt we could complain to authority. Mick, with a certain missionary zeal, had proposed to the leading hand of the mess, called 'Hookie', like most Leading Seamen, that he approach the Divisional Officer to get some better sleeping quarters for us and had immediately been shot down.

''Ave you seen the poncey Wavy Navy (R.N.V.R.) bugger who's the divvy officer?' he replied scornfully. 'Well you might as well piss in the wind as ask 'im. What's more this effing 'ulk is so full you couldn't swing your chopper let alone an 'ammick. An' what's more I 'ear it's going to get worse.'

He was dead right.

A few days after we had joined the ship, towards the fourth week in July just after we at last left anchor and berthed in the James Watt Dock, Greenock, we were going through the endless process of painting the ship's sides when several buses drew up alongside.

'Not another effing draft – they'll be stacking 'em in the chimney next,' observed the seaman sharing my painting stage. Then we made a double take. For the servicemen pouring out of the buses wore no familiar Navy blue but the R.A.F. version. In their scores they disembarked with their kitbags until around 100 were lined up on the quay. Whether it was our crew's upset at seeing these vastly unwanted arrivals or simply traditional enmity between the two Services wasn't clear but within seconds the catcalls were flying forth.

The jeers of 'Brylcreem Boys' were the least offensive of the jibes. Shouts of 'Just look at them brownhatters (gays)!' or 'Got your water wings?' and 'Watch your arses, darlings', poured down on the unfortunate Air Force men. It was the last kind of welcome anyone wanted to any kind of ship and for one as grotty looking as the *Lothian* it must have been totally dispiriting. Their first sight of their bareboard messdeck in the depths of the ship would have sent morale tumbling a few more degrees.

Exactly what they were doing aboard puzzled us for a time especially when we heard they were not passengers but part of the ship's company. In the meantime our astonishment was doubled by the arrival of some thirty Royal Corps of Signal men, again to be a proper section of the complement. Since we also had several dozen Royal Marines to handle the landing craft we formed a peculiar kind of Combined Ops although not at all like the fully integrated lot bearing that title. As events proved the four Services aboard *Lothian* preferred to remain segregated as far as possible, if only out of suspicion of one another.

We seamen were convinced this was just another mad idea from the nuthouse Admiralty or that someone in the R.A.F. and Army had got draft chits mixed up. What earthly use could all these Air Force men, mainly wireless operators and Ops Room personnel, and Army signallers be when we already had dozens of communications ratings of our own? we asked ourselves. It led to even wilder rumours about our future mission. None was more way out than that we were going to set up a secret base for ships and aircraft on some frozen chunk of Arctic.*

The bewildered 'Brylcreem boys' and 'Pongos' had no more idea than we had. The peculiarities of warship life were beginning to confuse them still further for hardly any had served at sea before. To our surprise we discovered they were all volunteers for sea duty, which immediately confirmed them in our eyes as being 'right soft erks'.

No time was wasted in taking full advantage of their innocence. All the hoary Naval chestnuts were pulled out to lead them further into confusion like sending them deep into the ship's bowels to

* Prior to D-Day an experiment had been carried out aboard the Headquarters Ship *Hilary* to improve the limited communications system in this type of assault vessel. As well as extending and improving the radio and operation room amenities R.A.F. and Army men were brought in to provide better links with aircraft and fighting units ashore. It was so successful that the scheme was extended to the L.S.I.(H)s *Bulolo* and *Largs* and all three ships were enabled to carry out their part in the Normandy Invasion much more successfully. The *Lothian*, which was ready too late for D-Day, was given the most sophisticated system of them all.

To find the men for this new role the R.A.F. formed the Headquarters Ship Unit and consequently put hundreds of them aboard five L.S.I.(H)s and several Fighter Direction ships. Its records for the time do not make it clear why a detachment was sent to *Lothian*, which would clearly not be able to make efficient use of it when operating with the Americans, who had totally different systems of radio communications – as events were to prove. But it appears the Unit may have believed the ship was destined for service with the British in South-East Asia. In the rush to put Force X together the Admiralty may not have informed the R.A.F. of the *Lothian*'s true destination.

find the 'Golden Rivet'. We would insist: 'Every ship has one put in when they're launched – worth hundreds of quid it is.'

When they did find out they were having their legs pulled they still couldn't understand why it seemed such an obscene joke to us. But a mateloe's interpretation of this ancient myth has purely phallic meaning.

None of this encouraged any shipboard comradeship, which was something we were to regret later on. And the R.A.F. and Army men were not as daft as we thought them. As ship's company they were entitled, if over twenty years old, to draw a daily tot of grog. Hardly any of them fancied the idea and some accepted the threepence a day granted in lieu. But the enterprising ones took the rum and then flogged it to the ratings for a much better return. It was strictly against regulations and the punishment was severe but it was an illicit trade that flourished.

But the eighteen- and nineteen-year-old seamen who formed the bulk of the deck complement had no compensations for being the lowest form of animal life aboard. Our meagre pay was too low for us to find much relief from having a 'pissy run ashore' and, I suppose, our heads were too weak to enjoy it if it had been possible. That did not stop us sampling the Greenock bars where we relieved frustrations in belting out bawdy Naval ditties. We had learnt to inject real emotion into our favourite: 'Roll on the *Nelson*, *Rodney*, *Renown*, this one-funnel bastard is getting us down.'

4

Arthur George

Memo to Board of Admiralty from C. C. Hughes Hallett, Captain R.N., Director of Planning, July 5, 1944:

> *If the Force [X] is to proceed at the end of July there is little doubt that a great deal has got to be achieved in a very short time and that a great deal of inconvenience has got to be endured by all the personnel concerned. It will need a strong personality to make the Force efficient and keep up morale of personnel.*

Finding ships had been difficult enough. Finding a senior officer to match the demanding description given was almost as great a problem. There were plenty of good top men about but very few had sufficient experience with landing assault forces. Those that did were still engaged with Normandy or had been detailed for the forthcoming Operation ANVIL *against the South of France. Choice of one with exactly the right rank reduced the options still further. Inhibited by its desire to appoint someone important enough to prevent the Royal Navy losing face the Admiralty ignored some worthwhile four-ring Captains. There were two Vice-Admirals available who had the desired qualities but appointing someone of such high rank could, it was deemed, run the risk of upsetting the U.S. Navy through overkill. The Flag Officer must be a Rear-Admiral it was therefore decided. In itself this was ambitiously out of step with normal procedure. Such a senior officer would normally command a larger, more impressive squadron than six converted freighters. A captain would be considered important enough and in Captain C. A. G. Hutchison, D.S.O., R.N., of the* Glenearn,

Senior Officer of the L.S.I.s, the Force did already have an experienced man adequate for the task.

For the rest of the first week in July, throughout the second and into the third the Admiralty searched for an Admiral who could be spared. There were certainly no volunteers to command such a makeshift collection of ships bound on such a dubious mission. In the end the choice rested on one man.

On July 20, only five days before the planned departure date, Rear-Admiral Arthur George Talbot, D.S.O. and Bar, was formally appointed Flag Officer, Force X.

It was forty years from the time when, only twelve years old, he had entered the Royal Navy cadet college at Osborne. For thirty years he had seen his career develop unspectacularly if steadily up through the ranks to Commander, part of the First World War spent aboard a monitor (a type of floating big gun platform). Yet 'Arthur George', or 'Noisy', as this determined officer with his powerful 'quarterdeck voice' became known in the Service, had his sights set on emulating a handful of his relations who had achieved prominent ranks in the Royal Navy. No less than five of them, including both his grandfathers, had become admirals. The Talbot family, through marriage, were related to the Earls Fitzwilliam, whose stately home at Wentworth, near Rotherham, South Yorkshire, was the 'longest' baronial home in England. Arthur George, whose father was the estate's Agent, had been born in a house in its grounds.

In 1934 he achieved his first plum appointment – as Captain 'D' of a flotilla of destroyers in the Mediterranean. He quickly made his mark as a leader of determination and zeal. Although it won him more respect than affection among sections of the Lower Deck it successfully captured the attention of their Lordships in London. When World War II began this Captain of stern jaw, compelling eyes and medium build, had risen to the important post of Director of Submarine Warfare.

It was a job he undertook with tremendous vigour demanding, as he always did, a high standard of enthusiasm and efficiency from his staff. Planning, reports and action had to be undertaken with the greatest possible accuracy. It was this, unfortunately, that led to a brush with his direct master, Winston Churchill. Attempting to paint a morale boosting picture of the Royal Navy's successes against the Germans, the latter boasted to the House of Commons in 1940 that it had sunk eighty U-boats. Hearing this Captain Talbot felt compelled to put the record straight by making out a report that only twenty-two had, in fact, been sent to the bottom. Churchill was furious. A bitter row ensued between the two men that was finally resolved some months later when Arthur George was sent back to sea – at Churchill's instigation, it was claimed.

But the action probably did his career good. From 1941 to mid 1943, as a Captain, Talbot had the rare experience of commanding three important aircraft carriers, Furious, Illustrious and Formidable, one after the other, seeing action from the North Cape to the Indian Ocean. It was aboard the latter that he received recognition for his endeavours by being raised to Rear-Admiral. Almost immediately he found himself appointed one of the Naval assault force flag officers for the forthcoming invasion of Normandy. He had no experience of this type of Naval operation but very few British Admirals did. What he lacked in knowledge he made up for in enthusiasm.

His determination to get the most out of the thousands under his command during the months of training from his base in Inverness sometimes led to bickering with junior commanders who felt they knew more about landing tactics. According to one senior officer a number of the juniors felt unhappy enough to form a deputation just before D-Day to seek the intervention of the overall Naval Commander, Admiral Vian. Hurt feelings, however, were smoothed over and 'Force S', which was to cover the assault on 'Sword Beach' sailed into action with Arthur George as its Flag Officer aboard the HQ Ship Largs.

Flying from her was Rear-Admiral Talbot's signal: 'Good Luck. Drive On.' The Largs *certainly enjoyed a big measure of luck. Just before reaching the beaches a German torpedo missed her by inches and another sank the warship closest to her. If the headquarters ship had been sunk not only might this vital part of the landings have been drastically imperilled but the whole story of Arthur George, H.M.S.* Lothian *and Force X might never have happened.*

But wearing a tin hat loaned by a senior Army officer whose daughter, Lucinda Prior-Palmer, was later to become well known to the British public as a champion horsewoman, Arthur George steamed on, braving the choppy Channel weather as much as enemy action. Ever since joining the Navy he had suffered seasickness, but so had Nelson.

His zeal for seeking out the fighting at close quarters was shown by the way he insisted on going ashore most of the four weeks or so his flagship lay off the beaches. According to former staff officers he would load his jeep with bread for distribution to Army units and be driven unhealthily close to the action. At one time, it is said, he was forced to take cover in a ditch when caught in the middle of a tank battle.

It was this determined Admiral who, shortly after returning from Normandy, found himself ordered to command the tiny, motley squadron known as Force X for a vague, demanding mission on the opposite side of the world. After the massive assault group he had led it was rather like asking Sir Thomas Beecham to give up his symphony orchestra to conduct a village brass band. It must have left 'Noisy', who might have expected a command in the forthcoming ANVIL *landings in the South of France or some other big operation, with mixed feelings. To add to it he had to serve under American control and his attitude towards those allies was known to be cool.*

On July 24, four days after his formal appointment, he flew north to Scotland to get his first sight of his flagship. Any misapprehensions he held must have been doubled when he saw her mongrel looks and trebled when a lightning inspection of her showed up the serious deficiencies in accommodating an admiral and his large staff for a lengthy period – especially himself. One look at the quarters reserved for the Flag Officer, which, while better than most aboard, were intended only for brief stays, was enough. He would, he told the Captain, be taking over the latter's much roomier cabins. But the dour R.N.R. veteran was having none of it. If the Admiral wanted his quarters then he formally requested permission to relinquish his command there and then. Perhaps, wisely, he judged it better to have no more to do with a ship destined for such a dubious mission. The fact remained that within a week the Lothian *had her third captain in less than a month.*

Acting Captain Christopher H. Petrie, D.S.O., R.N., hurriedly appointed as a replacement at a moment's notice, was as different as could be from his predecessors. This gentlemanly, fifty-five-year-old officer, who had joined the Navy a couple of years before the Admiral, proved almost reclusive, preferring his cabin to mixing with his officers. Perhaps age and a long, tough war had been enough for him. He had, in fact, retired from the Service before the war – as a lieutenant-commander but given, as was the custom, the farewell present of promotion to commander. He had for some years, according to some, been an orange-grower in South Africa, but in 1939 he had been recalled to the colours.

Most of his time had been spent in command of assault ships such as the famous Bulolo *and of H.M.S.* Glengyle *on Mediterranean and other operations, making him one of the most experienced captains in*

44

the technique of landings. But it had taken its toll and from somewhere he had suffered a limp. Being ordered to command Lothian *must have come as an unwelcome demand when he might have expected to coast the remainder of hostilities back into retirement.*

His experience, at least, could prove a vital asset, which was far more than could be said about the great majority of his officers. Apart from the Jimmy, with his many years of regular service, most were young, inexperienced Wavy Navy Lieutenants and Sub-Lieutenants – a high proportion very recently out of officer training school. Only four of these executive officers held watchkeeping certificates – an abnormally small number and a situation that was going to create serious problems in the months ahead. Equally, very few had much notion of other essential duties such as acting as Divisional Officers, which would prove an obstacle when dealing with discontent among the ratings. But they were all the Admiralty had been able to find at short notice and at a time when nearly all good officers were involved with Normandy. As one of Arthur George's staff said later: 'We not only got the scrapings of the barracks we also got the scrapings from among the officers.'

Not that Lothian *was short of officers. With all the extra ones needed for the complex Operations and Communications installations there was an abnormal number for a ship of her size – sixty among the ship's complement alone. And Rear-Admiral Talbot brought another thirty-five with him (later the total of officers was to reach 110 – more than one for every seven in the Lower Deck). But there was a very clear division between those manning the ship and 'Staff'. Only when sheer emergency demanded did anyone from the latter get involved in helping run* Lothian *although, in spite of their much smaller numbers, the Staff packed in more well tried experience.*

Apart from Arthur George's immediate personal officers such as his Paymaster Lieutenant-Commander secretary and his Flag Lieutenant there was an R.N. Captain as Chief of Staff and several 'straight ring' Lieutenant-Commanders, including a navigation expert, and a pair of Royal Marine officers, a Lieutenant-Colonel and a Major. To complete his entourage the Admiral also brought two personal stewards, five Marine orderlies, a battery of Writers for his office and various others such as his own signal yeoman.

Some of these, from Captain down to the lowest ranks, Arthur George referred to fondly as 'family'. Throughout his career he had always tried to keep his aides with him wherever he went, at sea or ashore. One of those who had been with him longest was his coxswain, a killick, John Jacobs, who not only 'drove' his Admiral's barge but also doubled up as chauffeur. For the marathon voyage across two mighty oceans with only, it seemed, the jungles and remote atolls of the South-West Pacific ahead there did not appear to be any call for him to perform the latter duty. But the Admiral was not leaving anything to chance.

Soon after Lothian *succeeded, at last, in finding a berth in the James Watt Dock, Greenock, the ship's company watched in amazement as a large Humber '4 by 4' (four-wheel drive) car was hoisted aboard and securely covered in tarpaulins and lashed down on the boat deck. Since there had not yet been any official disclosure of the ship's mission and destination it added to the wild rumours flying around. Cars meant roads and the only war zone with plenty of those was obviously somewhere in Europe. But that belief wavered as the mountain of stores being loaded grew ever larger. Surely there was far too much for just a short voyage?*

The amount being manhandled into the ship for the Staff could have satisfied many a whole warship or a civil service department. There were fifteen tons of cartons of forms and paper alone. All of it, like the huge amounts of ship's equipment, had to be carried down steep ladders into the bowels of the ship by tired, overworked seamen. Despite the many months she had spent under conversion in the shipyard someone had forgotten to install a proper hatch for loading stores. It was an oversight that was to cause the ratings much backache, loss of shore leave and the Navy plenty of despair later on.

For the Jimmy, Lieutenant-Commander Buckel, it was yet another great burden on top of the many he was experiencing as the senior executive officer responsible for ensuring the ship was made ready for sailing. The change of Captains had not helped since it meant more decisions falling on him. In most ships with so many men aboard there would have been a commander between him and Captain but because the Admiralty was strictly following manning procedures for a ship such as the Lothian *no such officer had been appointed. A request that the rule be bent because an abnormally large complement had been put aboard, particularly the R.A.F. and Army contingents, was flatly rejected.*

When he was not busy supervising loading the Jimmy was desperately attempting to fulfil Arthur George's orders that extra accommodation had to be provided in spite of the very brief time left before the Force would depart – only nine days from the day Lothian *entered dock. The ship turned into a bedlam as gangs of dockyard maties swarmed all over her, welding, riveting and hammering yet more bits and pieces on to her upperworks. A completely new Captain's cabin was erected as a separate structure abaft the bridge. Forrard of it another unit went up – made of timber and looking more like a large garden shed.*

Returning aboard after a brief leave Arthur George toured the flagship to see what had been added in his absence. At last he came to where this unnautical looking deckhouse stood. 'And what is that?' he asked sceptically.

'That, sir,' explained the Jimmy, 'is your office.'

Exposed to any rough weather it was no place to conduct or prepare for a landing or do anything in comfort but the Admiral was to use his day room for most of his work and the garden shed was where his Writers handled the outpourings of paperwork.

If the Writers were cramped and sometimes seasick their presence and that of all the many other additions considerably worsened pressure in the messdecks. Lothian *had been converted to carry around 450 officers and men and there were now another 300 over that amount. The worst congestion by far was in the seamen's messdeck although life in the others was also uncomfortable and unhealthy. But the messdecks represented more than just separate physical divisions. As time was to prove more and more they were just material parts of much wider splits. There were always distinctions between various departments in warships, such as between seamen and stokers, marines and bunting tossers, but normally all became welded together in one healthy shipboard spirit. In* Lothian *there were really several different ship's complements simply sharing the one hull.*

The major cause for this was the exceptionally big communications department with its many sparkers and coders who carried on an entirely separate working life (and socially, too); the R.A.F. and the Royal Corps of Signallers, who we regarded as 'passengers'; the sizable 'flotilla' of Royals aboard to man the landing craft and the number of Admiral's Lower Deck staff, who regarded themselves as entirely separate. It would have taken a major effort to form a single, well-knit unit of all these plus the usual ship's ratings and no one made any determined effort to do so.

Nothing at all was done to curb the animosity that directly resulted among the seamen from this much divided situation. They had not been in the Clyde long before they began complaining they were just slaves for everyone else aboard. A.B.s and O.D.s expect to do the dirty jobs,

47

the deckwork and the storing ship, but the presence of so many other men increased their work enormously. Since many of the seamen were making their first voyage to sea and were finding even simple tasks hard the bitterness being created was all the greater.

But there was one 'gripe' that almost everyone in the Lower Deck shared. In spite of the clear signs that the ship was going to go abroad and for a long time there had been no announcement of foreign-going leave being granted. Even in wartime, wherever possible, a few days at home were allowed before a foreign commission began. Had someone in authority thought of it soon enough Lothian's men could have been given some time to visit relations if only for a long weekend. Their Lordships had clearly been so desperate to get the Force to sea that it had pushed aside any such possibility. Now, in Greenock, even the Chiefs and P.O.s were complaining.

They approached the Jimmy. He, in turn, begged the Captain to grant some sort of leave. Following the upward procedure the Captain requested permission from the Admiral. But time was running out. Yes, men in separate 'watches' could, in turn, take 48 hours leave. For most, however, this could mean no more than staying in some Servicemen's hostel in Glasgow. With rail travel in wartime taking so long, most of the time, if not all, would be spent going to and fro. The break from the ship and her squalid conditions was welcome but much of the grievance remained.

If anyone had known just how far and for what reason they were going overseas the dissension could have been far greater but even by wartime standards the secrecy being maintained about Lothian's destination was unusually tight. It was not clear whether this was due to the Admiralty's fear about the enemy finding out. Or was it more about the ratings' reaction if they discovered they were having to continue a long war by being sent in an almost entirely new battle zone for the Royal Navy when hostilities in Europe were reaching their end?

5

All at Sea

'. . . Energetic steps [needed] to improve morale of the Navy
. . . so as to create a will to continue the fight until Japan is
defeated.'

Top Secret Memo from Director of Personnel
Services to the Board of Admiralty, May 8, 1944.

'. . . a line of thought in the Service which says: "We have
finished the German War now it is someone else's turn for the
Japanese War." '

Part of a Staff Officer's minute, dated May 10,
1944, discussed by their Lordships when planning
the sending of the Royal Navy to the Far East and
Pacific.

'If, however, the Lower Deck gradually discovers for themselves that there is going to be little or no demobilisation after
Germany is defeated, grave discontent may occur in ships and
establishments which do not possess the best officers.'

Signal from Senior Officer B4 Escort Group to
Commodore (D) Western Approaches, June 29,
1944. (Four days before the Admiralty approved
Force X.)

All around the raucous noise of ships being loaded and discharged
in the James Watt Dock told how the war effort in Europe was
being pressed to the full but aboard the *Lothian* over 700 officers

49

and men stood in almost awestruck silence. Above the din we had heard 'Noisy' Talbot announce our destination. In one short sentence he had killed all the 'buzzes' about our future. We had been miles off target. It was nowhere in Europe, nor some mysterious mission off Africa or even the Far East. Now we could hardly credit we were actually being sent all the very long way to a battle zone that we had cheerfully assumed was strictly Yankee territory.

The Pacific was the last place in our thoughts as we had heard the pipe: 'Clear Lower Deck. All hands except watchkeepers muster on the quarterdeck.' The latter was no more than this ex-freighter's after welldeck – not large enough to hold the ship's company in orderly ranks and many of us had to cling to guardrails or stays as we waited and wondered why we had suddenly been brought together. The hubbub of noisy speculation died away quickly as into view on the deck forrard and above marched the Admiral with the Captain and the braided phalanx of staff officers.

For most of us it was the first time we had heard what was to become his familiar bark. Wasting no time he proclaimed: 'You have all been waiting anxiously to learn where we are bound and the purpose of our mission. Now I can tell you. H.M.S. *Lothian* is flagship of the assault squadron known as Force X which has been assembled at the urgent request of the United States Navy. As from today we shall form part of its Seventh Fleet when we sail from the Clyde. Our destination is the South-West Pacific and our task is to assist the Americans in the war against Japan.'

If Arthur George expected us to cheer or leap for joy he must have been sadly disappointed. Our only reaction was one of stunned surprise. But before we had time to digest the news he went on to announce something more appealing. 'You will be happy to learn that en route we shall spend several days in New York . . .'

The rest of his words were drowned by a genuine outbreak of noisy pleasure. If there was one port in the whole wide world that mateloes in wartime would have wanted to visit more than any other it was this exciting city overflowing with all the luxuries that had become extinct in wartime Britain. Not to mention the women and booze. All that was all we young O.D.s could talk about as we headed back to the messdeck. It had blotted out our gloomier thoughts about having our war extended to the Pacific.

But not for long. Although we talked excitedly about the orgies of every kind we were going to revel in among the skyscrapers and bars and night spots seen on American movies, a growing sound of discontent was emerging among certain older ratings. Some were clearly furious at being sent so far from home and to a war they insisted was someone else's business. None were angrier or more frustrated than a trio of two A.B.s and a killick (Leading Seaman) who were holding forth in the centre of the messdeck.

One, a Welsh A.B., who had earlier made it abundantly clear to everyone prepared to listen that he should never have been drafted to the ship at all or even to sea since he had had two warships bombed and torpedoed under him, was demanding we take some kind of action to prevent us being sent.

'I tell you boyos they ain't got no right to shove us in with them effing Yanks. Let them buggers fight their own effing war. Where were they when we was catching a packet over 'ere at the start of things, eh?'

From his two oppos, a Scottish rating and the Irish leading hand, came almost equally virulent support. Too belligerent, perhaps. We eighteen-year-old first timers sympathised but were frightened off. There was no way we were going to stick our necks out and risk the undoubted wrath and might of Naval authority by something so audacious as a protest. From the time we had, as nervous civilians, entered the Andrew at the training establishment H.M.S. *Raleigh*, at Torpoint, across from Devonport, we had learnt that however harsh an order was we had to 'jump to it' without question.

There was a formal procedure for registering a complaint up a ponderously slow ascending ladder via Divisional Officer to First Lieutenant and, if important enough, to Captain, but even when a complaint was similarly shared by many it had to be undertaken individually. And becoming a 'Requestman', older hands had warned us, ran the risk of being regarded by authority as a troublemaker.

A few of us had put in requests since embarking in *Lothian* and the experience had left us doubtful of it achieving any good however valid our cause. They rarely got beyond Divisional Officer level and, already, we had a poor regard for the Wavy Navy Lieutenants appointed, theoretically at least, to ensure our discipline and our well being. They seemed scared, or inexperienced enough, to take decisions themselves or pass requests on up the scale. Seamen daring enough to ask for some basic improvements in messdeck conditions had been abruptly told they had no choice but to put up with the existing, desperately poor ones.

The protesting Taffy should certainly have known better than to suggest demanding anything of our superiors let alone a complete reversal of a sailing order. In the short time he had been aboard he had made no less than three requests to be sent back to barracks. He insisted he had, after he lost his last ship through enemy action, been promised a safe berth ashore because of war stress that was seriously affecting his nerves. He had got as far as the Captain who had firmly told him that there was insufficient medical evidence and that if he persisted the next time he came before him it would be as a defaulter.

When the Welshman had come steaming furiously back to reveal this to the messdeck he raised little more reaction than a few belly laughs. An old hand like him should have more sense, he was told. The truth was that because of his persistent griping about what he saw as a blatant injustice he was fast becoming regarded as a messdeck nuisance. We had enough gripes of our own and no one wanted reminding of these or any others.

Yet all we young O.D.s could think of as we at last pushed our bows out into the broad Clyde on August 3 was how we would stand up to a force greater than anything in the Royal Navy – the sea itself. We were green enough already not to want to be any greener.

Convoy U32 slowly assembled off the Oversay Light, on Scotland's West Coast, rather more tardily than its American Commodore liked. Most of the fifty-two vessels, mainly U.S. tankers, had arrived on time but not Force X. Five of the assault ships plus the *Lothian* had left the James Watt Dock and sailed down the Clyde only to find that the sixth was mysteriously nowhere in sight. On his flagship's bridge Rear-Admiral Talbot grew wrathful at seeing his first chance to display Royal Navy efficiency to his Allied partners-to-be ruined. Had not all the L.S.I.s been given their sailing orders, he demanded? Not quite. Someone had forgotten to pass them on to the absent ship. Fortunately her Captain had spotted the rest of the Force departing and hurriedly prepared to sail – but was forced to leave a few of her crew behind.

Like sheepish passengers arriving late for a coach tour the Force eventually tagged on to the convoy under the caustic gaze of the Commodore also peeved at a change of order forced on him by the Royal Navy's presence. Instead of the more direct crossing to New York that would get himself and the many other American seamen back home more speedily he had been instructed to sail further South. An Admiralty signal had requested a route that would reduce the risk of heavy seas to the minimum. It feared, it stated, that the four 'Empire' ships in the Force would run a serious risk of losing their landing craft, slung from davits over the sides, if they rolled as much as 15 degrees. In their high-out-of-the-water light state this was a distinct possibility. To lessen the danger the lower of the two tiers of L.C.A.s usually carried had had to be left behind to follow separately in a specially designated cargo ship.

The engineroom crews, mostly young stokers with no previous experience of any ship let alone the strange type of machinery and boilers in these converted freighters, were finding it difficult to get things right. The *Empire Spearhead* broke down temporarily but, at least, she and her sister ships could normally maintain convoy speed. Not so the *Lamont* which constantly lagged behind forcing the Commodore to slow down our progress. Once her steering gear collapsed adding further delay. By comparison *Lothian* performed reasonably efficiently in spite of some patch-up repairs but, like most of the Force, the inexperience of some engineroom hands could not prevent her committing one of the worst crimes of a ship in wartime.

I was working on deck when I saw great volumes of black smoke billowing from our funnel – enough to alert every enemy U-boat for miles around. The consternation on the bridge was matched by the fury with which one of our U.S. Navy escorts came tearing up. As she drew alongside her Captain bellowed to us over his loudhailer: 'Am I to be held responsible for your smoke as well, Admiral?'

It was, we discovered, a reference to the fact that because we were part of a Merchant Navy convoy Arthur George had decided to hand over Naval command to the escorts. The U.S. Navy commander seemed happy to have a sly dig at us for our blatant inefficiency – underlined by the way the lagging *Lamont* continued to be easily identified by constant smoke signals. Her Chief

53

Engineer was later to suffer stern retribution although for a more personal offence. His ship's Red Indian uprising symbol remained her identification signal long after he abruptly departed.*

Nothing marked the greenness of many of *Lothian*'s seamen so much as the way scores of us became useless with seasickness and remained so for a good part of our crossing to New York.

For once we were oblivious to our normal squalor, avoiding the messdeck, to find any corner where we could retch out of sight of unsympathetic P.O.s and officers who tried making us carry out normal duties. Being absent from one's watchkeeping station was a serious crime but we cared as little about that as we did about the prospect of the ship being sunk – we might have welcomed it, in fact. The forenoon of the second morning at sea several of us had found sanctuary in the large operations room, temporarily unmanned. It was a strange place to divulge confidences in between our nausea.

In our extremis all we could think of was home and loved ones, or the lack of them. Oggie, who, for once, couldn't bear the thought of food, moaned: 'What I wouldn't do to be back 'ome. I used to think my dad was dead stupid swallowing the 'ook (leaving the sea) to come back to a crummy Cornish village. Right now I'd give an arm to be alongside 'im.'

'All right for some,' muttered Scouse. 'My dad copped it in the blitz – a jerry bomb blew 'im and the rest of a busload to bits just as 'e was going on nightshift at the docks.'

It was the first time we had been told this tragic fact and it left us sympathetic and stunned – until sickness overcame us again.

Then it was Yorkie's turn to capture our barely sustained emotion. 'Didn't rightly know my da'. 'E got the wrong side of a threshing machine. Me mum brought me and my sis' up, like. 'Ow she did it an' kept farm going Gawd knows. That's why I wish real bad, like, I was 'ome. Jenny, that's my sis', joined t'Women's

* In his first 'Letter of Proceedings' to the Admiralty Rear-Admiral Talbot refers to the black smoke blaming 'inexperienced engineroom crews'. He also complained that the haste with which the Force had been prepared prevented exercises being carried out. In dealing with the problem of repairs that could not be done in Greenock he mentions sending his Staff Commander Engineer on ahead by air to New York to arrange for them to be carried out there. In the event shortage of time prevented most of this.

Land Army and left farm. Now Ma's got a 'ole flock of sheep to keep on't own.'

You could always tell when Yorkie was 'omesick. He lapsed deeper into the vernacular. Usually it just raised a laugh among the rest of the O.D.s as when he once told Oggie he was 'like dook guzzling in't scarp'ole'. Or, as he translated, like a duck grubbing in a puddle of rain. Now we just felt sorry for him, understanding his longing far more.

I felt the others' eyes, doubt clearly written in them. Scouse summed up the general opinion: 'I suppose you've 'ad it pretty soft ain't you?'

My middle-of-the-road accent plus a shyness about the cruder forms of Lower Deck life had already marked me as an outsider and I wasn't going to push myself still further to the fringe. I discreetly kept to myself that truth about being the son of a former Royal Navy Paymaster, now commanding a unit of the Sea Cadet Corps, in view of the average ratings' loathing for 'pigs'. I simply admitted I had been brought up 'just ordinary – nothing posh'. In an effort to encourage a little support I added that one brother was a seaman in the Merchant Navy. But I kept back anything about another one who was a War Correspondent or that all three of us had chosen journalism for a career. It would only have emphasised the difference.

Only Cockie and Mick were absent from our heart-to-heart, retch-to-retch chat although we knew where the former was. For all his boasting and his great air of being your real 'Jack' no one had succumbed more to seasickness than him – so badly that he'd been whipped off to the sickbay. We regarded that as an unfair advantage. 'Always was a jammy bastard,' swore Oggie. ' 'E told me 'is dad keeps a boozer in the East End, where all the crooks and black marketeers 'ang out. Says 'e could always lay 'is 'ands on all kinds of rabbits (illegal goods).'

'You can't believe a word 'e says – a real bullshitter is Cockie,' announced Scouse scathingly.

'Not like Mick – 'e's so effing 'oly it's a wonder 'e ain't a sin bosun (chaplain),' sneered Oggie.

'Be fair t'lad,' begged Yorkie. ' 'E told me 'e was brought up in't orphanage. At least we got some folks left.'

In that sad and sick frame of mind and body we endured our soul and stomach searching for a few minutes longer before we heard the Ops Room door bang open and a Wavy Navy Lieutenant appear. At first he looked askance but smelling, if not seeing our trouble, he softened.

Obviously not an executive officer but one of the strange breed of communications and cypher specialists he let us go with a gentle lecture. Our gratitude went only so far. 'A right poncey bugger,' was how Scouse summed him up later. It would take more than kind words to win our respect for officers we regarded as useless in almost every way.

This attitude was not improved when we had been at sea a week and were steaming west of the Azores. We heard our very first call to Action Stations. Still lacking proper sea legs let alone any warlike attitudes we reacted like a dormitory of schoolgirls suddenly finding a burglar in their midst. Apart from one brief emergency drill there had been no chance to get a proper grasp of our action stations and we responded with slowness and doubt. Only the fierce verbal whippings from the P.O.s got us, eventually, to our gun, radar or other posts. I suspect that if it had been an aerial attack we would have been sunk before a shot could have been fired or a radar wave brought to bear.

The multitude of officers we carried seemed in just as bad a predicament, dashing hither and thither and getting in each other's way. It was not the kind of scene to inspire eighteen-year-old O.D.s. As it happened the alarm resulted from the supposed asdic (sonar) contact with a U-boat by one of our U.S. escorts, backed by an alleged periscope sighting by one of the merchant vessels. Nothing further materialised except a heated dressing down of everyone from officers to Lower Deck by Arthur George. From then on until we sighted New York he made our life a misery with one set of emergency drills after another.

While it did smarten us up it did not inspire us with any do-or-die sense of duty or raise our morale. Returning to the dosshouse that was our messdeck after every drill we found our spirits tumbling yet again. The off-duty conversations still held a strong measure of discontent, especially among the disgruntled A.B.s and leading hands upset at being sent so far foreign. The younger seamen tried pushing all this aside with their dreams about the erotic delights supposedly awaiting in New York.

If we talked like seamen who had not seen a port or a woman for months instead of a bare few days it was more an indication of everything we had missed during four long years of war. It was incredible to us that we should soon be in a city with no blackout curtains, no blitz damage and boundless food and other abundant delights. The fact it would be the very first foreign port for most of us sent our expectations dangerously skyhigh. Older, wiser heads would have told us that we would still be treated as the lowest of the low in H.M. Navy with all the work and unbending discipline that incurred. Yet we acted more as though we were cruise ship passengers about to be treated to the highlight of a holiday voyage.

Of course we were not. Even emigrants had got better accommodation and food than we were experiencing. But our longing to escape our grim steel box of a messdeck only added to our eagerness to step ashore in the American city. Later we were to recall these almost uncontainable emotions and realise that this was the point where life in *Lothian* really started going badly wrong for us.

6

Statue Sans Liberty

If anything can be more impressive than the New York skyline approached up the Hudson River it can only be the added sight of some great ocean liner arriving. H.M.S. *Lothian* in her drab camouflage and mis-shapen superstructure was certainly not that. Nor did we have the benefit of any ceremonial, fountainous jet welcome, so often given to big passenger ships. But Rear-Admiral Talbot wasn't going to let the obvious disadvantages stand in the way of his efforts to create the best impression. No creeping quietly in to our berth as virtually all the hundreds of vessels did when entering wartime New York, warships included. No, our arrival was to be as ceremonious as he could make it.

From the moment that awe-inspiring sight of the great sky-scrapers hove into view the whole ship's company, including the R.A.F. and Army contingents, were lined up at attention along every inch of open deck space. Had we been in some mighty battleship or even a sleek destroyer the scene might have made a stirring impression on any watching Americans. As it was we must have looked an even odder sight – more like a tramp in a stolen dress coat. The catcalls from the crews of the two tugs that came to take our tow lines showed how peculiar they thought it was.

A Royal Marine band might have added more dignity to the proceedings but the Admiral had come up with a substitute for that, too. We ratings were stirring uneasily in the unaccustomed heat of the local high summer when we almost jumped from our skins. From the eyes of the bow came the loud, plaintive wailing of what seemed a soul in agony.

'Gawd, someone's murdering the cat,' gasped Cockie alongside me.

'More like a 'uman sacrifice,' whispered Yorkie.

It was neither. Standing there at the 'sharp end' was a rating manfully blowing a set of bagpipes, clearly a little out of practice but slowly working up to a powerful rendition of some Scottish lament, reel or pibroch.

The P.O. in charge of us looked shocked. 'Who the 'ell is 'e and who gave 'im permission to play that flaming thing?' he asked of the world in general.

None of us knew. Not until later. The culprit, as we saw him, was a New Zealand bunting tosser (signalman) of Scottish descent. In fairness he had brought his pipes along only for some reasonably private practice but Arthur George had heard of his talent and before the unwilling rating knew what was happening he had had himself appointed official ship's piper. Each time we entered any port he had to perform his one-man band act just as though we were some Scottish Regiment going 'over the top' in Flanders. It didn't stop there, either. Whether the Admiral had certain baronial pretensions or not, I do not know, but the Kiwi was detailed to march up and down piping outside Talbot's cabin when he was entertaining guests to dinner.

Our first sound of him, however, only added to our irritation. It was however more physical than aesthetic. As we stood baking in line under the hot sun we itched furiously. The reason was also the cause of our untidy appearance. In a misguided effort to smarten us up we had just been issued with so-called 'whites' – full-length drills that were, in reality, made of heavy grey-looking canvas material. They were as unbendingly stiff as they were immensely uncomfortable. As we perspired profusely under their weight the coarse cloth and sweat caused the uncontrollable itching so that we hopped about like a party of schoolchildren desperate to spend a penny.

Where these archaic uniforms had come from nobody knew. 'Postie', the ancient three-badge (good conduct stripes) A.B. who had come out of retirement for the war and had been given the easy-going postman's job, looked at them in amazement. 'I 'aven't seen the likes of these since I was in the 'ood (Hood) before the war,' he recalled. 'They must 'ave bin lying around in the slops (clothes stores) at Guz for years.'

If they had any virtue at all it was they could stand to attention on their own, they were *that* stiff. We begged Postie to show us how we could soften them up but he shook his head sadly. 'We used to stick 'em in a bucket with some caustic for days or tie 'em at the end of an 'eaving line and tow 'em astern to make 'em wearable, but you jest ain't got time for that.'

As we reluctantly donned them for entering harbour we knew what the knights of old must have suffered putting on suits of armour. But worse was to come. As the *Lothian* edged slowly up to berth alongside Pier 45 in the narrow canyon between dominating warehouses the seamen got the order to stand by the hawsers ready to tie up. 'What about changing into overalls?' enquired Scouse, like the rest of us, not believing we were being expected to handle dirty ropes in our new, supposedly best uniforms.

'Do what you're told – it's not my idea,' barked our P.O. Neither, apparently, was it the Jimmy's. Someone above him, and we could guess who, had insisted that wearing working gear would create a loss of smartness. That was certainly missing when we eventually completed mooring ship with the 'whites' blackened all over with stains from wet hawsers and oil. Out thoughts were just as filthy. Here we were poised on going ashore in this exciting city, eager to sample all the luxuries we had missed for so long, but likely to be refused due to the dirty state of our clothes.

Dinner that day was ignored as we desperately scrubbed and swabbed the uniforms with paint remover succeeding mainly in simply distributing the stains in a more even, greyer way. In the process we succeeded in adding wrinkles where there had only been stiff creases. Yet, we could have taken more time. Our assumption that we would be allowed ashore as soon as possible was quickly squashed. This time it was back into overalls and we were herded on to the quay to load stores . . . the first of a veritable mountain of them. That day and for the remainder of our stay in New York an unending stream of trucks arrived with their contents to be manhandled as we strained and sweated in what was the hottest local heatwave for fifty years, according to the city press.

I suppose the remarkable thing was that we were allowed liberty at all that first day in port. But it was past seven o'clock before we could step down the gangway. Our 'whites' (greys was a better word) looked no better but, fortunately, the descending darkness hid all but our general dishevelment. Our excitement was still running high but no longer matched by our energy. Storing ship had nearly exhausted us and wearing our heavy, uncomfortable uniforms in a temperature still in the high 80s, sapped much of our remaining strength. The fantasies we had held about whooping it up on Broadway slid from us as quickly as our sweat. Even if we had been in a fitter state there was still a major obstacle to overcome. A more poverty-stricken bunch of 'jacks' could rarely have gone ashore here. All we had been given in the way of cash was ten dollars per Ordinary Seaman.

In the messdeck beforehand we had miserably discussed what we could spend such a small handout on. 'Hookie', our Leading Hand of the mess, jeered: 'That won't even get you a stand-up bang-off. You'd be better off 'eading for the Sally Ann or one of them forces canteens where they gives you free scoff.'

It was a sensible solution yet hardly the glamorous notion we held of rubbing shoulders with 'gangsters and their molls' in some shady nightclub or bar. The idea that many held of getting 'rotten drunk' was also a non-starter unless booze was a give away price here. But with hopes still high we headed into the unaccustomed pleasure of brightly lit streets with no threat of bombs descending. Our aim was to find the servicemen's mecca of Times Square, the 'Stagedoor Canteen'. It was a measure of our naivety that we had no idea of how to get there and were nervous about taking strange public transport. For awhile we strolled along the streets gazing hungrily at the almost forgotten sight of shops filled with food and clothes. None of these entranced us more than a greengrocer's. For the first time in over four years we saw bananas. Forgetting any idea of booze and women we pressed inside demanding enough to keep a colony of apes happy. We must have looked like monkeys as we squatted on the hot kerbstone munching them for all we were worth.

Precious liberty time was flying by and we knew we must press on if we were to reach the truly bright lights but the saturating heat and our irksome uniforms slowed us to a crawl. It was then that another reminder of what we had been missing for so long in wartime Britain finally brought us to a halt. The drugstore has always been an institution in America and to us tired, thirsty mateloes the first one we saw looked as magnificent as the banqueting hall of the finest stately home. We descended on its icecream counter like pirates about to pillage a Spanish galleon. I don't know how many times we 'went round the buoy', but judging by the reaction of the audience of New Yorkers we attracted we must have set some kind of record.

It was only when our meagre money was exhausted that we struggled to our feet and headed slowly back towards our ship. Only Oggie was smiling, however, for the rest of us felt pretty sick. I couldn't help thinking what a lot of idiots we would have looked if we had vomited when we got aboard. Nothing unusual in ratings doing that but never through having one icecream over the eight.

We slept badly that night. The messdeck had become an oven that was cooking our overdose of fruit and icecream into a devilish banana split. As we slouched up on deck the next morning early to fall in for duty we looked a sad, dissolute lot. The officer taking charge of us obviously put the cause on the more obvious nautical sins. 'Look at you!' he snorted. 'You're a disgrace to the Royal Navy. You booze and shag yourselves silly all night and couldn't care less about being fit for work. But there'll be plenty of that for you I can tell you.'

It was blatantly unfair and, in the majority of cases, totally untrue. We stirred angrily and there were mutterings of protest – quickly subdued by the Petty Officers. But the damage had been done. We were not to forget those remarks and for weeks after they were to lie in our potentially explosive thoughts like a slow burning fuse. The officers, however, appeared oblivious to their danger. Not so much some of the P.O.s. Later that long, boiling and exhausting day I overheard a couple discussing the incident as they stood in the shade supposedly supervising us. 'He can't push these lads like that – H.O.s (Hostilities Only) got to be treated more gently,' one commented. 'You're right – 'e's asking for trouble,' added the other.

If we had been local longshoremen there is no doubt we would have gone on strike as we toiled in temperatures touching 100°F trying to make some indentation in the enormous amount of stores arriving. All the time we were hampered and had our labours doubled by that failure during conversion to install a hatch for loading. Every single item once it was swung on to the limited deck space had to be manhandled down two steep ladders through the messdeck and down through a tiny opening in the deck. It was physically impossible for us to cope with the ever increasing backlog which spewed over to create piles of crates and cartons along alleyways and as far back as the Admiral's deck.

As it edged its way there Jimmy did his utmost to prevent it actually spilling over on to this holy ground and more or less succeeded. But Arthur George was far from satisfied as we learnt from our Leading Hand, Hookie. ' 'E gave Jimmy a right bollocking. Told 'im the ship was a right disgrace and 'e wasn't doing 'is job proper. That weren't the end of it. Ole blood-and-guts was back again a few minutes later complaining there were dirty finger marks on 'is cabin door. "I suppose it's not possible for you to keep a clean ship," ' mimicked Hookie.

How anyone could possibly expect normal shipwork to be carried out when every single seaman was detailed for storing was a mystery to us but we underestimated the Admiral's determination to have a truly pusser flagship. That became obvious that afternoon when we heard Arthur George's loud growl to Jimmy on the foredeck. 'Why is that rating wearing his cap flat aback?' he demanded. 'See to it he's correctly dressed.'

We gazed up at the target of his wrath. There, sitting at the controls of the ship's crane helping bring in the stores, was a stoker with his cap tilted to the back of his head. It was clearly to avoid it rubbing in the sweat pouring from his forehead and if not correctly worn was practical. But a yell from Jimmy quickly had it replaced in orthodox trim. We nervously pushed ours into the right angle as well although having to wear caps at all was a nuisance. By now we were so hot that it would have been hazardous to strike a match anywhere near us. But our inner fury was even greater.

Somehow we had to find an outlet for our tired frustration at having to work so hard when such lurid temptations as New York could offer were just the other side of the pier gates. They fell, not unjustifiably, on the rest of the ship's complement but especially on the R.A.F. and Army contingents.

In our eyes they had always been 'passengers' spending most of their time loafing about with no real duties to perform. Now we had to slave away as we watched them stroll ashore shortly after breakfast with a full day and night to enjoy all the delights we were missing. We were barely less annoyed at seeing the rest of the ratings aboard getting their run ashore while we were still busily loading ship. We seethed with the injustice of it all, made heated protests to our P.O.s, who were sympathetic, but all to no avail.

That second day in port was worse than the first. Far worse. Storing went on after the first dog watch (4 to 6 p.m.) when we had hoped we would be let off the leash; throughout the second dog and on through the whole of the first (8 to midnight). Unbelievably we didn't stop until 3 a.m. The next time we turned to was 6 a.m.!

Had we been less exhausted and less dispirited, the trouble that was clearly brewing might have erupted sooner. As it was we had become like automatons – almost incapable of passing crude comments on the sight of officers all dressed up to kill striding ashore or being waited on by the cars of socialite New Yorkers. According to the buzzes that descended to us from the wardroom stewards, the British colony was providing them with everything from cocktail parties to nightclub orgies. That they were having a splendid time was not in doubt with Arthur George going still one better. That second day after registering his emphatic views about the state of the ship we had seen him come down the gangway followed by a steward bearing a suitcase and being driven away in an official black limousine. The buzz was that he was off to meet with his American Navy masters. But not only that. The Admiral, we learnt, had booked himself into a hotel for the rest of our stay.

In a way we could accept the Grand Canyon of a gulf between officers and men if only we had the opportunity to enjoy our own particular, if more earthy, pleasures. The chances of doing that in the last two full days we lay alongside were severely reduced by not being allowed liberty until after 6 p.m. one evening and 8 p.m. on the other. We had also, to a large extent, lost both our physical and mental will to whoop it up. Even donning those corrugated hard uniforms was a drudgery we would gladly have avoided. Exchanging one sweatbath of a messdeck for another in the humid, steaming streets of the city seemd an unwelcome choice. But we had, by some miracle, been granted an extra five dollars and as mean a pittance as this was we had a mateloe's usual desperate urge to spend any cash we possessed.

It was just enough to pay our bus fare up to Times Square and Broadway, which by now had assumed all the significance of a Holy Land Crusade. Perhaps we could also buy one of those cheap, tawdry souvenirs that seamen are easily hypnotised by (ours were either models of the Statue of Liberty with its Freudian significance for us or of the Empire State Building) plus a picture postcard or two. Not that we could send them home since it would have broken wartime secrecy about ship's movements but they were proof, at least, of any boasts we would later make to family and friends about having been there. But any thought of buying a drink let alone a fat, juicy steak was clearly not on. It didn't prevent our increasing hunger, far from satiated by the poor food aboard.

Shedding any idea of repeating our icecream marathon we wandered slowly back through the streets fringing Greenwich Village eyeing the gay scenes inside the various small eating places but having our watering mouths dehydrated by the prices demanded. It was then that Scouse spotted the board boldly positioned outside one of New York's typical firestone buildings. It read in fiery print: 'All Servicemen Welcome. Food and Friendship Happily Given.'

'Come on, what are you waiting for?' urged Scouse starting to make a dash for the place.

'But . . . but it's an effing Sally Ann,' Cockie pointed out protestingly. 'You ain't going in one of them for Gawd's sake.'

'Speak for yourself,' said Mick. 'There's nothing wrong with the Salvation Army.'

'Yes, what's more the grub's free,' said Oggie emphatically.

That did it. We trooped in, not a little bashfully, but certainly hungry. I was thinking how Hookie's advice had at last proved correct.

As tired and bedraggled as we looked we were received with loud cries of welcome by the smiling Salvationists clearly glad to have won over some of 'you English boys'. Would we like some coke or one of the other distinctly unhard drinks? Our great thirst overcame any latent effort at seeming more manly. The sight of batteries of hamburgers and frankfurters; lemon pie and large buns lowered any remaining religious resistance.

After wolfing enough to make even the citadel's soldiers glance anxiously at supplies we at last relaxed content. But not for long. 'Free' as the food had been advertised it was not without a certain price. Just as we were considering making our way back to the ship the Army Captain suddenly announced: 'Now boys I think it's time we gave our thanks to the Good Lord for all we have received.' With that he began intoning a prayer that was as long as our faces. Sheepishly we rose to our feet not knowing whether we were expected to clasp our hands in prayer or not. More embarrassment was to follow. After what seemed ages the Captain announced a hymn. Normally I enjoyed a good Moody and Sankey but not in front of a bunch of atheistic mateloes. Three hymns later and feeling more foolish than forgiven we emerged.

Cockie's first words expressed most of the feelings. 'If any of you lot of muckers says one effing word about where we bin I'll thump seven bells of shit out of 'im.'

It was not that we were ashamed of visiting a Sally Ann canteen but more that we did not want to lose face among other seamen we were sure had been living it up ashore in true hairy-chested Jack fashion. We need not have worried. Arriving back aboard before our liberty was up we found most in the messdeck had also returned and most remarkably sober. Some willingly admitted they had been too tired and too skint. The thought that they would face yet another's day's hard grafting from 6 a.m. had forced them back to get what sleep they could. Instead of the blissful time they had expected they seemed to be in a more bloody frame of mind.

As I turned into my hammock I remembered the parting words of the Salvation Army Captain: 'God keep you and protect you.'

It would need an even mightier power than his to do so I firmly believed.

7

H.M.S. Unsanitary

Like many of his seamen Rear-Admiral Talbot was not having a pleasant stay in New York. But for totally different reasons. The failure to carry out most of the urgent repairs and additions to his flagship was one. Sending his Commander Engineer ahead to ensure the vital work was done had largely proved a wasted effort. More disconcerting was clear evidence that Force X could not expect much help from the Americans even though it was part of its 7th Fleet.

Soon after Lothian *berthed he had flown to Washington, D.C., having sought a meeting with Admiral King so that he could better establish the role his force would play in the Pacific, especially its part in the approaching Philippines invasion. But although their talk had lasted nearly an hour Arthur George had had to come away no wiser and certainly no happier. King had been courteous but cold – even apparently puzzled as to why the British Admiral and his flagship should have been sent. He seemed impervious to the latter's suggestion that with all his D-Day experience and that of his staff they would be a great asset in Pacific assaults. All King would agree was that as the Force had come this far it might as well continue on its mission.**

Returning to New York, by rail, Arthur George found a more immediate worry. The lame duck Lamont *was in trouble again, only*

* Staff officers who accompanied Admiral Talbot to this chilly meeting spoke to me of King's reluctance and suspicion about the Force. One of them claims he was definitely mystified about the Force's intentions. Unaware of the signal he had ostensibly sent asking for six L.S.I.s, they were surprised about it in view of his reactions. Whatever the truth they feel he was probably forced, possibly by

more seriously. Undergoing brief repairs in the Brooklyn Navy Yard more mechanical mishaps had occurred.

To within a few hours of the Force's sailing time she was incapable of putting to sea. The day before, the 17th, her boilers had failed totally. There was not a drop of water or a light available throughout the ship. Her meagre ventilation system had broken down and her troop decks became stuffy, darkened dungeons. And this was how the first detachment of servicemen due to sail in her found conditions. All told some 800 men, mainly U.S. soldiers, were due to board.

It was hardly surprising Arthur George was angry. News of the Lamont's *dire state had been brought him by Britain's Resident Naval Officer in New York, who reported that on seeing the state of the ship the first body of men who happened to be a party of Royal Australian Air Force men 'hitching a lift' back to the Pacific had refused point blank to sail in her. Their action had, stated the R.N.O., been approved by an R.A.A.F. officer in Washington. But there was worse. Perhaps as a result of the Australians' refusal the G.I.s following on behind had also turned the ship down.*

Shortly after the Admiral received a request from the U.S. Army for permission to send one of its M.O.s for an official inspection of the Lamont *to see if she was really unfit. Talbot insisted on his own staff doctor being present. The American had no hesitation in declaring the ship unfit for trooping. The British officer was more cautious. Although, he explained, the* Lamont *could not be considered a 'bed of roses for trooping in the tropics' he felt the poor conditions were due mainly to the boiler and other machinery failures that were being quickly put right.*

But the more detailed report that the Admiral received from the U.S. Army after a second inspection made it quite clear that it wasn't just the temporary failures that led to its rejecting the ship: '. . . found inadequate toilets, galley, refrigerated stores, ventilation, recreational space, laundry for over twelve-hour trip.' The killing line at the end read: 'Vessel now suitable as cargo ship.'

Arthur George was forced to accept the American refusal although he

---

Roosevelt (with Churchill's persuasion), to agree some Royal Navy participation.

The Admiralty also seemed to be playing a very canny role where the Americans were concerned. Some of its distrust of what the U.S. Navy might do with the Force is evident in the special orders it gave to Admiral Talbot. These can be found in Appendix I.

considered their objections exaggerated.* He could have left Lamont
*behind since she no longer served any current useful purpose and would
almost certainly continue to prove a ball-and-chain on the Force's
progress towards the South-West Pacific. Yet he decided to proceed in
her company. He was convinced that if she could be got to the war zone
she could still serve some useful purpose. It was a decision he was to rue
almost at once and with growing reason in the future.*

We had paid our farewell to the Manhattan skyline. It now lay in a
haze behind us. But we still lay off the entrance to the Hudson.
Just six of the Force. The missing member? The *Lamont*, natur-
ally. Admiral Talbot paced the bridge impatiently as we steamed
aimlessly around at dead slow speed constantly glancing towards
the U.S. shoreline. At last a cloud of black smoke confirmed the
appearance of our lame duck. No other ship could reveal herself in
such a flagrantly unwarlike fashion. Her boilers and other machinery had been patched up – just.

Yet we still left some behind. About a dozen men had deserted
from *Lothian*, including two of the R.A.F. contingent. In the
seamen's messdeck we were surprised that not more of us had
stayed ashore. Only the fact that desertion in wartime and on
active service carried a very severe penalty could have stopped
some who we knew were desperate to leave. Later they deeply
regretted their missed opportunity. Surprisingly we had remarkably few defaulters due to overstaying their liberty or to drunkenness. Lack of shore leave and money could have been the only
explanation. In one way we were glad to leave. Getting to sea we
might at least derive some benefit from ocean breezes for in the
New York heatwave the messdeck had become even more unbearable.

---

* In referring to the incident in his Letter of Proceedings Admiral Talbot
added his opinion: 'I cannot refrain from commenting on the initial action of the
R.A.A.F., which seems to have precipitated the incident. In time of war such
action reflects little credit on either their service or our country in the eyes of the
Americans.'
   Further on he refers to an inspection he made of the *Lamont* in Balboa when he
'formed the opinion that her accommodation did not appear worse than any other
L.S.I.'. But subsequent signals from Talbot to the Admiralty confirmed there
were numerous complaints by American troops of conditions and lack of facilities
in the Landing Ships.

As Force X at last formed into some semblance of naval order, the L.S.I.s and their total of 4,000 G.I.s in line astern and H.M.S. *Lothian* to the centre rear of the twin columns, we gave a last look at the New York skyline. Would we ever see any civilisation again? Ahead lay a voyage of over 10,000 miles and while we were sad to leave the bright lights we were far from sorry not to have to suffer any longer the agony of those four tortuous days loading ship. But there was a constant reminder of them in the ship's even more unwieldy appearance caused by large piles of stores that still remained on the upper deck. It had proved totally impossible in the time to stow it all because of the lack of space and a proper hatch. Once again the Jimmy had been at the receiving end of Arthur George's irritation at seeing his flagship look more like a tramp vessel although the former could have done little about the problem. However, we saw it as poetic justice.

Yet we had been incensed by one particularly annoying incident. Just as we seemed to have finished our marathon loading several trucks arrived bearing what was for us a delicacy well worth exerting an extra effort . . . hundreds of cartons of orange juice. Not only was this an unheard-of luxury in wartime Britain but it would help relieve our thirst and risk of vitamin deficiency in the tropics. To our dismay the order came to leave it behind because the storerooms were already overflowing. Since most of our efforts had been given to loading such dreary items as dehydrated vegetables, flour and other basics we were infuriated. No sooner had the officers and P.O.s turned their backs than we hurriedly put as many of the cartons into the cargo slings as possible and had them swung aboard hoping they would go unnoticed among the mountain of stores on deck.

We had not reckoned with the problem of stowage once we put to sea. Nor with Arthur George's demand for smartness. Soon after sailing the order came down from on high: 'The upper deck must be cleared of stores at all costs.'

We sweated for hours trying to find somewhere for the massive amount, squeezing all we could into any nook and cranny as long as it was out of sight. But there was still a considerable pile left on deck. It was then that the Jimmy took what, I suppose, was the only action left to him.

'Heave them over the side,' he ordered.

If we had been told to throw loved ones or barrels of rum into the

70

sea we could not have been more upset. Among the boxes bobbing up and down in our wake went the precious orange juice. For days afterwards the incident caused bitter talk around the messdeck. A 'crime against humanity', Mick called it indignantly. Others put it more bluntly. It was one more grievance to lie smouldering inside us.

We were spared little time, however, to dwell on our miseries as the Admiral set about trying to mould us into some kind of recognisable fighting force – both in *Lothian* and in the rest of the Force. We needed it, we knew, but we found it hard to cope with the endless round of gunnery practices, fire drills and other emergency exercises in the growing heat as we steamed South. Tiredness turned into exasperation when Arthur George added several peculiar and, to us, quite unnecessary manoeuvres. Once he ordered the ship to heave to while two landing craft were lowered for the purpose of trying to tow the *Lothian* around in a complete circle.

What emergency this was supposed to cope with we could not guess and even the experienced ratings thought it odd. Viewing the Royals vainly attempting to carry out the towing Postie commented wonderingly: 'I've served under a few Admirals but they ain't done nothing like this.

'Mind you,' he went on, 'we 'ad a Flag Officer aboard a battleship I was on in the 'Ome Fleet and 'e got up to some queer tricks. 'E was for always ordering us to take the cutters and whalers away and row like 'ell after the ship while she steamed away from us. If we looked like catching up the bugger used to increase speed an' 'e wouldn't let us alongside till we was 'Arry Flakers.

' 'E used to say it was for the good of our 'ealth. Bollocks! 'E was just a sadistic old sod. But we got the better of 'im. The boat's crew I wuz in fixed it between ourselves to give 'im a right scare. As we wuz rowing after the ship one day an A.B. whips the bung out while the cox ain't looking and within minutes we wuz swimming around in the 'oggin. Mind you we 'ad lifejackets on.

'When we gets back aboard after being picked up we reports a man missing. Makes a real big show of it – says the missing rating 'ad an 'eart attack because of the rowing. They spend a couple of hours searching and then the bloke turns up aboard! Says 'e passed out when 'e got aboard and 'ad bin lying unconscious in the 'eads.

71

After that the Admiral gets shit scared the nut'ouse will 'ear about it and packs it in.'

We O.D.s would have liked to have tried some such ploy on Arthur George but he seemed far too impregnable. From what we could judge he seemed to be Flag Officer, Captain, Jimmy and every officer rolled into one. He certainly took a very close part in shipboard affairs. With Captain Petrie preferring to keep to his cabin; the Jimmy hopelessly overworked, hardly enough watch-keeping officers and the remainder either specialists or too green to count, the Admiral might have felt compelled to exercise more control than a Flag Officer normally does. He was also just as determined to keep the officers and men aboard the L.S.I.s on their toes with signals flashing out or hoisted from the yardarm all day long.

The more orders that went out to the ships the more they seemed to wander off course for few of these unwieldy ex-freighters were capable of reacting mechanically in the same way and time. Several times there were near collisions and even the normal business of maintaining station in line astern proved hazardous with ships getting too close or yawing off a straight line like the top heavy Empires. The only 'safe' vessel was the *Lamont* which kept lagging so much that she was usually out of harm's way. It was all a perpetual source of irritation to Arthur George, clearly determined to weld his command into something approaching smartness and aware that it was under the constant gaze of our four U.S. Navy escorts. Their Captains and crews could not have been impressed and they, too, must have become a bit irritated with the stream of commands that kept them always altering course and position.

Thankfully, on the third day after leaving New York, we received an emergency order from the U.S.N. command ashore to divert to Charleston, South Carolina, to take shelter from an impending hurricane threatening to head north along the Eastern Seaboard. None of us had any idea what this Southern Carolina port was like but it raised our spirits at the thought of at last getting a decent run ashore. At least we could be sure there would be no more stores to load. To cap our delight we were granted leave to begin soon after berthing. But the piped announcement added nothing about being given the necessary dollars with which to enjoy ourselves. In alarm a small deputation went to the

'Paybob's' office but were bluntly told no money was available. It was no consolation to us ratings as we stepped ashore that barely anyone in the Lower Deck had a cent to spend between them.

The 'Deep South' has its compelling charms but none of them could lift our deep despair. If there is a more foreboding sight than a mateloe letting off steam as he spends his back pay it is that of one moping miserably past bars and other tempting dens of vice completely broke.

This time we had no qualms about seeking out anywhere that offered free sustenance and would probably have volunteered to sing any hymn and not just the nautical version, either. But in the strange streets of Charleston we soon lost our way and appeared to be getting ever deeper into the rambling black sector of the city. At last we rested our tired feet and steaming bodies in those much hated 'whites' on a bench in a small, crowded square. The hordes of children and the groups of men standing around the corners eyed us curiously until one tough looking character made a direct approach. 'You sailors looking for fun?' he enquired.

'A beer would be more like it,' groaned Cockie.

'Sure, man, I can get you all the beer you want and plenty more besides,' the stranger replied.

When we admitted our total poverty he seemed to be unconvinced as though we were setting out to bargain but, to add encouragement, he announced: 'Where I'll take you boys the beer's on the house.'

We glanced at each other suspiciously but the offer was too tempting for us to hold back. Anyway we were in the proverbial 'beggars can't . . .' situation. Our limbs feeling less weary we followed our guide through a tangle of alleys until we found ourselves being led down some steps under an old wooden building. I had never been in a shebeen but that was what I imagined the crowded, smoke filled and altogether squalid atmosphere of the small room with bar we were now in must be.

'Hey, give these sailors a beer – they got a thirst like a mule,' our black saviour yelled at the fattest woman I'd ever seen. Within seconds we had our hands round cans of American beer and were making sure their contents were inside us before anyone changed their minds. Only then did we start peering through the haze to see exactly what we had been led into. The expressions on our eighteen-year-old faces must have said all. Apart from a couple of black men the seats and walls were totally occupied by women in skirts and blouses that told all.

While the rest of us looked startled Mick's face was torn into positive horror. He burst out: 'Let's get out of here – we're in a whorehouse!'

'For Gawd's sake keep your voice down,' begged Cockie, 'they'll effing well murder us.'

'No wonder they 'anded us the beer – it's a bloody come on,' moaned Yorkie.

But Mick was already half way to the door. Should we stay or run after him? It was an agonising decision but our minds were made up by the menacing looks now coming from the two men and the very stout woman, who was obviously the 'Madam'. In one mad dash we followed Mick outside, up the steps and down the alley while, behind, came bellows of fury.

We didn't stop running until we reached the first, more brightly lit street. Still glancing nervously over our shoulders we slowly got our breath back. It wasn't long before Cockie got his normal panache back as well. 'I mean if I'd got the dough I'd 'ave 'ung on – some juicy bits of black 'am back there,' he said. I'd noticed he had led our retreat for most of the way.

But most of us simply felt foolish. Once again we would never dare to repeat our American shoregoing experiences to anyone aboard. Yet our troubles were not over. As we began resuming our wanderings a U.S. Navy jeep squealed to a halt alongside us. Out poured a squad of patrolmen armed to the teeth with revolvers and long truncheons.

The Petty Officer in charge glared at us sternly: 'You Limeys know you're off-limits? Ain't you read your orders?'

We protested our innocence and our ignorance, which only brought scorn pouring down on us. 'By rights I should take you guys in but it's pretty plain to me you're greener than effing shamrock. What you want is an effing nurse not a whore. Don't you know a red-light zone when you see one?'

Feeling as shamefaced as nuns caught eating illicit cream cakes we trooped back towards the harbour while the jeep followed at a crawl behind us. It didn't go away until we passed back through the guarded gates. There was still three hours left of our shore leave although we noticed other ratings were also returning to the ship and having no money they had little choice. By the time we sailed the next morning not one case of drunkenness had been reported – a unique event for the *Lothian* and very nearly for any other warship in a U.S. port.

With the hurricane now reported to have altered course away from our intended direction we once more put to sea. Yet again we had to hang around while we waited for a straggler. This time it was not the fault of someone on the Admiral's staff nor engine troubles. The sudden signal to depart had been sent to all the ships except that when it reached the *Empire Spearhead* it had not been passed on to the Captain. Apparently assuming that the Force would be delayed longer than a day he sensed nothing amiss. Many hours later a second, more demanding signal did reach him. As quickly as he could he got his vessel ready and cast off. But in the process he had to leave behind a dozen men who had been sent ashore to collect some urgent canteen items. They never saw the *Spearhead* again for nearly two weeks when they were flown in to Panama.

When we heard about it later our immediate reaction was: 'Some bastards get all the luck.' We would have done anything to have got left behind. By then we had reached Panama and our reasons for desiring this so desperately had increased fourfold.

8

Down Spirits

Ships are more like women than just their gender. They bring out the best – or worst – in the men who serve them. Those that are stylish and shapely encourage their seamen to be smart while the dowdy ones with poor figures only raise a sloppy response. *Lothian* definitely fell in the latter category. Apart from the sheer physical difficulties in keeping ourselves clean and tidy we saw no point in wasting spit and polish on such a harridan as our ship. Unfortunately for us Admiral Talbot took a totally opposite view.

He had been too busy trying to improve our grave lack of seagoing qualities and our fighting capabilities to bother too much about appearances until we left Charleston and were now heading into the Tropics. Captain Petrie and the Jimmy had not shown undue concern, either, but probably because they accepted that in war and in our over-crowded ark any strict regard for the kind of pusser smartness found in more stately warships was a bit pointless. But Arthur George now felt something better was needed.

Until then we had simply turned to in the mornings in our overalls and, for lack of other suitable clothing apart from our heavy uniforms, had virtually spent the whole day working or standing watch in them. Suddenly we found daily orders insisting we had to observe the kind of 'bullshit' routine found in battleships or training establishments. Morning 'Divisions' and 'Evening Quarters' were introduced – formalities that took no account of our physical problems and proved just an extra irritation. But what annoyed us more was that only the seamen and not the other ratings had to endure them.

76

Griping profusely we would struggle into our hotly uncomfortable No 2s (working uniform), line up for inspection and then hurry back below to don our overalls again. The same tiresome ritual took place again in the evening. Since we had nowhere to keep our uniforms clean and tidy we would parade looking as though we had spent the night sleeping in them with the inevitable result that we were constantly being reported for our dishevelled appearance. But, usually, only when the Admiral put in an appearance and Jimmy or the Divisional Officers, who clearly felt Divisions and Quarters were a superfluous nuisance, had to take stern action.

We suffered it because we felt we had no choice but it was quite a different matter where another part of our daily routine was concerned. The ship's complement had, as was normal Navy practice, worked throughout the day from leaving Britain. But as we crossed the Tropic of Cancer, after heading through the scattering of Bahamian islands, we confidently expected a change to tropical routine whereby, because of the sapping heat, the afternoons would be a stand easy for all but watchkeepers.

No such change happened. Nor on following days. In the blazing heat of the afternoon we still had to turn to so as to carry out the painting, scraping and other grimy duties. Inside our thick overalls, there being no tropical clothing aboard (in the rush to get the Force away someone had forgotten this essential), we baked like spuds in their jackets. Anyone who tried lowering the top of their boiler suits to ease their suffering was immediately reprimanded. A notice in daily orders warned us that exposure to the tropical sun would cause severe sunburn and that anyone suffering in this way would be deemed to have got 'self-inflicted injuries' and therefore subject to punishment.

Seeing the officers all coolly dressed in sparkling white shirts and shorts did nothing to improve the already poor impression we had of most of them. It was pointless us requesting more sensible clothing but we did our best, unofficially, to demand what we deemed our lawful right – tropical routine. When we approached our P.O.s and Chiefs we found them unusually sympathetic listeners. They, too, they explained, had already requested the same – through the Jimmy. In turn, it appeared, he had asked the Captain to grant it. As seemed to happen a lot he had sought the Admiral's permission. Back down the chain, according to the P.O.s, had come the answer: 'Request refused. No tropical routine until the ship's company are brought to a greater state of efficiency.'

We failed to see how two or three hours off in the afternoons, particularly as Wakey Wakey would be much earlier under tropical routine, could make much difference to our standards. After all, we told ourselves, we had the long weeks crossing the Pacific ahead of us in which we could be licked into shape. Inevitably our dislike of Arthur George grew.

As much as we preferred our Captain because of his more gentle handling of us we felt it was time he should become more assertive. If anyone was going to stand up for us he was the only person as far as we could judge. Yet we had little hope of this happening. Although a Flag Captain had total responsibility and command of his ship and any Admiral was in some ways just a passenger we felt the two roles were overlapping in *Lothian*. Arthur George was often on the bridge and we had seen him give orders to the Officer of the Watch and others even when Captain Petrie was there. Only once had the latter taken umbrage, so we believed. During a tricky manoeuvre Arthur George had ordered a change of course, which was the Captain's direct prerogative. The latter had coldly pointed this out to the Admiral, politely requesting him to leave the bridge.

When we heard about it we broke out in laughter rather than sweat.

The 'sweat' part needed no underlining. At mealtimes and in off-duty moments we sat squashed up on our benches perspiring like customers in a steambath. The temperature in our 'oven' had averaged the nineties and the simple ventilation system that injected, but did not extract, also appeared to be getting heatstroke. Like most of the auxiliary equipment in the engineroom the air pumps were suffering from overheating. But our purgatory was an aphrodisiac for the ship's wildlife. We had always had some cockroaches – what ship did not – but from being occasional visitors easily exterminated they bred into armies in the hothouse conditions. There was no stopping them and they crawled, ran and explored everywhere. Scores must have been killed simply by accidental treading on them but hundreds more thrived. There was no escaping them. They climbed into the food fannies and one was lucky not to find one or more attempting swimming lessons in one's soup or nestling in the stew or hash. We pleaded for some antidote but among the mass of stores we had loaded there was not an ounce of insect powder.

If the 'roaches had any virtue it was simply that they were too big to miss, which meant we could avoid eating them. Not so another of our crawling menaces. It was Yorkie who first discovered it as he was acting as cook of the mess (the rating deputed to fetch and carry). As he was preparing to empty the remains of the soup fanny into the gash bucket he suddenly let out a cry and dropped the heavy steel carrier on the concrete deck. He got bawled out by Hookie but all he could say was: 'The bloody soup's alive.'

We all gawped into the depths of the fanny and, true enough, the bottom was a reeling mass of minute creatures. We stood back horrified and sickened to think what we had just eaten. Hookie peered himself but seemed far less upset. 'Jaspers – that's all they are. They comes in the flour they make the soup with. Won't do you no 'arm.'

That we disputed. We wanted nothing to do with 'jaspers', whatever they were. In fact it proved to be a Naval nickname for weevils, a revelation that did nothing to ease our nausea. Yet, in the months to come, we found we could stomach even these. Since they became an inescapable part of anything containing flour, and most of our dreary food did, we either had to eat them or starve. Usually it was both. We became so inured to these two loathsome insects that they served to ease our limited entertainment. Using the mess table as a Derby course we ran cockroach races and when that and our mainstay recreation of solo whist became boring we took bets on how many weevils could be tapped from slices of stale bread.

Our third and potentially worst enemy among the voracious wild life aboard had no entertainment value whatsoever. Much the reverse. My first traumatic experience of it occurred one night when I had come off the First Watch (8 p.m. to midnight) and was trying to get off to sleep in my hammock. I had, by this time, managed to escape the ordeal of lying on the dusty messdeck 'floor' but only by securing my hammock in the very narrow space over the top of our lockers with the securing ropes tied to the deckhead piping. It was more like mountaineering getting in and out but, at least, I no longer got trodden on. That night sleep proved more difficult than usual with the heat and the fug getting worse as we steamed further towards the Equator. I must have been only partly conscious when I thought I heard someone pulling at the 'nettles' (the lines between the canvas and rope) of my hammock. Half awake I raised myself and gazed blearily behind me. In a second I was very much awake. There, its twitching evil face just inches from my own, was as big a rat as I have ever seen.

My cry, let alone the appalling sound as I leapt from my hammock oblivious of the great drop below, must have woken the whole messdeck. The cries of outrage were almost as loud as my own squeals of pain from injuring myself on the hard deck. The small crowd of ratings who gathered around me seemed more concerned with having their sleep broken.

I tried telling them about the rat but was bluntly told to 'button your flap' (shut up) and I spent the rest of the night nursing my bruises and sprains on the deck, far too scared to get back into my hammock. Only later as the rats emerged more and more from the bilges and other dark crevices and became a constant threat to messdeck life did I get any satisfaction – from fear and discomfort of other seamen receiving these nightly invaders. If the rats were in search of food they could not have come to a less likely place. We were only too glad to ditch any greasy leftovers, and there was plenty of these, into the gash chutes on the ship's sides. Even if we had had any personal delicacies they would have been locked well away from thieving hands. As it was such titbits as 'nutty' (chocolate) and biscuits had disappeared from the small NAAFI canteen we had aboard and we were limited to the sparse, unappetising offerings reaching us from the galley.

If we sometimes regarded Arthur George as another version of Napoleon, and not only because of his stocky stature, we were wide of the mark on one important aspect. 'Boney' at least believed an army marched on its stomach. The Admiral, of course, had no notion of what we were eating, we told ourselves, or even he would have done something to improve matters. Or was that just wishful thinking? We knew there were large amounts of good food aboard – hadn't we sweated ourselves to death loading it in New York? Yet, as the days passed by, the quality and type of food served us got worse and worse. What, for example, we puzzled, had happened to all the fresh veg? All we were getting from the day we left New York was over-steamed dehydrated spuds, cabbage and carrots. Where was all the tinned fruit we had manhandled into the bulging stores? 'Figgy Duff' (suet pudding) was our standard sweet except for rare moments of madness when we were given Manchester Tart – a jammy affair with custard. And who was getting all those sides of beef and thick steaks? Lobscouse and stew that swam in grease and looked as though it had been bought from a back alley ship's butcher were our reward.

The answers seemed so obvious that as quick as we were to attach blame on our common enemy 'the pigs' we could not totally credit they could have completely collared all the best for themselves. Or, if they had, how could they enjoy it, knowing we were getting, as old Postie put it, 'the worst effing rations I've 'ad in thirty-five years in the Andrew'.

Yet as the reports rolled into us from the wardroom tiffies (stewards) of the succulent meals being served up three times a day to officers who, apparently, seemed unconcerned at their good fortune and our lack of it, what alternative had we but to think the worst? No longer did we simply simmer with contained wrath but began letting off verbal sparks not really caring who heard but stopping just short enough of ending up as defaulters. It was our only form of retaliation as we saw it then although not quite. We still had some sense of humour left. That had been raised from its sinking level in the first place by the sudden appearance on our 'menu' of what must have been one of the most obscenely phallic items of grub ever served to a rating. It was intended to replace the sausages that had vanished from the scene but whoever had concocted it must have had king size sexual aspirations. What appeared on our plates were very large, very hard salami type objects that were as inedible as they were redly suggestive.

Trying to eat them threatened our teeth as much as our digestion and there were various crude suggestions as to what could be done with them or to whom. In the meanwhile they made dangerous ammunition for inter-mess warfare – easily capable of raising a bruise when thrown hard. It was Cockie, appropriately, who came up with the best answer and the most effective way of displaying our disgust over our food to the 'pigs'. Coming down to dinner that night they found themselves confronted by a long chain of the 'sausages' festooned along the bulkhead outside the wardroom – all wearing Naval issue French Letters.

There was the inevitable investigation but not carried out with the severity we anticipated. The Jaunty questioned us sternly but I suspected he saw the humour of it as much as we did. He went away apparently satisfied with our emphatic denials but warning us that we would be 'first for the chop' (punished) if there were any more incidents like it. The officers had, we learnt, dismissed the joke as 'typical Lower Deck vulgarity' not appreciating the cry for help behind it. We still got served up the inedible 'bangers' for weeks to come until even they disappeared from worsening meals.

This episode was the first and last bit of light relief we attempted to ease our fast-growing sense of bitterness against officers we now regarded as being callous to the extreme. They could easily have made life more bearable for us, we assured ourselves, as we laid the blame for almost everything on their heads. When our worst problem occurred, however, we had to find a broader based enemy. Our loathing spilled over on to the Navy as a whole – right down from the 'nuthouse' that had been responsible in the first place for the conversion of the ship and her despatch to the Pacific.

In the tropical heat and in our furnace-like messdeck the one craving we most wished to satisfy was our thirst. Apart from the strong, well stewed tea and the 'kai' (cocoa made from block chocolate) during night watches all we had to ease our constantly dry mouths was water. It had never been very drinkable since it was mainly the kind evaporated from sea water (our freshwater tanks just could not cope with the many extra men aboard) but soon after leaving Charleston it began to taste even fouler. It also became as dankly dead as long-standing pond water. Drinking it took courage and a strong stomach.

It was the week I was Mess Sweeper and I was trying vainly to brush away some of the concrete dust without making it billow over everyone when Hookie ordered me to get up to the NAAFI and buy him a 'tin of Andrews'. It struck me as odd since most of us were suffering one of our bouts of diarrhoea at the time. When I returned with the liver salts I watched as he spooned a good dose into a mug of the putrid water and then began stirring it furiously. 'Learnt this dodge when we 'ad trouble with the water in a corvette I was in – it's the only way to 'andle it.'

Before he had finished drinking a procession had formed up to the NAAFI where the Canteen Manager at last found he had something worth selling. But the consequences of mixing Andrews in every time we had a drink also put unwelcome pressure on our Heads, which had been designed for half our numbers. It was just as well supplies of the salts quickly ran out.

But so did the water.

The first we knew of this disaster was when a pipe over the PA system told us: 'Due to a fault with the evaporators there will be a temporary loss of water for drinking. Sea water only will be supplied for washing. All Cooks of the Mess to report to slops for an issue of salt water soap.'

If it had been announced that we had run short of rum there could hardly have been greater consternation. Our next port – in Panama – was only three days away but even that was too long in the tropical heat. The news also spread quickly throughout the ship that far from being temporary the fault with the water supply needed extensive dockyard repairs. Not only had the evaporators been damaged but the linings of the water tanks had broken up – the cause of the foulness of the water. To replace these was complicated and could take weeks.

Once the initial shock had passed we tried finding what tiny consolation we could. After all the whole ship, as we thought, was suffering the same problem and as much as we turned our hate on the Royal Navy as a whole we were 'all up shit creek together' and best if we put a bold face on it. If the water system was so bad then we could expect a decent layover in Panama, where, by all accounts, the rum was strong and the girls more than willing. Such optimism, however, may have been more a sign of our deeper seated despair. It was not long before it had been overtaken by renewed anger when we discovered that fresh water had not entirely vanished from the ships. It was still available in the wardroom and for certain senior officers.

The seamen's wrath on being told this increased when a friendly E.R.A. (Engineroom Artificer) revealed he had just been servicing Arthur George's bath. We knew of the Admiral's passion for daily baths and also of his running battle with the Lieutenant (E) responsible for the water supply, which had often had hiccups that upset the Flag Officer's insistence on comfort and efficiency. Now, said the E.R.A., he was complaining that sea water was adding to the problems let alone spoiling his soak. He had to suffer it because by the time the steamy, jungly isthmus of Panama came in sight the whole water system seemed to have caved in.

No thirstier ships' company ever viewed approaching landfall with greater craving to 'have a wet run ashore'. The decks were crowded as we headed direct for the Canal entrance and a tropical rain storm broke over our heads. But hardly anyone moved, glad of the soaking on little washed bodies and stretching out tongues to lick the welcome fresh water off our faces. We even accepted the rigid formality of being paraded at attention since it was a means of extending our drenching although the Canal workers eyed us as though we were mad. Only the Kiwi in the bows trying to blow his soggy bagpipes felt frustrated. If he was playing a lament it was appropriate but neither he nor us could have known how more suitable an overture it was for sending us over the top.

9

Storm Brewing

As great a miracle of engineering as it had been when it opened almost exactly thirty years before we passed through, the Panama Canal had become no more than a brief break in the monotony of a long ocean voyage for the thousands of vessels now using it to reach the Pacific battle zones. Apart from refuelling, where necessary, the dozens of ships a day were hurried on with no chance of their crews having a run ashore. Not that they missed much. All that the harbours at either end, Cristobal and Balboa, had to offer were canteens and a few dreary bars. The only seductive attraction, Panama City, lay two miles from the second as well as being largely off-limits to Servicemen. The Spanish invaders, pirates and canal workers who had died by the drove from yellow fever and malaria had retaliated by leaving behind plenty of virulent V.D. The intense equatorial heat and 100 per cent humidity all added to the Canal Zone's distinctly unhealthy atmosphere.

Why any seaman would want to spend a night's leave there let alone stay longer might have seemed a mystery yet there was undoubtedly a deep longing among the *Lothian*'s deck ratings to linger. But was it because it was Panama or simply a case of any port in a storm? We would have wished for a more appealing sheltering place but we were, in Naval language, totally 'chock-a-block' (fed up). Almost everything had got us down and we could see no sign whatsoever of any improvement, rather the reverse. If the *Lothian* had sunk through colliding in the narrow waterways of the Canal we might have raised an almighty cheer.

'Morale' was not a word we ever used but if we had we would have said it was now non-existent. Yet we seemed to be carried along magnetically by the very drudgery we griped about. Any deeper anger remained smouldering like a bonfire of autumn leaves waiting for a fresh breeze. That was the potentially fiery state we were in as we endured the long drawn-out haul through the steeply ascending Gatun Locks, towed by mechanical mules, and then under our own steam through the lengthy Gatun Lakes before entering the last stretch in the descending Miraflores Locks. We had sailed straight into the Canal at 4 p.m. and it was midnight before we reached our berth at Balboa. All that time we had had to stand by or work on deck, much of which had clearly been due to excessive zeal by the ship's officers rather than from practical necessity.

Our only pleasure as we faced the task of tying up at the end of an exceptionally tiring, extremely sticky day was the sight of Arthur George performing a firework display on the bridge as a result of the antics of our Canal pilot who seemed to have far less seamanship than even we O.D.s. For nearly an hour we backed and filled off the jetty unable to get close enough for a line to be got ashore. It was nearly 2 a.m. before we collapsed into our hammocks, totally exhausted. At five thirty we were reluctantly roused by the Wakey Wakey and given strict orders to make the ship look 'less like a Bovril Boat (a sewage disposal barge) and more like a pusser man o' war'. We knew why that order had come. We were lying right under the windows of the U.S. Navy HQ and not exactly creating any challenge with our hull rusty and our mis-shapen superstructure also in need of champering up. Almost too tired to get the stages over the guardrails we began the long, hot task of repainting the sides. We were still at it during the afternoon although if ever a place demanded tropical routine it was Panama.

As we carried our pots and brushes back to the paint locker we were suddenly brought alive by the unexpected sight of the *Glenearn* leaving her berth and heading for the open sea soon to be followed by the four Empires, which had refuelled at Cristobal. There was no sign of the *Lamont* but that did not surprise us. We knew from her pathetic efforts to keep up with us crossing the

Caribbean that she could not go much further without being docked for repairs.*

But why were we still lying alongside with no sign whatsoever of departing? No official announcement of any kind had been made although there were plenty of buzzes flying around. We were going into drydock. No, we were having a patch-up job done and would sail the next day. We were having to wait for the *Lamont* or, the wildest rumour of all, we were being pulled out of the Force and being sent back to Britain – this last 'buzz' rising from the fact our four U.S. Navy escorts had sailed with the five Force ships that had left.

Yet it did seem as if our longing had been answered, if only temporarily. We looked forward eagerly to getting ashore and turning our back on the 'Loathsome', as the ship had been nicknamed, for several Heaven-sent hours. We should have known better. During our supper we learnt there would be little leave other than a visit to Balboa. Nearby Panama City was officially deemed 'unsafe' for us. As one A.B. interpreted it: 'That means the old man thinks we'll all get the clap.' He probably wasn't far wrong. No native female could come anywhere near the ship without being the focal point for unmistakable indications of how she could relieve the ratings' frustrations. Most of the women looked pleased about the prospect. I could see 'Rose Cottage' being extended to take in adjoining messes.

There could not have been a more overromantic title for such an uncharming place. It was my first experience of living at close quarters with a V.D. mess (it was the one just the other side of our lockers) and I still could not quite accept the sight of its four current occupants or, rather why they were so confined.

They had been the lucky, or unlucky as the case might be, who had been able to afford a woman in New York or Charleston. Now they were paying the torturous surcharge being extracted by the Sick Bay 'tiffies'. The injections were painful when applied by the most gentle hands and, according to the victims, no pain was spared when done aboard. The agony was probably considered

* Rear-Admiral Talbot reported to the Admiralty that the *Lamont* was running its engine bearings hot; that its refrigeration plant had broken down and that there were 'numerous other defects'.

justified as a substitute for the fact that in the Andrew, unlike the other Services, catching V.D. was not deemed a crime. Many in the Lower Deck considered it an honourable battle scar or even a necessary initiation into being a proper seaman. As our Leading Hand Hookie told us: 'You ain't a real 'airy-chested Jack until you've caught a real dose.'

But the prospect of us young O.D.s achieving nautical manhood this way looked like remaining academic in view of our restricted shore leave. Some of us would have been too scared, anyway, since we still had nauseatingly vivid memories of the horrifically detailed films shown us on the effects of V.D. when we were at training establishment. The emphatic notices now posted aboard about the extreme risk of contacting the disease in Panama added to those fears. Yet they also added to our growing feeling of being prisoners. But anything would have done by this stage. The intense heat and humidity had made us extremely irritable without our other problems and we found fault with one another let alone with authority.

Much of our off-duty time, and some working hours as well, was spent considering how much we could achieve improvements by fair, or foul, means. The fact that no one could come up with anything practicable added to our frustration. It was probably in desperation that we thought about what was blatantly a criminal action according to K.R.s and A.I.s (King's Regulations and Admiralty Instructions) but seemed the only way out of our predicament.

A Round Robin.

It was Taffy, the discontented A.B., who first proposed it to us although the notion might have come from one of his equally belligerent oppos. Sitting at our mess I had watched him trail round the other ones heatedly trying to persuade their members to support his cause. When he reached ours Hookie gave him an icy reception.

'Why don't you take a walk down the starboard gangway (there wasn't one) you Welsh git?' he told him.

Taffy was too worked up to take much offence. 'Look lads, I know I goes on a bit about things but me and a few others 'ave been chatting it over and we think it's 'igh time we stuck our necks out an' got them idle bastards on top to do something about this shit'ouse they calls a messdeck. There's plenty more that's wrong as you boyos know effing well. An' it ain't going to get no better that's for sure.'

Hookie was not impressed. 'What you mean is that you want us to do your dirty work for you. I seen your sort before – always 'iding be'ind while the rest of the muckers get jankers.'

This time Taffy grew angry. 'That ain't right! There's no other fucker in this messdeck oo's bin on requestmen more than me. An' I might just as well 'ave pissed in the wind. No, it's time we mucked in together an' showed them pigs we mean business.'

Just what was he suggesting? we demanded.

When he revealed it was a Round Robin there was a frozen silence. As green as we were, we knew such an action was totally forbidden – any request had to be individually made. Hookie put the situation into down-to-earth perspective.

'That's all y're asking – 'aving us stuck with a conspiracy charge!' he sneered.

'So what!' retaliated Taffy. 'If every Jack signs it, all in a circle like, what the effing 'ell can they do about it. Can't shove the lot of us in cells, can they?'

To ram home his point he added: 'An' where in fuck's name are they going to find replacements while we're stuck in this effing dump?'

The argument may have held flaws but we, listening eagerly, were not looking for any. To us it seemed as good a way as any out of our troubles. Even Hookie felt it was worth testing further.

'An' oo else 'ave you got to sign it?' he demanded dubiously.

'There's plenty of the boys,' he announced airily.

We insisted on names.

The Welshman rattled off nearly half a dozen and then, obviously feeling it was not enough, added the fact that 'all them ex-Pongos goes along with it'.

But he had pushed his luck a bit too far. The former soldiers he referred to were yet another strange part of the *Lothian*'s weirdly mixed up complement. There were around a score of them who, until a short time before joining the ship, had served in the Black Watch and Staffordshire Regiment. According to their story they had taken advantage of a fairly new scheme whereby soldiers could volunteer for the Navy and, fed up with being Pongos they had gladly made the switch. In our eyes, however, they must either be mad or have some evil reason for leaving the Army. As far as the first part went the score were, as a result of their unhappy experience in *Lothian*, their very first ship, inclined to agree with us.

Few in the messdeck had griped as much as some of the ex-soldiers, particularly several of the Scots, tough Glaswegians, who were also often under punishment for minor acts of indiscipline. They were considered a nuisance by the killicks and older A.B.s and even we O.D.s kept clear of them. Taffy's mention of them brought an icy reaction. So it seemed to have done wherever he had sought backing. The Round Robin proposal foundered quickly.

In the next day or so, however, we could see Taffy along with his closest mates still persisting in raising some kind of active response from among the seamen. They were being given fresh ammunition all the time. Part of this came when we learnt that the reason for us being left behind by the rest of the Force was so we could have repairs done to our freshwater system. That was certainly welcome but what disturbed us was the fact that the work would only be of a temporary kind. According to the stokers we would be lucky if the repairs would last us all the way across the Pacific as almost everything to do with the machinery and the tanks was in need of urgent replacement.*

It seemed inconceivable to us that a shipload of 750 men would be sent on such a long voyage, likely to last five weeks, with months of active service in a war zone where proper repairs would be impossible. As we had already found out to our cost the lack of drinking water, let alone the difficulty of getting properly washed in seawater, was a major hardship no one would suffer if they could possibly avoid it.

* In referring to the water problem in his Letter of Proceedings Rear-Admiral Talbot stated: '*Lothian*'s fresh water system had given trouble ever since leaving U.K. and had now broken down completely. The electrical pumps had burnt out.' He added: '. . . it was found impossible to make *Lothian*'s fresh water system good in less than fourteen days. I was forced, therefore, with the choice of accepting this estimate, leaving *Lothian* behind and transferring my Flag to *Glenearn* or attempting a 'patch-up job' within a limit of four days and then sailing at 16 knots to catch up the Force before they reached Bora Bora, our next stop.'

He concluded this section: 'I decided finally on the latter course.'

Of all the decisions he had ever taken during his long, often distinguished Naval career this may have proved the one he regretted most.

Our anger fell on Arthur George. No sympathy was wasted on the fact that the ship was already well behind schedule and that the Admiral had somehow to push on. As far as we were concerned the ship, indeed the whole Force, should never have been sent in the first place. The messdeck P.O., trying to soften our wrath, suggested it was the U.S. Navy that was forcing us to continue regardless but we had heard what had happened to *Lamont* in New York and believed the Americans would do the same to us given half a chance.

If we needed a much higher target on which to express our frustration, higher even than the 'nuthouse', we could, according to the buzz which had been around since leaving Scotland, find it in none other than Winston Churchill himself. It was he, in conjunction with Roosevelt, said the rumour as it came all the way down from the wardroom, who had insisted on a British Naval force being sent to the Pacific as soon as possible. But it never got further than being shipboard gossip.

However much, or little, truth there was in any of these assumptions, and the correct reason may have included a bit of each, we felt like pressed beef being squeezed into submission under a massive weight of authority. Something more emphatic than simply complaining among ourselves was essential. As on most occasions when we young seamen felt lost for an answer to a serious problem we leaned on Hookie. What would he recommend? Did he go along with the more determined action Taffy had been urging?

He pondered over the questions as he rolled himself another 'tickler' (cigarette made from cheap Navy issue tobacco). At last he answered: 'You gang together like what 'e says and you'll end up deeper in the shit. They'll throw the 'ole of K.R.s and A.I.s at you. No, if you wants to complain you got to do it pusser like – each man puts in 'is own request chitty.'

Hookie licked the cigarette paper into shape, lit up and then added dourly: 'But I'll tell you this. If Jimmy or the Old Man gets an' 'ole lot of requests all griping about the same thing they'll claim it's a put-up job. Won't get you nowhere except, maybe, a bollocking. I seen it 'appen before.'

So what was the point of protesting officially, we argued?

'That's just it,' retorted our Leading Hand. 'They've got you by the balls, ain't they? Maybe if we was on an 'Ome Station we could

91

raise some shit right up to the nut'ouse but 'ere in this effing piss'ole we're knackered. 'Oo's going to give a monkey's fuck what 'appens to us, especially as we're lashed up with the Yanks.'

In righteous indignation Mick suggested our best ploy was to complain to the U.S. Navy, although he couldn't propose how. Hookie sneered: 'Can you see Arthur George letting the Yanks poke their noses in as to 'ow 'e runs 'is flagship? Gawd, talk about sucking a fish's tit! (trying the impossible).'

We had gained nothing from consulting our mess mentor but he had, at least, put our situation into some kind of proper, if despairing, perspective. All we could hope for now was a miracle. There were no avenues of escape and the Welshman's suggestion could only end up in us being squeezed into a tighter jam. That evening he and his Scottish and Irish oppos were still trying hard to raise support. The next morning they were given fresh fuel to fire their cause when, as the seamen were working ship, we saw the whole R.A.F. contingent piling merrily into coaches alongside. We had only one interpretation for this – the 'Brylcreem boys' were being given a special outing when we had to work ship.

Not since joining the ship had I seen such an open display of protest from the ratings. We crowded around P.O.s, Chiefs, Leading Hands demanding to know why we were not receiving such favoured treatment. It brought the Jimmy hurrying up. Demanding silence he explained: 'The R.A.F. have been given permission to go on training manoeuvres. They have not been granted liberty.' He was very emphatic and we returned reluctantly to our labours still feeling we had been hard done by. That frustration exploded when we saw the Air Force men return and learnt that they had, in fact, enjoyed a sightseeing tour of Panama City.

A highly dangerous situation now threatened. As small as the incident might have looked in retrospect it had all the explosive potential of a hand grenade tossed into an ammunition dump coming on top of our mass of other grievances. The First Lieutenant must have appreciated the risk, or at least that we had a genuine cause for protest in view of what he had told us. But he had been, as we later found out, misled himself. The 'manoeuvres' had been a ruse by the R.A.F. Squadron Leader in charge to get his men the shore leave they felt they deserved. This revelation did not improve relations between the Navy and R.A.F., which had always been sensitive. But it resulted, to our surprise, in us being taken on an excursion by coach to Panama City.

The American servicemen watching us board the buses must have received a peculiar impression of Royal Navy men. We behaved more like schoolchildren given an unexpected half-day holiday. The ship's officers seeing us look so happy might have mistakenly believed we were an unusually content mob of ratings. Even we forgot, for a brief while, our weeks of torment as we were driven through luxuriantly tropical countryside although most eyes and gestures were concentrated on any native women we passed. By the time we reached the capital the local jungle drum network must have signalled the city to expect a latter day version of Henry Morgan buccaneers out to rape and pillage.

But we were only being allowed out on an extended leash. Our route took us deliberately clear of the native quarters concentrating on the Spanish additions. However beautiful was the architecture and however historic the atmosphere they could not have been so entrancing to most as some down-at-heel bar, especially one packed with girls. But the local whores had not been slow to discover the Navy was in town. As we were led reluctantly into the cathedral a covey of them followed on behind trying to negotiate a quick deal. Yet they could not have been more out of place inside this ornate monument to Christianity than a crowd of sex-starved, irreligious mateloes with a spiritual thirst demanding something far more potent than Holy Water.

In the fast descending dusk I spotted several seamen sneak away and thought it surprising more did not follow. Were we younger ones just plain cowards or were we simply overawed by such alien surroundings and too heeding of the stern warnings of personal risk we might run? Our Spanish-Indian guide had been frighteningly descriptive of the muggings that were, he claimed, commonplace and particularly of the V.D. menace. 'Better you get keeled by the Japs than get seepheelees from the girls 'ere. For sure eet weel make your peeness fall off.'

The endless number of churches were a safer if far more boring bet. In the third, perhaps the fourth, I saw Mick standing in front of a painting of the Virgin, which we had been told possessed miraculous powers. Like a good Catholic he crossed himself and appeared to be saying a short prayer. As I stood admiring his courage at doing so in front of so many amoral seamen I felt a nudge in the ribs and heard Cockie's snigger: ' 'E'll need more than an effing miracle once we gets back aboard.'

I had to agree. The prospect of returning to the ship killed any joy the trip had provided. It was a far more gloomy atmosphere in the bus on our return journey from the carefree one when we had set out. If anything some of our frustrations had been increased. Perhaps we felt more like children allowed to press noses against a sweetshop window but forbidden to buy anything inside. What I felt certain about at that moment was that it would take far more than a short coach excursion to relieve our deeply bitter feelings.

10

Mutiny

September 1, 1944: the brief war reports printed in H.M.S. *Lothian*'s Daily Orders showed that on all Fronts the Allies were advancing towards victory. Armies were pushing deeper into France, north through Italy and island hopping towards the Philippines. Air Forces were taking a heavy toll of enemy resources from Europe to the Far East. At sea U-boats were being sunk and shore installations shelled. Everyone, everywhere, it seemed, was totally engaged in winning the War. All, that is, except those aboard *Lothian*.

We were distinctly apathetic as we toppled out of our hammocks very early that morning. The same daily orders stated we were due to sail from Balboa that afternoon to resume our protracted voyage to the South-West Pacific but none of us seamen viewed the prospect with anything other than loathing. The 'patch-up' job on the water system had been completed yet it had not got rid of the foul taste and we had been warned to use supplies carefully. The many other problems such as bad ventilation, steambath messdeck conditions, rotten food and so on were as disturbing as ever. Our spirits could not have been lower.

Like automatons we turned to wash down decks and the high humidity and the sappingly draining heat did nothing to shake us out of our lethargy. Yet I could feel something stirring among us. Like a breeze rippling in across the sea I saw whispers of conversation roll from one small party of men to another, gathering pace as it went until it reached my little group.

Approaching us came 'Lofty', an O.D. from another mess.

Speaking quietly he said: 'You 'eard the chat? The griff going round is that we all got to stand by to stir up a bit of action.'

What action and when? we queried him keenly. Urging us to keep our voices down, he answered: 'Don't ask me but it's no duff gen. It comes from them killicks and A.B.s what's been planning something. Just you pass the word on.'

Personally I thought it could be just another example of a wild buzz backed by some wishful thinking. Yet I could see it was taking a grip on the other seamen and we passed the news on as we had been asked. By the time we went below for breakfast, which featured the obscene bangers, there was a tense air of expectancy all around. It heightened as we saw the Scot along with Taffy and an Irish Leading Hand, who was generally regarded as being more on our side than on authority's, going the rounds of the messes. Eventually reaching our own the Scot, looking well pumped up and flushed, asked, almost demandingly: 'You lads are with us, ain't you?'

As we had no idea what we were supposed to be with our replies sounded pretty feeble. Tell us more, we insisted. All he would say was: 'You'll get to know soon enough. There's too many big ears around. Just you wait for the signal.'

Taffy added his word. 'Now don't let us down, boyos – it's one for all and all for one, isn't it?'

Was it? I wondered. I began to feel a disturbing, empty sensation in the pit of my stomach. Something ominous that I did not feel I was capable of handling was about to happen and I was not sure I wanted to get involved. I looked around at the other O.D.s as if seeking some assurance that they shared my uncertainty but they seemed more excited about the prospect of trouble than nervous. No good looking towards Hookie for moral support, either. He seemed to be intent on keeping his opinions to himself.

I wondered if he was just playing it safe, sensing it would do him no good at all to assert his official role when most of the messdeck seemed to be working up into an agitated state of dissent. Leading Hands always had an awkward task that almost demanded a split personality. Although they had a lot of responsibility they had to live right alongside the junior ratings sharing all the same problems and relying a great deal on their goodwill to make their own lives bearable. Similar N.C.O.s in the other Forces usually had the space to avoid most of this pressure but there was barely room for that in a crowded warship. Still, I wondered if Hookie, and the other killicks, would honour their rank and shortly report what was brewing to the P.O.s for the news to find its way up the scale at least as far as the Jimmy. It seemed, at that stage, almost inevitable, and I could see the awesome might of Naval discipline come crashing down on anyone mad enough to challenge it. I could see no way that any planned disruption would not be quickly discovered if only through gossip being passed on by 'arsehole crawlers', those messdeck menaces always ready to impeach shipmates in order to wheedle a superior's approval. As we returned on deck to resume our work I put forward the possibility to some of the others.

There was qualified acceptance but Scouse did not think it mattered. 'Those boys, Taffy and the rest, 'ave got too steamed up to give a fuck. If you ask me they're looking for all the trouble they can get. I bet you that if we told them to jag it in they'd still kick up shit.'

I sensed he saw little wisdom in joining in any protest although he would not say either way. Cockie, on the other hand, was all for it. The rest of our six could be classified as 'Don't Knows'. Yorkie summed up their general attitude when he said: 'I'll do what t'rest of lads do. If they wants t'join in I'll stick by 'em.'

Mick, who I felt might have moral objections, surprised me. 'I'll go along with that,' he joined in. 'It's got to be all or no one.'

Was I willing to risk my neck? I asked myself. Perhaps it was just plain cowardice but I was more scared of being an odd man out. I, too, would probably follow the herd.

Similar thinking must have been taking place among the other seamen and I could see that many were performing their duties at go-slow pace almost as if already responding to the call to action. So far there was nothing blatantly open about it although it was puzzling the few P.O.s around. They kept ordering us to 'jump to it' but as soon as their backs were turned work all but came to a halt. It was obvious neither they nor the officers, including the Jimmy, had heard that trouble threatened. Perhaps they dismissed our unusual reluctance as being an example of 'sailing day fever' with no one keen to begin a long ocean crossing to an unknown fate in a war zone.

By the time we reached our mid-morning stand-easy break it

seemed clear that no one in the messdeck be they killicks or just O.D.s was going to inform on us. Were the former really on our side? I wondered. If so then they would lend plenty of muscle to whatever action was planned. Although nothing had been revealed it now seemed hardly necessary to raise the tense interest of the ratings. They all seemed of one intent. During the past weeks I had seen how they could instinctively respond with a single mind, almost like a flock of birds which automatically follow each other's movements. Existing so tightly together also created an almost telepathic understanding between us. No one needed to spell out why some sort of demonstration against our poor treatment was, perhaps, our only answer to it and nobody did.

Anyone entering the messdeck during that break would have been left in no doubt that we were about to explode so great had the tension become. But it was rare for P.O.s and officers to visit our sweatbox unless they had to and our highly charged emotions were allowed to boil up unchecked.

Yet I also sensed an almost fatalistic attitude among the seamen. It was as if they were accepting a call to retaliate against their masters as an inevitability. The way they were responding to some vague urging that lacked the fiery pleading that I thought had to be an essential part of any uprising seemed to underline this impression. No one appeared over-concerned about whether it would succeed – an unlikely prospect – let alone the certain severe punishment that would follow. It all had a frighteningly eerie compulsion that made my stomach churn again.

But the mounting tension was also making some impatient. On either side I heard cries of: 'What are we waiting for?' and 'Let's get something effing well done.'

But no one took the lead either for or against. If the leading seamen were going to assert their authority then surely now was the time yet I noticed that hardly any of them were present – an unusual occurrence at Stand-Easy. Were they trying to keep their yardarms clear (free of personal trouble) by putting themselves at a safe distance? Just as surprisingly there was no sign of the trio of prime movers in all of this. Could they have turned yellow or had they been collared by P.O.s and officers more aware of the trouble than we thought? The buzzes flew around the messdeck. Then an A.B. I had previously seen in close company with the Scot and

Taffy appeared down the ladder bearing a message from his oppos.

He went from one part of the messdeck to another telling the ratings to bide their time. He told us: 'The lads got it all under control. You won't 'ave to wait long. Just wait 'til you see them at dinner then get ready to lend an 'and.'

Delay, we all knew, was dangerous. With the men all ready to rise up why hang about? came the demand. The A.B. insisted it was too soon; that any action needed to be closer to sailing time. The seamen had to be content with that.

Although the situation looked, for a moment, like getting out of control no one seemed anxious to take command. If, as the rest of the forenoon dragged by, they could have got hold of the three principal agitators they would have demanded immediate action but we were forced to assume they were lying low to avoid being fingered. If they had been hiding it did not stay that way for long. When we had reluctantly resumed work and I, with a small party, was on the wharf going through the motions of getting a few late stores embarked we saw the three walk boldly down the gangway and head straight into the U.S. canteen. The pipe to dinner was still some minutes away and they were blatantly committing the crime of being absent from their place of duty.

Any second we expected to see the Jaunty or one of his Crushers march after them for we failed to see how the Officer of the Watch or one of the P.O.s could have missed witnessing such open defiance. But not a thing happened. It almost looked as though it was being deliberately ignored. But why? I wondered. The answer could have lain in what occurred a few moments later. There was a bustling of activity at the head of the gangway and we saw the full Bosun's Party line up and the unmistakable figure of Arthur George in his full regalia appear accompanied by Captain Petrie, similarly smartly uniformed. Shortly after several official cars drew up and out stepped half a dozen senior U.S. Navy officers up to Captain's rank along with one R.N. Commander we recognised as the Resident British Naval Officer in Panama. We simply stood there gawking lazily at the procession as it headed up the gangway to be piped aboard. As they followed the Admiral in the direction of his cabin I saw him snap something at the Officer of the Watch. A moment later he was storming on to the jetty demanding to know why we had not stood to attention.

His dressing down completed he marched stiffly back aboard leaving us feeling far less disturbed than he had intended.

' 'E'd really be two blocks (fed up) if 'e knew what the boys was up to,' sneered Cockie. 'I bet the ole Admiral really tore 'im off a strip for us spoiling 'is bit of bullshit.'

'Ay, well Arthur George's going t'feel chock-a-block 'imself when balloon goes up,' added Yorkie.

The pipe to dinner ended that conversation and as we headed for the messdeck, our appetites whetted more by the thought of the drama we expected to play out than the meal itself, I could not help wishing I was sharing with the Admiral and his high flown guests in what would undoubtedly be their far tastier and more filling meal.

If I ate anything that dinnertime or if anyone did I could not recall. Our minds were totally concentrated on what open act of protest we were to be led into. Tension was still running high although it now appeared more a tightly suppressed kind as though we had been overwound. If our mess was any indication hardly anyone was prepared to risk passing any kind of comment on what was to happen or should happen. That messdeck tele-pathy told us that nerves were too near breaking point to risk saying the wrong thing. Even the Leading Hands, who had now reappeared, seemed to be in a similar fragile state of high tension.

As if for reassurance we kept looking around at the other messes to see how their occupants were reacting – only to find them staring back at us. Every so often our gaze was directed towards the ladder as we anxiously waited for the ringleaders to appear. The news that they had so openly visited the canteen had quickly spread raising doubts among some sceptics about the trio's true intentions but bringing admiration from others who regarded the action as proof of the agitators' determination to flout authority.

Personally, and I probably was not alone in this, I half expected to hear the heavy tread of the Jaunty's or G.I.'s (Gunnery Instruc-tor's) boots pounding down the steel ladder to have us all up for even thinking about disobedience. But we must have been pro-tected by some great mystical force or those responsible for ensuring discipline were proving incredibly lax for it was the three agitators who came hurrying down below. Whether it was just excitement or possibly because they had been drinking some of the

American beer on sale at the canteen along with their tots but they had worked themselves up into a high state of fervour.

His face almost scarlet the Scot jumped on to a bench and called out: 'O.K. lads. Are we all in this together?'

There was a nervous hesitation. Then came a resounding roar of approval that could have been heard up on deck.

Stirred up even more by the almost unanimous response the Scot burst out: 'I don't 'ave to tell you what it's all about. They've been treating us like cattle and if we don't show them we ain't going to stand for it any more it's going to get effing worse.'

Again a mighty bellow of support.

Waiting for the din to subside 'Scottie', as the messdeck was now shouting out his name, went on: 'All me and my oppos is asking you to do is just stand fast when you 'ear the pipe to stations (for seagoing). We don't want no one to move. Just you sit tight an' let us do the talking.'

Someone cried out: 'Talking's no effing good. They'll just piss all over us.'

Scottie yelled back: 'Just let the buggers try. When they see we ain't going to take this effing boat to sea and the Yanks start asking questions they'll soon come round, just you wait and see.'

A sceptic retorted: 'What's to stop the pigs getting the buntings and pokers (signalmen and stokers) to handle the ropes?'

The Scot had an immediate answer for this. 'No one ain't going to scab on us. If they try that one on they'll 'ave the 'ole ship be'ind us.'

Until then I doubted if many of the seamen had given much thought to how the remainder of the ship's company would react. Most might have taken it for granted that because the complement had become so segregated we would be bound to be on our own. Yet Lower Deck sympathies were, when it came to the crunch, for fellow ratings and not for officers. The rest would support us morally, at least, and possibly actively, I thought.

But some were now demanding that we try and get everyone behind us from the start. This time it was Taffy who stepped forward to reply. All his Celtic passion aroused he cried out: 'As soon as the rest of the boys see we're making a stand they'll be be'ind us all the way – jest you wait and see. But first we got to show them we mean business. Anyone 'oo don't back us up deserves to get all that's coming to 'im.'

It sounded like a veiled threat of intimidation and Taffy may have gone a little too far. But Scottie, who seemed to have a natural talent for controlling a crowd, applied more psychology. 'Anyone who's not with us just step up that ladder. No one's going to force you to join in.'

He must have known what the reaction would be. No one was going to let his messmates down or, at least, be seen to be doing so. Not even the killicks and badge A.B.s moved. The great majority were clearly showing support. But the intense noise suddenly died away to be replaced by an uneasy silence as the pipe for us to turn to after dinner brought an icy note of authority into the messdeck.

Would anyone break ranks? I wondered. Like most I had taken it for granted that our action would start right away but some must have thought we were not being expected to begin our protest until the actual order to prepare for putting to sea. The confusion may have been due to the fact that we had all expected the ship to sail immediately after dinner but, for some reason our departure was being delayed for this pipe was just the normal order to start afternoon work.*

A small number began moving slowly towards the ladder only to be shouted back by the rest. Scottie appeared to be losing control yelling out for everyone to carry on until seagoing stations were called. But he was underestimating the extent to which the seamen were now behind the call to demonstrate their grievances. Having made up their minds the majority were not going to budge. A deafening crescendo of noise arose as men bellowed out their support and began hammering mess tables as though they were a form of tribal war drum. Facing the inevitable the trio of ring-leaders joined in while we all waited for the din to bring the inevitable confrontation. If anyone had had fears about such a dramatic display of disobedience they were now showing full-blooded determination to express their anger.

* The cause of the delay in sailing was a decision by Rear-Admiral Talbot to entertain his U.S. Navy guests before departing. The ship was nearly ready to leave when they came aboard.

11

Armed Defiance

The drama of our revolt needed no emphasising. We did not have to be told we were committing a crime grave enough in peacetime let alone in war. It had needed someone to excite our anger into action but we were almost solidly behind it. Then our mounting tension was nearly forced towards panic. The messdeck lights, which had never been brilliant, suddenly dipped creating an eerie semi-darkness. I heard Oggie cry out: 'Christ – they're trying to screw us down.'

Like many of us he interpreted the cut back in power as a clear sign that the officers had found out and were already retaliating. For a few moments the consternation grew until Scottie yelled out: 'Don't panic – it's only the gennies (generators) being cut back.'

From time to time the engineers conserved on fuel by reducing the supply of electricity to parts of the ship where it was least needed. They must have taken it for granted that we had returned to duty and the messdeck was all but empty. Slowly a kind of calm returned while we began raising our courage again to face the inevitable investigation that must soon begin. It took just a bare few minutes before the first figure of authority appeared down the ladder.

It was the Buffer (Bosun), normally a breezy character more inclined to jolly us along whenever we were reluctant to hurry. He must have sensed something was drastically wrong for he looked nervously wary as he peered into the gloom. There was nothing lighthearted about the order he barked out: 'Jump to it. The pipe went ten minutes ago. What . . .'

But he was cut off in mid-stream by a bellow of 'Fuck orf'.

The jeer was instantly taken up all around the messdeck – fierce enough to send the Chief scuttling back up on top. Whoever he would report to would be left in no doubt about our total disobedience. Such an easy first victory, however, boosted our confidence. We were ready for whoever should appear next. There was a sterner sounding tread to the pair of feet that came down the ladder a few minutes later. This time it was another P.O. but the ultimate in disciplinary rank – the Jaunty. His head had barely appeared when he was met by another fusillade of angry catcalls. It drowned out his first attempt to issue a command but, at last, at the top of his powerful voice he screamed: 'Get topsides at the double. I don't want any man disobeying my orders.'

A group of A.B.s nearest him began moving forward menacingly while the rest renewed their shouting. It was threatening enough for the Jaunty to turn quickly and hurry back up the ladder. Victory No 2. Yet we knew these were easy successes compared with the much tougher battles that would now follow. I sensed a certain nervousness among my fellow O.D.s as they became more aware they were being drawn into what might prove an over explosive rebellion. I turned to see how Hookie was reacting, puzzled that he, like other killicks, had shown no sign of trying to quell the disobedience or, at least, point out the trouble into which we were steaming at full speed. He seemed to be avoiding taking sides and, probably, faced by such a powerful show of wrath no Leading Hand thought it safe to buck this onrushing tide of emotion.

It was also difficult not to be caught up and carried along by it – more so when someone broke out into that hymn of revolution, the 'Red Flag'. In seconds it had been taken up all around in an anxious fervour to display support and boost spirits. As much as it added a more rousing, political dimension it also introduced a touch of black humour.

Few of us knew the correct words but most had grasped the more bawdy Servicemen's version. There was something ironic about hearing us 'workers' singing 'The Working Class can kiss my arse, we've got the foreman's job at last.'

Easily raucous enough to be heard up on deck it must have scared anyone considering coming below to force us into submission. All the courage he possessed was needed by the Jimmy as he stepped down the ladder next. For a few moments he stood stiffly tense at the bottom waiting to see if the din would die down. It only seemed to swell – until a loud cry from the ringleaders gradually brought it down several octaves. 'Let 'im 'ave 'is say – then we'll 'ave ours,' called out the Irish killick.

Wasting no time the Jimmy began telling us just how serious an offence we were committing: 'You are guilty of a very grave crime. You are not just disobeying orders but you are doing so in a foreign port in time of war and under sailing orders.'

From the semi-darkness someone yelled: 'Tell us something we don't know,' but the more subdued murmur showed that the First Lieutenant was making an impression. Hearing our guilt spelled out like this was awesome. None of us younger ratings had ever dared say boo to an officer and here was one with the full gold braided might of the Royal Navy behind him laying down the law as sternly as he could. Perhaps the more determined saw the effect he was creating for they began raising a loud chant that drowned out the rest of his words. Once more a number stepped forward aggressively and seeing how it was useless to go on talking let alone the danger of being assaulted the Jimmy turned hurriedly back up the ladder.

Part way up he turned and said firmly: 'I'll give you five minutes to think about it and then pipe hands to take in stores and prepare for sea. I expect every man to obey.'

This offer, which seemed almost like a reprieve, was the last thing we had expected. If he had told us we were all going to be clapped in irons I think we would have been less surprised. Perhaps he was trying to take the steam out of our outburst knowing it was useless to try force while we were secure in the messdeck or that making threats against us would only rouse us to greater fury. Whatever his thinking he seemed to be offering us a way out. But not to Taffy's way of seeing it.

'Don't let the Jimmy fool you, boyos,' he burst out. 'Once 'e gets you on deck they'll 'ave you good and proper. Even if 'e don't the old man or the Admiral will 'ave you by the bollocks.'

We could see the truth in that. None of us needed telling how Arthur George gave the First Lieutenant the run around or of the former's passion for discipline and retribution. Personally I didn't think the latter was the kind to set a trap and I, like many in that boiling, stinking steel box, was becoming desperate to go on deck.

We had a far more pressing need than any thought of backing out on our insurrection. In the mid-day heat and with so many men, well over 100, packed tight in the messdeck, our temperatures raised higher still by our emotions, we were becoming debilitated almost to the point of nausea. The more desperate put it to the ringleaders that we take advantage of the offer if only to get a few minutes of 'freshers' (fresh air).

At first they turned it down bluntly but as they saw there could be a risk of losing us altogether they partially agreed. Anyone who wanted to get a breather could do so but they had to get back below as quickly as they could. The screech of the bosun's call piping us back to duty brought the matter to a head. A few of us moved towards the ladder uncertainly not wanting to be thought of as deserters to the cause but as some more pressed on behind we climbed up glad to get into the open yet nervous about the risk we were taking.

There was, to our surprise, little sign of a reception party – just a few P.O.s, who seemed to be trying not to look as though they had evil intentions. It was almost as though they had been ordered not to antagonise us and when we had assembled in untidy small groups on deck they issued their orders with unnatural restraint. Slowly we moved off to our parts of ship still half expecting to be arrested at any second. The fact nothing happened was possibly more unnerving. It was as though two warring armies had broken off for a teabreak in mid-battle and were soon to be trying to bayonet one another.

Gradually this tenseness died away – only to be replaced by another anxiety. As my working party looked around we saw that comparatively few had left the messdeck. If we did not get back there quickly not only would the rest of the seamen think we had reneged but there might not be the chance to rejoin. 'If we 'ang around on deck the buggers will put a guard on the ladder and we'll be cut off,' insisted Cockie.

Yorkie posed another question no one else had wanted to air. 'What if we jag it in and let the rest get on with it?' he asked.

It was Mick who killed that notion. 'We've gone this far – let's see it through.'

With our P.O.'s back turned temporarily we sneaked our way back to the hatchway leading to the messdeck. From other parts of the ship others were following suit. Suddenly from behind we

heard the G.I. bellow: 'Get back to work you men or I'll have you.'
It sent us tumbling down below double quick. As we landed in the
messdeck a great cheer welcomed us. The others were convinced
we had ratted. The fact we had not appeared to give them greater
heart to carry on. As I sat down at my mess I wondered whether I
was more courageous than I thought or simply lacking courage in
not wanting to risk the finger of scorn being pointed at me or, more
likely, the fists of fury.

My thoughts were interrupted by Hookie sounding dour words
of warning. 'You lads got away with it once but they'll still 'ave you
for all this. There ain't no way any of us is going to keep 'is
yardarm burnished bright. The effing wonder is they ain't 'ad the
Royals in by now. It's always been a slack ship and no one don't
know their arse from their prick. I bets you they're all 'aving a
confab not knowing what the effing 'ell to do next.'*

So why hadn't he or the other killicks gone topsides when they
had the chance if he felt like that? we queried.

'No effing use any more, is it? We'd scuppered ourselves
already. My 'ook's (Leading Seaman's badge) is gone for sure and
if I know the Andrew they'll 'ave a few crossed 'ooks, crowns and a
bit of gold braid off a good few before they're through. No one, not
even the old man, gets away with 'aving this sort of trouble.'

His prophetic words of warning did not have the full effect he
had intended. The thought that our superiors would also suffer
was distinctly cheering. If nothing more than that was achieved it
might be all worthwhile. Another thing that bolstered our confidence was that we could not see how they could possibly hope to
operate the ship if all the seamen were locked up. We were the only
Royal Navy warship for hundreds, probably thousands of miles,
and finding a replacement crew would be impossible. Anyway, we
assured ourselves, we had done nothing more harmful than refuse
to turn to – no bloodshed or violence of any kind.

* News of the mutiny certainly came as a shock to the senior officers. That was
clearly the case with Admiral Talbot in that he had thought it totally appropriate
to invite the local U.S. Navy commanders to lunch aboard at the time. It proved
intensely embarrassing to him and to Captain Petrie, who was also a guest. When
the First Lieutenant wanted to tell him there was a mutiny he had to surrepti-
tiously send a message into the lunch to get the Captain outside. Then Petrie had
to extract the Admiral in the same discreet way. Returning to his guests Arthur
George had to find an excuse to get them to leave the ship as quickly as possible.

Our wishful optimism vanished as suddenly as a drop of water spilled on a red hot hob. From out of the gloom we were astonished to see Taffy, looking wilder than ever, emerge waving an automatic rifle above his head. Oblivious of the alarm he was causing he shouted: 'This 'll show the bastards we mean business. Jest let them try getting rough and they'll get some of this up their jacksies,' he added ramming a clip of ammunition into the gun.

Behaving more like a triumphant big game hunter exhibiting a severed head he paraded what could now be seen to be a Lanchester around the messes. Any approving cheers that brought were counteracted by gasps of dismay. Total disobedience was one thing – doing so at the point of a gun was another, far more frightening prospect.

''E ain't going to fire that thing is 'e?' Oggie begged of our Leading Hand.

'Taffy's just talk but he's effing raving mad if 'e thinks 'e's going to scare 'em with that. The bloody Royals will blow 'im to bits . . . and some of us as well,' Hookie sneered. But I could see he was worried.

Some wondered where the Welshman had stolen the gun but there was not much mystery about that. As Gunner's Yeoman he had keys to the rifle locker and the Lanchester was small enough for him to hide beneath his boiler suit. It proved, however, that he and his oppos had planned everything ahead and with more determination than a few beers and their tots of rum could provide.

There was no time to consider what our serious reaction to this vicious turn of events should be. Once more we heard steps descending the ladder and all eyes focused on who was going to make a fourth attempt to bring us to order. Would the Captain himself dare to confront us, the others having failed? we wondered. But once again it was the messdeck P.O. This time he had no chance to address us before he was almost swamped by the ringleaders and a pressing crush of their closest supporters. Whatever he was trying to say, whatever message he might be bringing was blotted out by demands that he go away and bring back some senior officer who would listen to our complaints and be prepared to put them right. In the mêlée Taffy could be seen still waving the gun furiously. The sight of it must have been enough for the Jimmy, who had also appeared before quickly returning on deck. Forcing himself clear the P.O. scampered after him, desperate to escape unscathed.

We were now left in two minds. While we took some confidence from the fact that no one seemed anxious to bring force to bear on us, which might indicate our complaints were negotiable, there was the thought that this softly, softly approach would change dramatically now it was known it was, ostensibly, an armed revolt. Opinions swung one way and then another but I could tell that some younger O.D.s like myself were fearful of brutal retaliation that might cost us more than a loss of liberty. Hookie did not help by telling us to 'steer clear of the ladder and get your 'eads down if them Royals come charging down'.

Scottie, Taffy and Mick may have believed in the same threat, for the trio had taken up a position at the head of the ladder where they would have a few seconds warning of any assault being launched. Only now the Welshman had hidden the Lanchester beneath his overalls. Our opinion that something alarming was about to happen became more fixed when the last remaining glimmer of electric light vanished altogether. The messdeck was now in total darkness. At long last they were beginning to tighten the screw on us. More pressure would surely follow, we told ourselves, as authority tried softening us up preparatory to a frontal attack.

Yet, it seemed, the talking was not yet over. From the head of the ladder we could hear the Scot's loud voice as he apparently became engaged in a heated argument with some unknown officers or P.O.s. Through the pitch blackness we could hear him insisting on our grievances being discussed before we would return to duty. Then, abruptly, the arguing broke off and the three came tumbling down the ladder as fast as they could.

For a moment we feared that it was a sign we were being attacked but no one followed and I could hear the sighs of relief around me. In the uneasy silence that followed we heard Scottie explaining that an attempt had been made to trick the three of them into being arrested.

Someone, he said, had suggested they go up to the Jimmy's cabin to 'talk it over – what sort of stupid cunts do they think we are? They'd 'ave collared us for sure. When they saw it was no effing good I could see they might make a grab for us so we got below double quick.'*

The three seemed revitalised and far from scared by their apparently narrow escape although the same could not be said for the rest of us. Once more we were suffering the heat and tension to the point where individual enthusiasm was weakening. It seemed we had been in the messdeck all day and not just a couple of hours or more – a feeling heightened by the darkness. All many of us had left now was only the spirit of messdeck camaraderie and we fell back on it more and more. To keep it going we once again broke out into bawdy singing. The appropriate 'This one-funnelled bastard is getting me down' was followed by our own version, repeated, of 'The Red Flag'.

That was bellowing forth when the Jimmy suddenly appeared again. The revolutionary battle cry stopped short but not the emotion it carried. A deafening roar of unsuppressed fury broke over the First Lieutenant's head. I half expected him to be driven back by such a massive show of anger, more so since he knew that one man, at least, was armed. His courage was undeniable as he forced his way through a shoving, hostile bunch of seamen and, whether for his own safety or to obtain a better platform, scrambled agilely on top of one of the tiers of lockers. There, as loud as he could, he yelled for silence. It seemed minutes before he could get enough response but, possibly having shouted themselves hoarse, the messdeck at last quietened enough for him to be clearly heard.

Perspiring profusely and in a tense voice that showed the strain he was having to suffer he told us: 'I order you to return to your duties immediately. You are committing the worst crime possible. You are guilty of mutiny and mutiny in time of war. Your offence could not be more serious.'

The background noise died almost completely. We were all fully conscious of the gravity of our disobedience yet this was the

* The Jimmy later told a Court of Inquiry that he was with the Messdeck P.O. when they confronted the Scots ringleader at the top of the ladder. He confirmed that a suggestion had been put to the Scot that he go up to the First Lieutenant's cabin but that it had come from the Petty Officer, who wanted to find a way of getting the seaman arrested more easily. The ringleader was later to claim it was the Jimmy who suggested it and the argument over who did so was to play a highly controversial part in subsequent official proceedings.

very first time anyone had officially told us we were guilty of mutiny. The very sound of the word was chilling. It might even have been enough to have made many of us accept that we had gone as far as we dare. If the Jimmy had gone on to state how he wanted us to go about responding to his order there could, perhaps, have been a partial collapse of the mutiny at least. But he was robbed of our attention and any support by a sudden yell from near the ladder of: 'Watch out! The Royals are coming.'

We turned to see the Captain of Marines half way down to the moment Taffy dashed from the mob in front of the First Lieutenant, his finger on the trigger of the Lanchester, which he was nant, his finger on the trigger of the Lanchester, which he was poking menacingly in the direction of the Marine officer.

I could see the expression of fear on the Captain's face, standing out against the light filtering down from above, as Taffy began climbing the ladder shouting: 'Get back up before I use this on you.'

There was no need for any further urging. The officer ran back up faster than anyone had before him. A few seconds later he was followed by the Jimmy, more slowly, but just as defeated. In the din that followed Taffy's violent outburst he could never have continued speaking. Nor would there have been much point. To have got us back to work he would have needed more of our trust than we were now prepared to give as a result of the Marine appearing. That, we interpreted,* was part of a plot in which the

---

* If we had known at the time how far the Jimmy, Lieutenant-Commander Kenneth Buckel, was risking his career in trying to end the mutiny as peacefully as possible we would have been on his side. Prior to coming down in the messdeck at physical risk to himself, he had received direct orders from Rear-Admiral Talbot to call out the Marines and have them launch an assault on the messdeck. The Lieutenant-Commander later made out a report in which he stated the Admiral had given him an order for the Marines to open fire down the hatchway to the messdeck. Believing this would obviously lead to many being killed and injured the Jimmy decided instead to make one last attempt to persuade the men to end the mutiny and at the same time order the Marines to assemble on the after welldeck ready to come forward should he 'be kidnapped'. He was anxious that they should not be seen in case it inflamed the seamen's tempers further.

The appearance of the Marine Captain was in direct contravention of his orders, Buckel later told a Court of Inquiry. He considered it as a major reason why his effort to win the men back failed. He could well have been right.

First Lieutenant was simply trying to hold our attention while the Royals made an assault. We were almost grateful for the Welshman's action even if it went beyond what many of the seamen thought wise. This seemed confirmed by the news that armed Marine sentries with fixed bayonets had now been posted at the top of the hatch. Mutineers we might be but we were now also prisoners.

12

Flight Ashore

The cautious sparring was over. The first violent blow in retaliation for our audacity had just been thrown. And it could be a knockout punch. A loud clang from on top told us they had battened down the messdeck hatch. Now we knew what it was like – as if some of the ex-convicts did not know already – to hear the foreboding sound of a cell door being banged shut.

Yet a gaolbird was allowed to breathe and one of our only two small sources of fresh air had been cut off. The ventilation system, which worked poorly, did nothing to take away the foul fug that was almost gassing us. How much longer, we wondered, before authority would rob us of even this tiny lifesaver?

It was not the only worry we had. Others were now being heatedly argued about all around. What were we going to do for food? All each mess had were a few crusts of bread. There was a thin trickle of water but that, also, might be switched off. It was obvious we could not fight on for long. Indeed! Would we be allowed to survive at all? The fear was genuine for in the saturating heat and with oxygen being rapidly eaten up our existence could be counted only in hours.

It all added up to one major question. Should we now admit defeat and surrender? Yet no one wanted to put it into words. Having gone so far it would be a shameful waste of our courage and a pathetic return for the heavy punishment we would suffer. We had so far achieved nothing more than cause our superiors embarrassment. The chances of them answering our plea for better conditions were thin.

There was very little objection when Scottie paraded around the messdeck urging us to stand fast and continue the fight. 'The bastards can't keep us battened down for ever,' he insisted. 'There's no one to work ship if we're all effing well down 'ere?'

In his passion to continue the mutiny, however, he had overlooked one distinct possibility. A shout from a killick quickly made him aware.

'I'll tell who will take 'er to sea – the pigs and P.O.s. An' once they've got us out in the 'oggin (sea) we're fucked.'

It brought a rumble of support and created further agitation among the already anxious ratings. Another loud cry insisted: 'We're fucked anyway if we stay down 'ere. Let's get on deck before the buggers make it effing worse for us.'

This produced a much greater roar of approval to which the Scot responded fully. 'O.K. lads if that's what you want we'll 'ave a go. But I don't want no one shitting on his oppos if we gets on deck. Get on the fo'c'sle and make effing certain no one 'andles them 'awsers. This boat stays in port until we gets satisfaction.'

The prospect of escaping from what had begun to feel more like a coffin was enough to whip up our fervour once more. Yet I could not help feeling that the chances of getting the hatch unbattened were very slim – not without our abject admission of surrender. I reckoned without the determination of Taffy. Leading the way he climbed the ladder and banged on the hatch as hard as he could. Then, as loud as possible, he yelled: 'Open up. We're coming out.'

Wisely he hadn't said why – simply leaving the Royals to make their own assumption. Whoever was in charge must have believed we were giving in or was not prepared to risk we were not for we heard the hatch being unscrewed and a few moments later blinked in the bright light that shone down. I saw the head of the Captain of Marines peer uncertainly down and then snap back quickly as Taffy literally charged up followed by the other ringleaders and a press of mutineers.

If the Captain had any thoughts of trying to stop us he didn't stand a chance. We forced our way past his squad of armed Marines, who seemed totally overwhelmed by the determined torrent of seamen pouring as fast as they could in the direction of the fo'c'sle. A corporal made a vain gesture to try and block our way but was abruptly shoved aside and I heard a rating bellow: 'Get back you sodding bastards.'

If we had been ordered to abandon ship we could not have got on deck more quickly. In what seemed seconds around 120 of us were streaming on the foredeck. Moments later we were gathered around the coils of hawsers and the winches forming an impenetrable barrier to anyone who tried to get near them to take the ship to sea. The mutiny was now well and truly out in the open and our belligerent display of disobedience there for anyone to see.

After the pitch blackness of the messdeck I felt as exposed as if I was under a searchlight. The sun beating down on the bare steel deck made it too hot to stand and we slumped on to the ropes to ease our burning feet. I wondered how long we could withstand the scorching rays on the rest of our bodies. But our spirits remained boosted by being in the open air and at having escaped from our suffocating prison below. Also, for the time being, we seemed to hold the whiphand. No one could take the ship out now.

Yorkie was not so optimistic. 'Bloody fine targets we make standing 'ere,' he sighed. 'Them Royals can pick us off just like dooks. Did y'see their rifles was loaded?'

We had and had been trying not to be frightened by it. I looked around to see if Taffy was displaying his Lanchester, worried that the sight of it might lead to mass slaughter. But he appeared to be unarmed. I asked if anyone had seen what he had done with the gun.

' 'E's got it all right,' announced Mick. 'I saw 'im stash it inside his overalls before 'e went up the ladder . . . 'anded the clips of ammo to some A.B. for 'im to 'ide.*

But I was relying more on the hope that the Admiral or Captain would do anything than have the Royals fire and create a slaughter in front of the dozens of U.S. Navymen who had now gathered on the quayside and were craning out of every available window in their offices. We must have looked a dramatic sight crowding the fo'c'sle in a mutinous group with the Marines poised with bayoneted rifles on the deck overlooking us. Yet there was no sight of Arthur George or the Captain. What was also obvious was that

* A Leading Seaman later called as a witness to the official inquiry stated that to try and prevent bloodshed he had persuaded the A.B. to hand him the clips of ammunition, which he then hid under the canvas cover over some hawsers. It proved to be vital in saving lives. There is no doubt the Marines would have been ordered to open fire if there was any sign of the Lanchester being used.

there was hardly anyone else in view. As we discussed this absence we agreed that the rest of the complement must have been told to stay in their messes or well clear of us to prevent being contaminated.

It made us feel all the more exposed and certainly a bit let down. The three ringleaders, for that is what they would certainly be regarded as when the time of reckoning came, had hinted that we might get support from the stokers and bunting tossers but that they were waiting for us to make the first move. Perhaps, we tried reassuring ourselves, they had also mutinied but were being forcibly kept in their messdecks. But we had little faith in this hope. We were too well aware of how abnormally segregated each Lower Deck department was in *Lothian*.

A sudden movement among the Royals concentrated our attention on them. Their Captain was issuing some kind of command. A few moments later they had vanished from sight. As they went we gave them a rousing jeer as though we had won some kind of victory although it was more to raise our own flagging spirits. I wondered if their departure was some kind of psychological warfare – aimed to put us off our guard or weaken our determination. Whatever it was it certainly made most of us feel more exposed and uncertain.

The 90 degree temperature, our total exposure to the tropical rays and our painful thirst was also starting to weaken our resistance. I only had to glance at some of the depressed looks on the faces of seamen around me to know they were hoping it would soon all be over. A few of the O.D.s began wondering aloud whether there would be a surrender. Scouse, who had never been fully behind the mutiny, put his feelings more firmly: 'We should jag it in. We've done all we can. There's no way we can stay up 'ere much longer. I don't know about you lot but I'm fucked already.'

Cockie turned on him violently. 'You just ain't got no guts. That's just what the pigs want – to get some of you shitty arsed lot to jag it in so they'll 'ave less of a scrap on their 'ands when they 'as to get rough. We stick together, see, or I'll effing well shove this fist down your throat.'

The pair of them sparred up and were within an inch of hitting each other when Mick, who was bigger and tougher than both, moved in between them. 'It's you two who'll get thumped if you

116

don't stow it. That's just what the pigs want to see – some of us 'aving a scrap.'

Reluctantly the two moved apart but still clearly hostile. I blamed the heat and the tension more than anything. It was a wonder tempers had not frayed sooner. It was some time since we had been given an outlet for our worked up emotions and we only had one another to turn on. But the chance to show a shared rebelliousness appeared from out of the alleyway. There, stepping towards us, marched none other than the Captain followed by the Jimmy and a couple of P.O.s.

If it was meant to be a show of fearsome authority it was a failure. Seeing the Captain appear for the first time in our presence since the mutiny began was taken as a sign that our protest was, at last, being taken with the seriousness we believed it merited; that he had shed his normally reclusive role and come to us to hear our grievances.

The ringleaders obviously thought he was on some kind of peace mission. When a few jeers broke out they yelled for silence. 'Give the old man his say,' insisted Scottie.

Advancing to within a few yards of us the officers and P.O.s halted. Seeing he had our full attention the Captain spoke out loud and clear – but not co-operatively. 'I order you to return to duty at once. You are committing mutiny in wartime and any man who disobeys will be severely punished.'

We remained silent but now more from surprise. Surely the Captain did not think his four shiny gold rings were going to make us come crawling back on their own when we had come this far? Perhaps he would offer some consolation. We waited expectantly.

But he became more determined we should surrender. Raising his voice angrily and displaying a fierceness alien to his usual subdued nature he called out: 'I shall take this ship to sea whatever you do. If you don't turn to immediately the officers and Petty Officers will man the hawsers. Any attempt to stop them will be met with force.'

This time there was no stunned silence. From every part of the packed crowd of mutineers rose a defiant rejection. I almost felt sorry for the old man as he came under raucous verbal attack that looked like erupting into a physical one at any moment. Shouts of: 'Try it on – if you effing well dare', 'Piss off' and 'You and whose effing army' flew around his head. Not since Captain Bligh had a Royal Navy ship's commander been shown such a mass display of bloody minded disobedience.

If he had deliberately set out to raise our wrath and force the mutiny into a more belligerent pitch he could not have done better. I could only imagine he had temporarily lost his grip; that such a usually benign, yet brave, man found that quelling a mutiny beyond his experience and personality. Or was he simply obeying a command of his Admiral?

With such clear evidence that firmness had failed he should, probably, have gone away to decide on some better alternative. Unwisely he persisted. Sticking his ground in spite of the fist waving mob, his temper rising, he shouted as loud as he could: 'I *shall* take the ship to sea – without you if necessary.'

He should definitely have stopped there but as if he was trying to emphasise his determination he added the fatal last words: 'As far as I'm concerned you can walk ashore.'

Rarely could such loosely meant words have been taken so literally. Without realising it the Captain had suggested to the ringleaders an escape route from the tight corner we were in by staying on the fo'c'sle. As he turned to march angrily away Taffy called out: 'You 'eard 'im! Let's get on the jetty boys.'

Wasting no time he, Scottie and the Irish killick moved speedily aft towards the gangway. There was a momentary hesitation by the rest of the mutineers before several dozen of them decided to follow. I and most of my messmates found ourselves caught up in their dash. Should I or should I not take this most mutinous of steps? As grave as our crime already was deserting a ship was still more calamitous. But there was no time to think as we were swept along through the alleyway and on to the gangway.

As we jostled to get down my already parched throat went agonisingly drier as I saw the Royals poised feet away with rifles at the ready. I almost froze to the spot at the thought of what they might obviously do next but the crush behind sent me almost tumbling down the gangway. No one was going to hang around to make a point blank target. The next few minutes became a blank – my mind refusing to acknowledge the danger and the drama of my actions. I could have been anywhere – not just stampeding blindly on to a burning quay in Balboa.

When, at last, I was able to force myself to accept what was happening I found my situation more fearful than I had expected. At a rough count there were now only about sixty seamen gathered around – half had clearly remained aboard either out of choice or had been prevented from coming ashore. We were still a sizable group but I felt dwarfed by the bulk of the ship towering above and the buildings behind us. It was obvious, too, that we were outnumbered by the excited clusters of spectators, mainly U.S. servicemen, who were standing around as though they were watching a real life cops-and-robbers thriller.

Like us they could see the lines of Royals now formed into two separate parties one above the other on the main and boat decks – all armed. Here and there on other parts of the decks were small groups of officers and P.O.s staring sharply down at us although of the Admiral and Captain there was no sign. No sign of any action either. The minutes passed agonisingly and slowly we mutineers edged closer together as the tension grew and we anxiously sought the reassurance of one another's presence. High above I saw the hawks that were a familiar part of the Panamanian sky wheel in languorous but sharp-eyed motion. Were they flocking together more and more? My imagination was working overtime.

The hot sun had dipped but was still strong enough to make us run with sweat although some of that could be fear. I had lost track of time but it must have been approaching 5 p.m. The mutiny seemed to have been taking place for far longer and I could not believe it could continue for much more. This time we had nowhere else to go. Whether he liked it or not Arthur George must have requested the Yanks to prevent us leaving the quay. The ringleaders must have accepted they had reached the mutiny's physical limits for they had become unusually silent.

The rest of us were too stunned by our own audacity to do more than just stand and wait for the inevitable stern repercussions. We did not have to wait long. Within ten minutes there was a bustle of activity at the head of the gangway down which we had anticipated the Royals would probably come armed to the teeth. But we made a double take when who should nervously ascend but some dozen or so Royal Corps of Signallers. They were, by our coarse standards, a very decently peaceful set of soldiers who did nothing more violent in the line of duty than man radios and other communication equipment. Just why they had been ordered to force us back seemed a mystery at the time although later I felt

119

someone had decided it was wiser in front of the Americans to keep the trouble in as low a key as possible. In fact it turned our mutiny, for a few moments, into low comedy.

As the Signallers got closer we saw they were armed with nothing more vicious than standard Army issue entrenching tools. Whether it was thought they were going to beat us about our heads into submission or what but it brought forth our first laughter since the revolt had begun. Encouraged by such a feeble threat the ringleaders and some dozen or more mutineers advanced on the soldiers, grabbed their wooden weapons and then heaved these into the harbour.

The sergeant in charge could only stand and look on with the puzzled expression of any Army commander who cannot decide whether to advance or retreat in the face of the enemy. He took what, sensibly, was the best action. He ordered his small, scared squad to march back aboard. They went with our cheers at achieving a real victory. But we knew it could not be for long.

Yet, whoever was giving the orders, was still clearly trying to avoid a more violent confrontation. Next down the gangway came a solitary officer. We recognised him only vaguely as a Lieutenant-Commander navigation specialist on the Admiral's staff. All he brought with him was the Naval bible we all could recognise – the thick volume of K.R.s and A.I.s.

Was he going to stand there on that boiling hot quay in front of the large crowd of Yanks and Panamanian longshoremen cat-calling while he read out the Articles of War or some section of the regulations that covered our crime? It seemed a remarkably pointless action if he was. We had already seen off the Jimmy (three times), the Captain and the Signallers and some formalised rhetoric was not going to make a solitary bit of difference. In seconds we had seen off this precocious attempt. As the Lieutenant-Commander opened his bible the ringleaders burst out into the Red Flag again with the rest of us helping to drown out any possible attempt to get his voice heard. Seeing how useless it was the officer turned on his heels and, saving any further loss of face, walked stiffly back aboard.

This second success should have raised our morale yet, as far as myself and some others around me felt, it began evaporating rapidly. The heat, the tension, the thirst and the sure knowledge that we could not hold out much longer made us begin to pray for some way out of the desperate spot which we had dug for ourselves. Around me I could hear other young seamen suggesting we should 'jag it in'. Many of us might have done had we not feared being regarded as cowards almost as much. We looked towards the hard core of rebels hoping for a sign they were relenting but it was obvious they were determined to hold out as long as they could.

Our attention reverted to the gangway down which we were now sure the Royals would advance in a no-nonsense effort to crush the mutiny. But, once again, a solitary figure appeared. Not an officer this time, nor carrying anything. But in an almost mad hurry. Virtually running down the gangway almost as though he was escaping from the ship came the figure of a killick we knew as one of the more helpful to us O.D.s. There was a rousing cheer from those who believed he was coming to join us in our stand but it quickly ceased when the Leading Hand jumped up on to a bollard and began loudly appealing to us to end the mutiny.

As passionately as he could he urged us to return aboard. 'You've made your point lads. There's no good standing around here. All it'll get you is a bigger dose of jankers.'

To us younger ones immediately in front of him, whom he was intent on persuading, it was the answer to our despair. From behind, however, the more rebellious tried to drown his appeal with jeers and chants. Shouting above the din the killick pressed on: 'Use your loaf lads. The Royals will be down among you any time – guns and all.'

Seeing he had won our attention he added: 'Don't worry. You haven't fought for nothing. They'll put your grievances right.'

With that he jumped down and calling out: 'Follow me lads', led the way towards the ship. Whether we were just desperate for any way out or because he seemed to speak with conviction and some authority I didn't know but we flocked behind him. Afterwards I asked myself, and others wondered, too, if he had been sent by the Captain or someone in command in a more human attempt to win us back. That, we were to discover, was far from the truth – as was the Leading Seaman to his cost. He had brought back all but seventeen of the mutineers on his own initiative but in the unsympathetic eyes of Naval authority he had committed a crime.

Our thoughts as we slowly climbed back up the gangway, however, were torn between the grim punishment we presumed lay ahead of us and whether we were really as treacherous as the boos and taunts of the men we had left all alone on the quay suggested.

13

Last Stand

They stood on the dusty, sun-baked Central American quay 5,000 miles from home defying one of the world's most powerful Navies. Just seventeen bedraggled, sweating men. Their last stand was as hopeless as their cause. It was as inglorious as many other defiant final battles in their Service's proud history had been heroic. But then, they were fighting their own side.

Trapped between ship and the portside building they shouted, sang and waved their fists as recklessly as rebellious convicts in a high security gaol. On three sides American Navymen watched in wide-eyed fascination. On the fourth, aboard *Lothian*, a bustle of activity showed the decisive ending to the mutiny and the Royal Navy's moment of shame was about to take place.

Minutes later the Royal Marines, tightly clutching loaded and bayoneted rifles, descended the gangway led by their Captain. As the mutineers clustered closer together in a defensive circle the Royals moved into position around them, arms held out at the ready. Standing between, the Captain demanded the rebels surrender and follow his men back aboard. The only response was a concerted jeer and cries of 'Come and get us'.

The tension, already high, grew even greater. Those who had witnessed the scene and later described it to us mutineers now confined to the messdeck after earlier returning aboard felt almost certain the Royals commander was going to order his men to open fire. Instead he told them to move in closer in a tighter circle.*

As they did so the seventeen closed ranks and thrust their fists up showing every sign of being prepared to fight it out. It brought

* The Marines had been sent ashore with orders to open fire if the ringleader Taffy had attempted to use his stolen Lanchester, the Court of Inquiry later held,

the Royals to a nervous halt. This was the kind of close combat they had certainly never been trained to undertake nor seemed overwilling to handle when it involved men supposedly on the same side. But another barked command and the Marines' discipline made them advance still nearer.

They were almost face to face when the mutineers flung themselves at the Royals, struggling to grab their rifles from them, regardless of the danger of being bayoneted.* Yet it proved little more than one last defiant gesture. In seconds the seventeen had given in, standing there defeated. The mutiny, the first in the Royal Navy since Invergordon, as far as anyone aboard could tell, and involving more violence and indiscipline, was over.

Tightly guarded by their armed escort the rebels were brought back into the ship. But still showing some spirit. As they were led right aft to where a temporary prison had been hastily made ready in the former stewards quarters they were still yelling out protests. From the Americans clustered on the quay came an answering cheer. It was to be the last comfort the seventeen would enjoy for a long time to come.

It would have been little cheer to them to know how the rest of us sitting around the messdeck waiting anxiously for our fate to be decided were also suffering an attack of conscience. Had we not left them in the lurch, we berated ourselves, they might have had a better chance of extricating themselves from their nearly impossible situation. Now they would face the worst penalties. But would we be much better off? Even if we had given in earlier we had still committed the most serious offences in the Naval Discipline Act.

---

was told. Witnesses, however, stated that the Welshman had been seen to throw the gun into the harbour between the quay and the ship's sides. Another version was that it had been put down a gash chute.

* The War Diary of 498 Flotilla, Royal Marines, which served in H.M.S. *Lothian*, stated: 'A case of mass insubordination occurred. A number of seamen refused duty on sailing and moved on to the jetty. 498 Flotilla under the command of Captain J. V. Bales were issued with ammunition and posted at special places. The three ringleaders and fourteen other ratings were placed under armed sentry by the Royal Marines. The seamen tried to obtain the Royal Marine rifles but were unsuccessful.'

Although all other references to the mutiny are missing from official files placed in the Public Record Office this brief mention appears to have been overlooked.

While we only had a hazy idea of what the ominous sounding legislation contained no penalty seemed too high.

Imprisonment, we felt sure, was a certainty – only the length of our sentence in any doubt. Yet would even that be enough to satisfy the fury of our masters? An appalling thought crossed my mind as I am sure it did in some of the others. Only the sudden rumble of the main engines followed by the unmistakable pitching of the ship leaving the berth took the grim thought away. So they had got the ship to sea. Was it the officers and P.O.s who handled the ropes, as the Captain said, or had the seamen who had chosen or been compelled to remain aboard at last given in and turned to obediently?

The answer to that came shortly afterwards when the rest of the men came back down into the messdeck. Defensively, I felt, some explained that after seeing the rest of us arrested they felt it was useless carrying on. Neither did they want to add to the punishment which they were sure they now faced. I could not argue with the sense of it but it still left us more mutinous seamen feeling they had been selfish. Cockie put it more bluntly: 'Talk abaht "Fuck You Jack I'm Inboard" . . .'.

Sympathy is a rare emotion in a messdeck where everybody is suffering some hardship and we should not have looked for any now. But it proved hard to accept we were obviously being expected to face our future ordeal without a word of regret from the rest especially when some of them took it too lightheartedly for our liking. Messdeck sick humour bred out of our misery with teasing remarks such as 'Watch out for them sharks when they make you walk the plank' or ' 'Ave you 'eard that keel'auling's still allowed for mutineers?'

We put up with most of these but one was too frighteningly close to the anxious thought at the back of our minds. It was the messdeck sweeper who joked: 'I jest seen the Bosun greasing down some ropes – got a funny sort of noose on them.'

I saw Yorkie almost turn white. No longer the phlegmatic oppo who had stood by us on the quay showing no trace of fear he turned fearfully towards Hookie and asked, almost pleadingly: 'They don't 'ang you from the yardarm any more, do they?'

Although the rest of us had resisted posing the same question our attention was just as great as Hookie gave his considered reply: 'No, I don't think so but then there ain't been a mutiny in the

Andrew since Invergordon – not in wartime neither. Gawd knows what the Admiral or them buggers back in White'all will do. I wouldn't put it past them as far as them effing sods back aft is concerned, especially Taffy. 'E'll be up for armed mutiny for sure.'

More hopeful than certain Oggie butted in: 'They can't 'ang us all or they won't 'ave enough seamen to 'andle the ship.'

Hookie wasn't impressed. 'Don't you effers think you're going to get away with just a kick up the arse. You'll be effing well screaming for mercy before they're through with you lot.'

Cockie protested angrily: 'Why just us! All the rest of the effers was in it with us, you killicks included.'

Our Leading Hand turned on him nastily: 'You want to stow it before someone uses your 'ead as a fender. It's up to every Jack to get out of this shit'eap the best way 'e can. But don't you worry there won't be many who don't get the chop. I told you before there'll be 'ooks and every other effing thing dipped before they're through with us. I'll be lucky if I'm just an A.B. doing jankers.'

We wished now Yorkie had not put his question. Even if hanging did seem a remote threat Hookie had made other punishment seem worse than we had first contemplated. The rest of that evening we sat around restlessly barely taking our eyes off the messdeck ladder down which we constantly expected the Jaunty or some other figure of doom to come stamping with orders for us to be placed under closer arrest.

Had we been calmer, better able to think straight, we might have appreciated the reality of the situation in a way which would have cheered us a little. In such an overcrowded ship room of any kind was at a premium not least the official cells. With only four of them they could obviously not cope with dozens of us. Nor would there be much use turning the whole seamen's messdeck into one big cell as some suggested might happen. There would be no way of preventing the risk of further rebellion from us and to batten us down would only cause suffocation. But the fact the ship was now heading, so we understood, to rejoin the rest of the Force with Arthur George apparently still set on carrying out his fighting mission was the greatest pointer in our favour. Even if the seamen who had not walked ashore were allowed to perform their normal duties there would still be far too few deck ratings to handle all the necessary round-the-clock work for the four weeks the Pacific crossing would take. Such vital tasks as radar watchkeeping and manning the helm could not be carried out by anyone substituted from other departments.

Such rays of hope as these were unable to shine through our total conviction that no Captain or Admiral would take a ship into a war zone manned by mutinous seamen even if their revolt had been squashed. Yet as we turned into our hammocks for a largely sleepless night and there was still no sign of any further action being taken against us we were left wondering if the unbelievable might not be a possibility.

At 5.30 the next morning as Wakey Wakey forced us, bleary-eyed, to face what we felt sure would be our day of reckoning we were in no rush to stow our hammocks and get washed. After all, we told ourselves, why hurry when most of us would still be confined below? When the messdeck P.O. appeared demanding to know why we were taking so long we assumed this was just his usual show of authority. It was only when he began insisting we 'turn to double quick' that it began to sink in we were actually being told to resume normal duties.

Once it had we needed no more urging. Getting back to work, even if it was washing down decks, seemed like a miraculous reprieve. The fresh, early morning ocean air lifted our spirits higher still and the sight of the broad expanse of empty sea all around with many days of that still to come added conviction to our growing hope that we could continue to enjoy our unexpected freedom for some time to come. When, at breakfast, we were told that we would also be expected to carry out our usual watchkeeping as well we, at last, realised the Admiral had been forced to accept the impossibility of keeping so many of us locked up. Would he be compelled to also show us greater leniency in the inevitable punishment we should have to face sooner or later? But our optimism was not so great as to make us believe that.

The seventeen tightly guarded by armed Royals back aft could have had no such wild dreams. If they were suffering some virulent contagious disease we could not have been kept further away from them with the whole poop out of bounds to us. It was not the only part of ship where we were forbidden to tread. More Marine sentries blocked off alleyways to parts of the midships superstructure where the Admiral's staff had offices. In one of

127

them, we learnt, most of his officers had been in constant sitting
ever since we had left Balboa, breaking off only for meals. All we
could glean was that they formed a Court of Inquiry into the
mutiny under the Presidency of the Chief of Staff, Captain
Duckworth.

It would, explained the older hands, decide who was to blame –
not just us seamen but anyone, officers, Chiefs or P.O.s included –
for letting it happen. The Court would also recommend what
action should be taken against offenders. That would almost
certainly mean court martials. But we could only guess. The tight
secrecy being observed went far beyond anything we had ever
known. The steady stream of witnesses from Captain down to
ratings being called were all sworn not to divulge a solitary word
outside the Inquiry with the threat of punishment if they did.
Whether any of the seventeen were brought before the Court
I do not know but none of us others who had walked ashore
were.

That first day after the mutiny crept uneasily by without us
knowing what was going to happen yet expecting an early decision. But we had to face up to clear signs that while we remained
aboard, even working normally, we were to be treated as lepers.
There had always been an uncomfortable atmosphere of segrega-
tion aboard but now we could see that the dividing lines between
us and the other ratings along with the R.A.F. and Army were
being drawn more tightly. Other department officers and P.O.s
were ensuring there was no mixing wherever possible and to our
regret we could sense the stokers, bunting tossers and the rest were
not objecting. From what we had earlier been able to tell they had
been sympathetic and appreciating we were fighting to improve
the bad conditions they also suffered but with our failure they
regarded our action as adding to their problems, for even tighter
discipline was being applied all round.

Although we were sailing through warm, sunlit seas a black
cloud descended over the *Lothian* that cast ever deeper gloom and
suspicion. It was not just confined to the Lower Deck. A state of
fragile tension could be seen building up between the ship's
officers as such and Arthur George's staff. Their relationships had
always been stiffly formal and now with the latter apparently
sitting in judgment on the former we could see a wide gulf
developing. The tight secrecy of the Inquiry, which affected our

128

Left: Author Bill Glenton, aged eighteen, photographed in a Glasgow park shortly before H.M.S. *Lothian* sailed on her secret mission to the South-West Pacific. Barely a month later he was a mutineer.

Below: H.M.S. *Lothian* at anchor in a South-West Pacific harbour – something she was to do in many others as she became a "Ship in Disgrace", unloved and unwanted.

Left above: H.M.S. *Clan Lamont*, the "lame duck" of Force X. Rejected by the U.S. Navy, her greatest distinction in the Pacific was her wicked reputation for "making smoke".

Left centre: H.M.S. *Glenearn*, a Landing Ship with a fine reputation. She was the only vessel in Force X of proper fighting efficiency and of any comfort.

Left below: H.M.S. *Empire Mace* with landing craft lowered – but not for action against the Japanese. Like the other Empires, her craft were used briefly for training Allied soldiers – until the L.C.A.s were proved unsuitable for the Pacific campaign.

Above: H.M.S. *Empire Arquebus*, typical of the hurriedly converted "Liberty" type ships pressed into service with Force X. Like the rest of the force, she was made to take a behind the front line "trampship" role by the U.S. Navy.

Above: H.M.S. *Empire Battleaxe* – a name that belied hers and Force X's rejected roles. This "Battleaxe" got rust, not blood, on her blade.

Below: H.M.S. *Empire Spearhead* – all dressed up for action but with nowhere to go. The G.I.s she and other ships in the Force brought from the U.S.A. for the Philippine landings were switched to American L.S.I.s.

Admiral Ernest King, Chief of U.S. Naval Operations in World War II. Although this almost anti-British commander requested Force X to aid the U.S. Navy in the Pacific, he clearly told its R.N. Flag Officer he wanted little to do with it.

The Many Faces of Admiral Talbot

Right above: Rear-Admiral Arthur George Talbot, D.S.O. and Bar (later Vice-Admiral retired with C.B. decoration). One of the three main R.N. Commanders off the Normandy beaches, his appointment as Flag Officer Force X was like a symphony orchestra conductor being sent to lead a brass band. The photograph shows him on his appointment as Rear-Admiral in 1943.

Right below: "Arthur George" posing in full glory with his Secretary Paymaster Commander Nevill Porter (to his Right) and Flag Lieutenant Ian Forbes Watson.

Far right: The other face of Arthur George here seen on the bridge of H.M.S. *Lothian* during her unhappy mission. The problems have clearly taken their toll.

A thinner, more thoughtful Bill Glenton, photographed in Sydney, N.S.W., exactly a year after sailing from Greenock in H.M.S. *Lothian*. He was a stone and a half lighter and like so many of his shipmates had been in hospital or otherwise invalided – "due to Allied not enemy action".

officers almost as much as us, was definitely upsetting them. They took exception to the way the staff seemed to be acting entirely behind their backs and they felt it went far beyond normal divided relationships in a flagship.

A friendly sparker passed on the news that all outgoing and ingoing signals between the staff and the outside world were now being by-passed the ship's communication staff and marked 'for Admiral's Staff only'. He, other sparkers and even their signals officers were prevented from being present when staff signals were transmitted.

From wardroom stewards came the news that socialising between ship's and staff officers had almost stopped even at mealtimes. That puzzled some of us who regarded all 'pigs' as being happy to share the same trough. But 'Pop', the other of our two three-badge A.B.s, did not find it strange. He had served on a C-in-C's staff in the dim distant past and considered himself an authority on such matters.

'No more than you'd expect,' he told us firmly. 'I seen it afore when the orficers on the flagship got theirselves up a creek. The staff didn't want nothing to do with them. They cut themselves loose in case they went down with the ship as well. The further our lot can put between theirselves and the mutiny and the court martial the better it's going to look for them.'

It cheered us a little to think we could be dragging down officers with us but Mick was indignant. 'It's not right them staff officers should get away with it. They knew what was wrong with the ship as much as anyone. Anyway if the Admiral wasn't so pusser we could have put up with things better.'

But it sounded too moralising for most of us. We certainly could not see an Admiral having to take any blame and however much moral justice was in our favour we knew the Andrew took a far less human approach to such major crimes as committed by us. Yet a strong sense of injustice grew within us. It always existed in O.D.s like ourselves. We were the lowest of the low and could be stamped on by everyone, we believed. We did not even have a ship's cat on which to pass the kicks.

Inevitably as we tried to adjust to our despair we should vent our feelings in the only way left to us – on one another. Bad feeling bred as rapidly in the messdeck as the cockroaches.

Those of us who had walked ashore could not help reacting

accusingly against those who had not. The messdeck became split into two factions – even separate messes. Tempers, which were never easy to curb in the cramped, overheated conditions, flared more abruptly than before in the tense, divided atmosphere. Freud would have had a field day but fists were the only psychiatry that counted among the seamen. The first time they flew was after Cockie, still nursing a grievance from his earlier row with Scouse, began taunting him for deserting the rest of the six by remaining aboard.

The Liverpudlian had just come off the last dog watch and was about to sit down when Cockie sniffed the air with great exaggeration and loudly asked who had created 'the effing stink'.

Scouse tried ignoring the jibe so Cockie persisted: 'You know what I think it is – it's what you get from a stinking scab.'

This time the insult struck deep. Baring up to the Cockney like a little terrier the short Scouser demanded he come up on deck where he could sort him out. Bristling angrily he shouted: 'I ain't going to be called a scab by some big mouth coward.'

The insult was enough to make Cockie lose his temper. In a flash his fist shot out landing full on Scouse's nose. As the blood spurted they wrestled one another to the deck. Seconds later Hookie had grabbed both of them by the hair and was twisting it until they screamed to be let free. Shoving them away the killick raised his own brawny fists and holding them up menacingly to their faces told them: 'If you want a fight 'ave it with me . . . I'll knock seven bells of shit out of both of you.'

Then, turning to the rest of us he said threateningly: 'That goes for the 'ole effing mess. You're up shitcreek enough already. I don't want no more stupid fuckers calling each other scabs. You just stow it until they give you something to really gripe about.'

It was brutal but effective. No earnest counselling by some social worker could have got across so well the uselessness of falling out among each other. Not that it ended the feud between Scouse and Cockie or brought the former properly back into the fold. Few of us were to exchange more than a passing word with him and, virtually sent to Coventry, he was soon to request a transfer to another mess.

For the rest of that evening we had little heart left in playing cards or hanging around the mess. Before turning in or going on watch most of us went up on the fo'c'sle to soak in fresh air and feel the greater freedom of the endless expanse of Pacific. It was there we found Postie yarning away to some other O.D.s. He enjoyed acting the ancient mariner and the more he could make us nervous with his tales of what he called ' 'ard ships' the more he enjoyed it.

Inevitably he was asked what he thought was going to happen to us after the mutiny. 'I thought as they'd have done something by now. You only 'ad to show what they called "dumb insolence" in the old days and they 'ad you doing jankers double quick. Course it's typical Andrew not telling us nothing until it suits them. But, since you arsk me, I'd say one things for sure an' it could be 'appening right now so as you wouldn't notice.'

He was deliberately trying to work up our interest and it was all there. He went on solemnly: 'A "Ship in Disgrace" – that's what we'll be if we ain't already. They done it before when there's been trouble aboard some warship although it was before my time. Once their effing Lordships put that on a ship's chitty there's no going back to an 'ome port until they've made you do your punishment. An' they send you to the worst places they can find – up some stink'ole like the Persian Gulf. What's more the rest of the fleet steers clear of you as though you'd got the clap.'

Surrounded by such a vast ocean with no other ships for company and bound for one of the remotest, uncivilised corners of the globe we needed no convincing.

PART II

14

For Those in Peril...

The cheerful air of close Anglo-American co-operation that had marked the Quebec Conference between Churchill and Roosevelt and their Chiefs of Staff in September 1944 had suddenly turned sour. The British Prime Minister's offer of a mighty Royal Navy fleet to aid the Americans in the Pacific had been instantly taken up by the President – but not by his Naval Chief of Naval Operations. Admiral King at first refused to have anything to do with it. In his unbending view the U.S. Navy had successfully taken on the Japanese fleet without such British help and could easily continue to do so until total victory was achieved. His antagonism was openly and fully expressed – as was the argument that followed with his own top Admirals opposed to him. Faced with being the only opponent to the plan he was eventually forced to accept it – very reluctantly.*

King showed no such objection when the Conference discussed the vital date for the next major Pacific amphibious assault – the biggest the world would see after Normandy. The invasion of the Philippines, if successful, would be the final blow against the enemy apart from landing in Japan. It was scheduled originally for November but heartening reports from MacArthur plus his eagerness to step up his increasingly fast 'leap frogging' advance across the South-West Pacific showed it could be done sooner. It would also be an almost 100 per cent

---

* Admiral of the Fleet Viscount Cunningham in his autobiography *Sailor's Odyssey*, referring to King's objections at the Conference, stated that the following day the U.S.N. C-in-C '. . . was resigned to the use of our fleet in the Pacific, but made it quite clear that it must expect no assistance from the Americans. From this rather unhelpful attitude he never budged.'

American campaign. The U.S. Navy Commander gave his complete support to the date being advanced a month.

That day, September 13, the Americans immediately intensified their softening up operations around the Philippines, sinking scores of Japanese merchant ships and shooting down numerous enemy aircraft. Two days later the U.S. 7th Fleet achieved a victorious landing on the last stepping stone before Leyte – on Morotai in the Moluccas.

Some 2,000 miles south of Leyte Gulf in the comparative safety of the big natural harbours at Hollandia, Dutch New Guinea, and at Manus in the Admiralty Islands, hundreds of landing ships and tens of thousands of troops were being assembled for the invasion now just five weeks away. It would take half that time for Force X to complete its Pacific crossing and join up with the 7th Fleet. There would be barely time to refuel, restore and carry out urgent repairs before setting out again on the long voyage to the landing beaches. Already weeks behind schedule Rear-Admiral Talbot could not afford to delay any longer.

Force X swung at anchor in the beautiful harbour of Bora Bora in the French Society Islands. Just six of the ships: H.M.S. *Lamont* still lay under repair in Balboa but the *Lothian* had at last caught up with the rest – on September 13, the day before reaching the island. It had been planned just as a brief, few hours refuelling stop but it was now the 15th with no sign of a quick departure. Neither was there any indication of the punishment we had spent anxious days wondering about – almost the reverse. Early this morning we seamen had been surprised at being told we not only could go ashore but *had* to do so. Some of our happiness at escaping the ship and feeling firm land under our feet had been taken away when we discovered it was going to be a route march kitted up in webbing, gaiters and heavy bell-bottoms but it couldn't destroy our overall pleasure.

Yet we were puzzled, too – both by the officer's obvious haste to see us off the ship and by what seemed to us an unnecessary delay to what we all knew was a mission rapidly running out of time. Any doubts that created in our minds vanished rapidly, however, as we marched off led by the ship's Warrant Gunner and tailed by our G.I. (Gunnery Instructor) along a winding dirt track beside the water.

The fresh new sights and smells were desperate relief from our stinking, hot messdeck. But we had not been marching for ten minutes when our surprise returned with greater impact than before. The heads of nearly 100 men turned sharply as one, as a loud explosion echoed across the harbour. From one of the muzzles of the twin forrard 4-inch gun of the *Lothian* sprouted a balloon of smoke that slowly drifted away in the calm warm air.

For a moment we were speechless and then Oggie burst out: ''Oo the 'ell ordered gunnery practice in 'arbour?'

'Practice my arse'ole,' snapped an older A.B. behind. 'You know what that is, don't yer?'

We didn't and said so.

'Effing Court Martial gun that's what,' came the reply. 'Crafty effing bastards – so that's why they sent us ashore. Get us out of the effing way while they weigh off them other poor sods.'

A bellowed order from the G.I. abruptly ended anymore chat and we marched on rather more morosely than before sharing the obvious thought that if the seventeen or some of them were being dealt with now then we could expect our court martial to follow, probably the next day. It also explained why the Force was still in harbour. Whatever immediate demands the war made Arthur George was going to put retribution for our mutiny first. To hold a court martial he needed a Captain of another R.N. ship to sit in proper judgement and this would be his last chance for that before the Force reached a war zone where such a court would be both more difficult to stage and doubly embarrassing in front of the Yanks.

The apparent closeness of our own trial and the rapidly increasing heat slowly began to turn our march into a punishment on its own, if not a deliberate torture. We yearned for a drink from the coconuts high above our bent heads and suffered frustration seeing the tempting bananas and paw-paws in small plantations. But there was to be no relief yet, so we thought. Then, suddenly, came the order to halt.

A ripple of almost happy excitement coming back through the column to us near the rear indicated it had to be due to something exceptional. Normally only two things could raise our spirits as quickly as this – booze or sex. Both seemed far too remote to contemplate. Yet it proved to be the latter. Coming towards us as we were ordered to stand aside from the narrow track was a crocodile of schoolgirls shepherded anxiously by a pair of middle-aged nuns, possibly French. Whatever charms they held they kept

137

well hidden beneath their flowing white habits and none of their Polynesian charges, although maturely developed for their age, could have been older than fourteen. Yet, if they had been a chorus line from the Folies Bergères they could not have roused more passion. They were, after all, the first females we had seen for two weeks and this was the closest we had got to the opposite sex for much longer.

Despite all the efforts of the Gunners and G.I.s nothing could stop our lusty calls and wolf whistles. I could well understand the nuns' alarm and desperate efforts to hurry the girls in their neat black tunics as fast as they could. If we seemed like a horde of voracious Vikings, the native girls simply smiled broadly and lapped it up. Had they been older or more attractive they could never have expected to arouse male fervour as much as this. And they showed their pleasure in unmistakable if totally unexpected display. As they reached the end of our line and almost as well drilled as Can Can girls they bent forward and with a flip of their skirts exposed the brightest, whitest knickers we had ever seen.

It was so surprising it left us stunned. But only for a moment. As one man we raised a mighty cheer that could have been heard back aboard the *Lothian*. It also raised our sunken morale. For the rest of our route march we stepped out more lightheartedly and the memory of that bawdy act of appreciation was to prove a ray of joy in the dark weeks to come. Teasers they were but for us they seemed more like angels of mercy.

The simple truth was that, however brave a front we tried putting on, we felt very much alone in our troubles believing the whole world was against us or, at least, totally ignorant of our conflict – even the ratings in the rest of the Force. Confirmation of just how carefully news of the mutiny had been kept from the other ships came while we were still ashore. As we waited for the landing craft to take us back aboard we were able to have our first contact with seamen from a couple of the L.S.I.s – their boat crews waiting at the same small jetty. The tight discipline we were under raised their curiosity. Hadn't they heard of the mutiny, we queried? Their astonishment said enough.

They had suspected something unusual had happened especially when the *Lothian* had anchored rather further from the rest of the Force than seemed normal and there had been little of the usual busy to-ing and fro-ing by boats between a flagship and other warships in port. The firing of the court martial gun had also whetted their interest but this had been assumed to be the trial of some individual who had stepped just a bit too far out of line. That would certainly not have surprised them if conditions aboard their own ships was any indication, they suggested. This time it was our turn to be surprised. Just why, I didn't know, but we had assumed life aboard the L.S.I.s was far better although it could have been due to our belief that because they were carrying U.S. servicemen usually far better treated than ourselves the ship's complement would also be more well off.

No, it had been the reverse, these other seamen insisted. The Yanks had been expected to cope with the same food, or lack of it, and same difficult conditions of living as the ratings. Not only was much of the food alien to the Americans but it was far worse cooked than they had been used to. Before the L.S.I.s had reached Panama the threat of serious trouble from the troops had become evident. Many had marched on deck and ceremoniously dumped meals over the side.

They had sent deputations to their officers, who, in turn, had demanded action from the Captains. High on their priorities, we heard with disbelief, were ice-cream machines – an unheard of luxury for us. Yet, to keep the Americans happy, a signal had been sent ahead requesting the machines be installed as soon as the ships reached the Canal Zone. Extra icewater fountains had also been ordered. Once fitted they had restored greater calm, if still an uneasy one, among the G.I.s – helped by an improvement in their rations. Now, however, it became the turn of the mateloes to object. They did not see why they should not also have a share in the luxuries. At first they had been curtly turned down and then, unexpectedly, the Captains had given way allowing them ice-cream plus slightly bigger meals. Now they had heard of our mutiny the seamen wondered if it didn't lie behind the abrupt change of heart.*

As much as we had been glad to learn we were not alone in our

---

* The dissatisfaction over food between the ratings and Americans on board the L.S.I.s continued to get worse judging by a signal sent later by Rear-Admiral Talbot to the Admiralty. In it he stated: 'Now that ships of Force X have American personnel on board most invidious comparisons are being drawn between standards of messing in British and American ships of the same Fleet. This is having an unfortunate effect on morale and discipline.'

139

suffering the news that it might only have been other ratings who
benefited from our revolt added to our depression as we headed
back to the *Lothian* and the prospect of our trial. As we came
alongside I began to understand how the convicts felt at starting a
long sentence in one of the old Victorian prison hulks. If there had
been a few bodies of mutineers swinging from the yardarm I doubt
if any of us would have been *that* surprised. But whatever harsh
sentences had been passed at the Court Martial there was no
apparent sign of anything unusual happening as we crossed the
head of the accommodation ladder and curtly saluted the quarterdeck. Nor was there any indication of where the seventeen now
were.

The whole atmosphere aboard was one of artificial calm with no
one outside the messdecks able or willing to discuss the trial. Most
of the other ratings had also been sent ashore (for swimming and
other relaxation – not a route march) while any P.O.s who had
remained in the ship were deliberately saying nothing. That day,
nor for weeks ahead, did we discover what the punishments had
been.

It would be normal practice for the lower deck to be cleared to
hear the warrants of any convicted man read out before he was sent
from the ship but no such formality took place. In fact the
seventeen had immediately been taken under Marine escort to
other ships in the Force for imprisonment in their cells until they
could be sent ashore to some convenient military prison.

Considering the enormity of the offences – the Welshman had
been armed, making it worse still – punishment such as handed
out seemed incredibly soft treatment. The Naval Discipline Act
included death by hanging for mutiny. All fourteen got ninety
days cells each.

Yet, if we thought they had got off extremely lightly then the
trio who led the revolt must have believed God, if not Arthur
George, was on their side. Their sentence for using armed force to
prevent one of His Majesty's warships from putting to sea on

He continued: '. . . I have ordered ships to raise standard of messing as
temporary measure while serving with American Fleet . . . up to a maximum of
3s 3d (about 16p) a day.'

While this may have been the case aboard the other ships there was no visible
sign of any improvement in *Lothian*'s messdeck catering.

active service in wartime was just one year's hard labour apiece.*

Among us in the seamen's messdeck were at least three who had served as much if not longer for far less serious offences. There was only one conclusion reached by us ratings: Arthur George or the Admiralty were deliberately playing down the mutiny to avoid embarrassment especially where the Americans were concerned.**

But face-saving only went so far. Before leaving Bora Bora we saw the Jaunty, the Buffer, a couple of P.O.s and half a dozen killicks sent from the ship – all brought down a rank and all unwitting victims of the mutiny.

Those being summarily dismissed from the ship must really have been angry at this odd turn of events. None, I suspected, could have felt quite as unfairly untreated as one of the killicks now heading for one of the other ships to start his regular Naval career again as an A.B. He was the one who had suddenly run ashore to persuade most of us to end the mutiny – an action we had half believed was officially prompted. Now we knew differently. When, later, we learnt he had been dipped for 'treating with mutineers' our dislike and distrust of the Admiral and any other senior officer we considered blameworthy, increased even more. There was, we told ourselves, no mean trick of which they were incapable.

Hookie had been absolutely correct when he had warned that no one could expect to escape being made to pay for our rebellion. He was living proof of it later that day when we returned to the messdeck and found him sitting with his 'housewife', busily snipping away the rank badges on his various uniforms. In other

---

* The three were kept in cells aboard the *Glenearn* until landed in Townsville, Queensland, to serve their sentence in the military prison there.

** In the opinion of certain ex-staff officers in Admiral Talbot's command the reason for the light sentences was due to a conscious decision to treat the mutiny more as a 'strike against bad living conditions'. This seems surprising in view of the Royal Navy's notoriously tough attitude towards mutineers and when one considers what happened at Invergordon – in peacetime. Our revolt was mutiny pure and simple and resulted from more than messdeck hardships. A more credible reason could have been the fact that the incident happened well away from Britain and the rest of the Royal Navy with sufficient chance of it being glossed over. It was also important to strictly limit the number of seamen severely punished in view of the great difficulty in obtaining replacements so far from Royal Navy bases.

parts of the messdeck it looked as though all those killicks who had not been sent from the ship were going through the same demeaning process. As O.D.s our sympathies were, at the best, formal for we could never see ourselves losing our place at the bottom of the totem pole however far others slid down it. Yet we were genuinely distressed when we found that our two oldest hands and, certainly, best liked A.B.s, Postie and Pop, were having to remove the three stripes that represented between them well over forty years' faithful service to the Andrew. This, we angrily agreed, was the meanest punishment of all. True, the two veterans had stayed with us right up to our gathering on the fo'c'sle but then so had everyone else. They had not walked ashore and it should have been obvious they were guilty of no more than messdeck unity, we told each other.

Amazingly the old ex-badgemen accepted their loss philosophically. 'Can't expect to 'ave good conduct badges when you've bin in a mutiny – we should 'ave 'ad a go at stopping you young H.O.s getting into trouble,' explained Postie.

What about the loss of the extra pay that went with the badges? we persisted.

Postie shrugged his shoulders. 'Where we're going among them South Sea islands you can't buy a fart in a bottle so we ain't going to miss it all that effing much.'

Such a willing acceptance of their loss was, we interpreted, a clear indication of how the Navy could grind one into being a cowering serf if one served it too long. Thank God, we assured ourselves, we were just H.O.s with a comparatively brief sojourn in its tight grip. If part of that time had to be suffered in gaol then it could not be much worse than our present unpleasant situation. Sticking out our chins, metaphorically, all we wanted now was for the long wait to be court-martialled to end.

Yet the Royal Navy's law of retribution could, when desired, work in a perverse direction away from those committing the crime. Instead of learning about our own trial we heard of one planned for the very officer who had been closest and most determined in trying to prevent us carrying on our mutiny.

For several days we had suspected that some kind of punishment was to be inflicted on that Jimmy as much as we, younger seamen, were puzzled by the signs. Half way from Balboa to Bora Bora as we lined up for the loathed, unnecessarily formal morning

Divisions only the seamen had to attend we found ourselves being inspected by another straight ring R.N. Lieutenant-Commander – from the Admiral's staff. Of our regular First Lieutenant there was no sign then or for several days to follow. The buzz quickly spread that he had been relieved of his executive role while the Court of Inquiry, still meeting intermittently after two whole days of intensive discussion, considered whether he was in any way responsible for the mutiny being allowed to happen.

This, of course, did not surprise Hookie. 'As I told you it was bound to 'appen. They got to stick the blame on someone and as Jimmy 'e's bound to be on a collision course. Of course, if 'e'd stopped us 'e'd be an effing 'ero. But that's the Andrew for you – 'anding out medals one second and sticking you in the rattle (cells) the next.'

But even he did not think the Jimmy would end up suffering more than just being transferred to another ship in the Force. 'Ole Arthur George won't want us getting cocky thinking we'd got 'im put on a charge.'

That was where the oracle was, at last, proved wrong.

Via the ship's grapevine came the news that Lieutenant-Commander Buckel was to be court-martialled.

Just as nothing had been explained when he had been replaced so no official announcement of his trial was made. We had to guess what the charges were but even the older hands found it difficult understanding, other than in general terms, what he was being blamed about. So far as most of us were concerned the only puzzle we were anxious to solve was why we still awaited a decision on our formal weighing off.

We were still in a dilemma when the *Lothian* and the rest of Force X with its four U.S. Navy escorts sailed from Bora Bora on the 17th. Like most of my messmates I had only a thin grasp of what was right and proper in the conduct of a task force but it seemed incredible that here we were on the final stages of going into action with a flagship manned by seamen awaiting sentence, no Leading Hands in direct charge of us, an executive officer awaiting court martial and with both Lower Deck and officers split into unhappy factions.

As we attended compulsory Sunday service that morning after leaving harbour I found greater meaning in the words of the seamen's hymn: 'For Those in Peril on the Sea'.

15

The Enemy – But Who?

'September 28: Passing through Solomons. No sign of the Japs ashore. Hard to believe there is a war on a few miles away. There is more war aboard here!'

The entry in my rough diary kept hidden in a grubby notebook in a corner of the radar office summed up my sad feelings but little of the continuing struggle aboard. Neither could any of the earlier, brief entries give more than a hint of all that happened in so short a time.* It was hard to credit it was only eight weeks since we had left the Clyde; that we had steamed 12,000 miles, further than any Naval assault force, as far as I knew, had gone before in World War II or any other war.

And the only scrap we had got into was with the Royal Navy itself.

If anyone among the majority of seamen had any desire left to uphold the honour of the Service it must have been buried very deep. Another entry stated how low morale had got. Not just among the seamen. Ratings in other departments seemed to have been infected by our depression. Even the R.A.F. and Army detachments seemed listless as though now more convinced they would have no worthwhile part to play aboard.

* Diaries were banned aboard ships in wartime but I wrote mine up in the shorthand I had learnt as a trainee reporter. If the Japanese ever got hold of it they would have had more difficulty translating it than I sometimes had.

144

Arthur George and the ship's officers were trying to create a greater sense of urgency among the complement with frequent practice Action Stations and other emergency drills but many of us, especially the mutineers, believed them to be largely wasted effort and an unnecessary burden. We ratings awaiting punishment about which nothing had still been revealed considered we would not be in the ship much longer to make our training worthwhile. Few aboard thought the Americans would even want the ship.

It was generally accepted that the U.S. Navy was, at the best, lukewarm in its regard for us. Following the mutiny right in front of its gaze we felt sure it would now treat *Lothian* with about as much fondness as a cowbow looks upon an angry rattlesnake. The Americans in Balboa would surely have signalled news of our revolt back to Washington, confirming, if he heard about it, Fleet Admiral King's dislike of the Royal Navy. Equally the report would have found its way to the South-West Pacific and the staff of the 7th Fleet. They would hardly welcome us with open arms.

There was also visible evidence that Force X's effectiveness as a combined unity was being watered down – apart from the problems besetting the *Lamont*. On the 25th September the Empire's *Arquebus* and *Battleaxe*, escorted by the U.S.S. *Machias*, had broken off to head for Noumea, New Caledonia, and Espiritu Santo, New Hebrides, to land their American troops at established bases. They were, we understood, to be held in these rear areas for some undisclosed reason.*

Would we also be shunted sideways? we asked ourselves. Present indications rather suggested it. From the sparkers we learnt they were puzzled by the fact that, apart from a few routine messages, there was hardly any radio contact with the U.S. 7th Fleet – far less than they had expected now we were entering the war zone. In their opinion the 'Yanks' were ignoring us. This convinced us more than ever that *Lothian* really was being treated as a 'Ship-in-disgrace'.

As we steamed closer to our final destination in New Guinea,

---

* The two ships and, eventually, others of Force X were used by the U.S. Navy in a secondary role, well away from the U.S. advance and in locations where we had little chance of seeing them again. This could have been a deliberate U.S. Navy tactic to put down the 'limey admiral'.

145

where 150,000 Japanese were still entrenched and the Aussies were fighting a tough battle trying to winkle them out, such thoughts were overtaken by an awareness that we might, after all, be going into action ourselves. The reduced squadron had gone over to a zig-zag course as an anti-submarine measure and we had closed up at secondary action stations, watch-on-watch-off.

I found it grim enough in the small radar office when I stood watch when we had a four-watch system with up to half a dozen operators on each turn. Now with others crammed together in temperatures that touched 110 it was rarely below 90, it became a question of which collapsed first, us or the equipment. Fortunately for our state of health it was the latter. I was on watch one night when there was a blinding flash and we were driven outside by the smoke and acrid smell. All we could do was to send for the young R.N.V.R. Sub-Lieutenant Radar Officer and leave him and a couple of mechanics to try and put the mess right.

Dragged from his bunk the Subbie was still in his pyjamas having shown what we thought was remarkable determination to get our radar operational as soon as possible. Someone else had a quite different opinion. Hardly had the officer got down to sorting out the trouble when a messenger arrived demanding his presence on the bridge. As we heard from a quartermaster afterwards he appeared there in his pyjamas looking more as though he had been sleeping in the scuppers only to find his presence had been demanded by none other than Arthur George, extremely concerned about the breakdown.

One sight of the young Sub-Lieutenant brought down the Admiral's wrath. Why was he so disgracefully and improperly dressed? he thundered. He must immediately return to his cabin, get into uniform and report back to the bridge to be severely reprimanded. This the despairing Subbie did. And he despaired even more when he had returned to repairing the damage. Within minutes his once crisp white uniform was covered in oil and smoke stains.

Perhaps Arthur George was suffering the strain brought about by the mutiny and the inherent problems of Force X. Yet there was a more basic cause: he suffered from insomnia.

It was common knowledge aboard that he slept little until the night was nearly over. Frequently he would pass the hours away dictating signals or appear on the bridge during the Middle

Watch, normally a time when the Officer of the Watch could relax more than usual. With Arthur George around he had to be constantly on his toes. But those last couple or so hours around dawn were very precious to the Admiral, at last finding some sleep. After the mutiny he must have regretted his decision to, at last, permit tropical routine to be introduced. Under its earlier start for the day Wakey Wakey was piped just after dawn, around 5.30 a.m. And the noisy bustle that created brought an end to his brief period of escape.

Arthur George's solution was simple but surprising. He ordered the time of 'dawn' to be put back.

A notice appeared on the wardroom board stating that from henceforward dawn was always to be at 0600. That might have been practical if the ship had been stationary but as we were constantly passing through different time zones it threw the setting of the many clocks and watches in the ship into confusion. Changes to them had to be made more than once on most days to cope with the Admiral's notion of sunrise. But the decision succeeded in giving most of us a rare chance for laughter.

The new spread of how some unknown officer had daringly written on top of the Admiral's notice: 'Look out God – He's after your job!'

Behind the comment lay some of the bad feeling that existed among the ship's officers at this time. They must have felt they were almost as much on trial as the mutineers as tighter discipline all round was applied. We knew from the wardroom stewards that a stricter watch was being kept on drinking among officers. Not that it wasn't generous enough – nine tots a day was allowed on their wine bill. But, occasionally, some exceeded it if only through standing rounds. Now their bills were being closely studied by senior staff officers and more than one officer reprimanded for going 'one-over-the-nine'.

Action such as that only cheered us tot-less under-twenties up and most older ratings, too. The massive gap between Lower and Upper Decks as far as alcohol was concerned had been too long in existence for us to gripe about it normally but in our unusually restricted circumstances we now saw it in a more callous light. But we were staggered when we learnt that someone in the wardroom had been suddenly confined to his cabin. This was nothing to do with drinking, however.

If there was one person aboard who held a particularly vital post it was certainly Mr. Pattison, the Warrant Telegraphist. Warrant Officers were a peculiar half-way appointment between officers and men but still unusually important. Like this one they had great regular service experience as well as often being highly trained specialists. In Mr. Pattison's case his technical knowledge of telegraphy systems was high enough to have had him made largely responsible for seeing that *Lothian*'s sophisticated communications set up was installed. If anyone was to suffer confinement to their cabin it would, more likely, have been one of the officers proper.

At the time we could only glean a little of what had led to him being kept in his quarters with a Royal on sentry outside the door. Somehow he had upset the Admiral. Whatever it was, the incident passed over fairly quickly. Shorly afterwards Mr. Pattison appeared going about his normal duties. But it left the 'sparkers', who had a very high regard for their Warrant Telegraphist, upset. As we were largely a Communications ship they believed they held a specially important place aboard. Perhaps it was the fact that their department looked like becoming even more vital now we were entering a war zone that partly led to the Admiral relenting.*

* Years later when I asked Mr Pattison (now retired from the Royal Navy) what had happened, he explained that he had been one of several heads of departments called to the Admiral's cabin to discuss the latter's scheme for overcoming manning problems caused by men being under arrest. Arthur George suggested that men from other sections, especially the communications one, should undertake seamen's work. When it came to Mr. Pattison's turn to give his view and to be frank he replied that his men were already stretched too far especially as they were having to be retrained in American radio methods. Then, perhaps too emphatically in view of the wide gap in rank, he said he thought the idea 'ridiculous'.

Arthur George's reaction was, says its victim, explosive. Warrant Officers had no right whatsoever to accuse Admirals of being ridiculous. For his audacity he would be confined to his cabin.

A couple of days later Mr. Pattison was told by a senior staff officer to apologise so the affair could be concluded. With little choice he did so to Arthur George. But the matter did not end there. When the time came for Rear-Admiral Talbot formally to sign the Warrant Telegraphist's half yearly report that would go to the Admiralty and had a big bearing on an officer's career he did so in red ink. It was, paradoxically, a black mark as only black ink signified an approving comment. The same report contained a glowing comment of approval from the Captain.

Whatever had happened it confirmed our feeling that Captain Petrie, who seemed surprisingly uninvolved in the incident, was definitely taking a back seat, whether by choice or compulsion.

We had never seen much of him and now we saw still less. Almost the only time for most was when he made his Saturday morning rounds when we were compelled to try and make the messdeck look as less like an underground air-raid shelter as possible. I could tell from his tired look that he was suffering the effects of the ship and everything that had happened in her. Even his limp seemed worse.

The quartermasters and bunting tossers, who had more chance to see him on the bridge, reported that Captain Petrie was unusually subdued, especially whenever the Admiral was around. Messdeck conversation homed in on the subject of how long we thought it would be before we had Captain No 4. If the Jimmy could be relieved of his job then we saw it as just one more step before the Captain could suffer the axe. Perhaps nothing dramatic but the chop nevertheless.

In a way we would be sorry to see him depart. Although he came within our all round condemnation of officers aboard he had always acted courteously and justly. He also won some sympathy from us because we sensed he and the Admiral had fallen out and that, in our eyes, was a recommendation.

My mess had been busy tearing officers' reputations into verbal shreds when Hookie, unusually thoughtful, butted in: 'Gawd 'elp us if we ever 'ave to fight the Japs. The way you lot is griping about the pigs you'd think they was on the other side.'

Pointing a warning finger around at us he went on: 'Let me tell you skivers a thing or two. When it comes to the crunch, when there's effing shells, torpedoes, bombs and Christ knows what flying around you got to depend on the officers whether you 'ate their guts or not. I wouldn't say this lot could piss against a wall without getting wet but they're all you got. So just stow your griping an' put up with them.'

I would not say his words of warning had much effect on us for we were too far gone in our disdain and despair. It needed something far more alarming than just words. And we quickly got it.

It was sometime in the Last Dog Watch, around 1830, when those of us off watch, idly sitting round in our messes, were suddenly quelled into rigid silence by the noise and reverberation of an explosion. We were steaming between Solomon Islands and New Guinea and it took no explanation to make us acutely aware it could be due to enemy action. But we just sat there showing no more reaction than shocked uncertainty. Even when the alarm bells rang and the pipe 'Hands to Action Stations' sounded we hesitated.

But Hookie and the other older, more experienced hands, were rushing for the ladder. 'Get off you effing arses,' someone yelled, 'This ain't no effing exercise.'

Like stampeding lemmings we dashed for the upper deck and our stations but unable to resist gazing around to see where the explosion had been. But the Pacific seemed to be living up to its name. Then, on our port quarter, I saw one of our escorts steaming at full speed in a distinctly purposeful manner. A moment later the sea behind her bubbled up like a massive cauldron and erupted in a waterburst. For a moment we stood hypnotised until a bellow from the bridge sent us scurrying on.

Apart from the minor and only suspected submarine incident crossing the Atlantic none of us young seamen had had any close contact with war at sea and just the sound and sight of a depth charge being dropped was enough to scare many. Common sense should have told us that no submarine would risk trying to torpedo us while under attack itself but we could not focus our thoughts that well. Only as time passed by and the sound of depth charges got further away did we relax.

Later, when we had been stood down, we joked about it, libelling the American Navymen as having got panicky and attacking what we argued had been no more than a big shoal of fish. But, I suspected, the latter had acted more coolly than many of us would have done in similar circumstances. It was, however, a useful, salutary lesson. As well as showing us we were far from ready to take a warship into action it had also taught us that there was something more to war than just fighting one's own officers. In minutes it had done more than Arthur George had done in months.

It had even pushed aside our thoughts about what punishment lay ahead. Yet those came flooding back as we got our first view of the towering mountains of New Guinea rising above the steamy jungle. Were we to be weighed off and sent to some unthinkably horrid prison ashore here? Surely Arthur George was not going to wait any longer to see we suffered for our wickedness? If he had not done so yet it was because he needed to get the ship across the Pacific, we told ourselves. Perhaps a fresh crew of seamen were waiting to take our place.

But the only men we could see as we berthed alongside in the small, but frantically busy harbour of Finschaven were hundreds of Aussie troops and a few U.S. Navymen. It was for those aboard who had never been closer to a battle base than in the cinema a compelling sight. We were fascinated by the dust covered, sunburnt soldiers bound to and from the exhausting task of trying to end the Japanese grip in the Owen Stanley Range; the small mountains of arms, ammunition and other fighting stores and the overall air of single-minded concentration on winning the war.

It contrasted sharply with our attitudes and made me, and probably most aboard, realise there might, after all, be some valid point to the discomforts we had gone through to get here.

I think that if we had been marched ashore there under arrest as mutineers we would have been ashamed. These troops we could see were risking their lives while we had fought to stay in Balboa, even though it was not from cowardice. Yet we were spared any such embarrassment. The only command we seamen got to go ashore was to load stores. Not a word about punishment.

After so long an ocean crossing we were desperate to stretch our legs on dry land and we lined up restlessly as the process of disembarking seemed to be taking unusually long. Craning his head Cockie gasped in surprise. 'Eh! They're 'anding out Frenchies. Cor, d'they expect we're going to 'ave a bang-orf with a bit of black 'am?'

His assumption was wide of the mark yet understandable. From the box that had been used for the contraceptives compulsorily handed to ratings when we were in the U.S.A. the quartermasters were dishing out small packets of a different kind – mepacrine anti-malaria tablets. There was no such refinement as water to wash the foul tasting things down although that was not the reason we came, in time, to hate them. No one warned us that a side effect would be to turn us a pasty shade of yellow. In a peculiarly sick kind of way this was the start of a very colourful period of our lives but we had no hint then of just how much the South-West Pacific was to turn us into ailing walking rainbows.

151

It took just the thirty hours we stayed in the port for us to appreciate how unhealthy a place New Guinea was. The intense humidity that slowed us to a crawl and called for courage beyond the normal devotion to duty to go down into the messdeck made us glad to get back to sea. As we stood around the upper deck gratefully gasping in fresher air we saw that the seven little nigger boys were now down to just two. Only the *Glenearn* now remained with us as we steamed West towards what was the final destination on our voyage from Britain, the three that had continued to Finschaven with us having been diverted to other island destinations.

We were bound, stated daily orders, to Hollandia, in what was Dutch New Guinea. It was, went on the brief announcement, a main base for the planned invasion of the Philippines, now just a short time away. In spite of our delays we would be reaching it in time to take part. After steaming 12,000 miles in two months, a mutiny, court martial, innumerable technical problems, unending discomfort and the apparent loss of five of the seven ships, there just had to be something worthwhile at the end of it all, we told ourselves.*

Arthur George certainly believed the occasion merited the pomp of an important event. As we sailed, just our two-strong, very shrunken Force, into the massive natural harbour of Hollandia, he had us lining the sides and the bagpiper playing some martial air in the bows. A brand new Rear-Admiral's flag with its two red balls flew from the masthead.

But if we had been a couple of stragglers rushing to join on the tail of a Lord Mayor's procession we could hardly have created less impression. We were totally lost among the hundreds of American L.S.I.s, other warships and supply vessels that packed the anchorages. As we watched almost in awe of an invasion fleet which in a single port outnumbered any that had assembled for D-Day we realised exactly how insignificant we were.

Mick, standing beside me, expressed it neatly. 'What did we have to come all this way for and have all that trouble when the Yanks have got all this lot?'

* In his official report to his C-in-C Navy at the end of our long voyage from New York the Commander of the U.S.S. *Sandusky*, one of the four escort vessels, stated: 'It is believed by this command that this convoy is practically one of the longest in the history of naval warfare – almost half way around the world.'

No, it had definitely not been worth it. The day before we had been given clear reason why. With peculiar timing, considering we were on the very point of joining an invasion, our punishment for the mutiny had been announced.

16

Jimmy for the Chop

We were too exhausted by the heat to appreciate the irony of it but it was there clearly enough. Almost the only thing the mutiny had achieved was the introduction of tropical routine. Now, as the rest of *Lothian*'s company enjoyed its afternoon stand-easy, we who had stormed ashore were being forced to work in the body-sapping intense humidity of New Guinea.

The American servicemen relaxing in the shade of the palms gazed on us in disbelief as we were marched in our heavy overalls from the jetty at Hollandia towards the U.S. store huts hidden in the jungle. Even the Japanese further into the mountains must have been taking time off from the war in such a steambath climate. Working in the New York heatwave had been bad enough; still worse in Panama but here it could only be described as torture. And punishment it certainly was.

Only two days into our sentence we were only just beginning to appreciate the extra suffering it meant. We had barely, in fact, got over the surprise of suddenly being weighed off. Breakfast was just over when the Crusher who had temporarily taken over the dismissed Jaunty's duties had appeared in the messdeck and ordered those of us who had rebelled ashore in Balboa to dress in our No 1s to be marched before the Captain. It was obviously not for a court martial yet we felt it was to tell us we were to be so tried.

In our massed group we were lined up on the Captain's deck as Petrie, looking tired and grey I thought, sat behind a table under the canvas awning. The familiar 'off caps' order that heralded all defaulters ceremonies came and the Jimmy stepped forward.

Perhaps because we had been caught off-guard after such a long delay from the time of the mutiny or because his words were blurred by the lapping of the sea against the hull as we steamed at full speed but it was a good few seconds before we realised he was actually reading out the charges against us.

'. . . being guilty of conduct prejudicial to good order and discipline in that, on September 1st, 1944, had disobeyed the orders of superior officers and had . . .' Whatever was said next failed to register in my mind numbed by the fear of what was to happen to us. Was it to be prison and, if so, for how long? How the Hell had I got myself into such a mess?

The agony seemed to go on for ever as one by one we were ordered to step forward and plead. I doubted if many grasped exactly what they were being charged with but the 'Guilty's' rolled out like the sound of a train rattling over the lines. As I awaited my turn I could not maintain the strict 'eyes front' order my gaze wandering off to the deceptively peaceful looking New Guinea coast. A weird escapist thought entered my head. 'What would any Japs watching us think if they knew we seamen faced a greater danger from our own side than from them?'

But my eyes swung sharply back to the Captain as he began speaking. There was little emotion in his tones yet he held our attention as tightly as if he had been an Assize judge sentencing a mass murderer. We had undoubtedly, he said, committed an offence that justified the sternest punishment. Mutiny was the worst possible crime in wartime and the Naval Discipline Act laid down the most severe penalties.

In spite of the great heat I felt a chill run through me. We had not then learnt what punishment the seventeen had suffered and nothing too severe seemed impossible. Captain Petrie continued in a way that emphasised this. We had acted shamefully in a manner that had brought disgrace to such a fine Service and we must suffer the consequences.

Then, as our spirits touched rock bottom, he suddenly lifted them. 'It is clear that you, all young ratings and nearly all in your first ship, were led by those who have already been sentenced for their more active part in this unhappy event. For that reason it was decided you should not be court martialled but be tried summarily by myself.'

And, suddenly, it was all but over.

There were the sentences of course yet as stiff as they were there could rarely have been so many seamen at one time receiving them that felt so relieved. We had all expected much worse than those read out – all the same.

'Six months second class for conduct, six months second class for leave.'

We had heard of 'Two and Two' even if it was not understood. The Crusher later spelled it out. For 180 days we would suffer punishment drill and extra duties. During all that time we would not be granted shore leave of any kind. Had we been in home waters we would have been considerably more downcast but out here in the remote South-West Pacific the loss of leave would not be such a hardship. The extra drill and work was going to be difficult to bear considering all our other problems yet so many of us were involved it would be a burden well shared.

If, as we imagined, we were soon to be involved in an invasion then we would be too much engaged at our Action Stations for there to be time to spare for punishment. So we cheered ourselves up. But a niggling worry remained. Just why had it been decided to have us weighed off immediately prior to joining the U.S. assault fleet? It was hardly likely to boost our already seabed-level morale.

Perhaps Arthur George – we always assumed he was behind everything – felt it would be worse if we went into battle not knowing our punishment. Whatever the reason the timing of it all looked deliberately planned. There had to be an ulterior motive we told ourselves – even for not gaoling us. That seemed obvious the very next morning when 'Clear Lower Deck' was piped and we mustered to hear a warrant read out for some unfortunate A.B. gunner who had been caught asleep on watch. As bad a crime as the Royal Navy deemed this it was hardly as heinous as our mutiny. Yet we heard him sentenced to ninety days in prison.

We watched him being taken ashore under escort – to be flown to Lae in Papua-New Guinea, where the Australians had their military prison. Our feelings were mixed. Perhaps, after all, we would have been better off joining him – no prison could be that much worse than the *Lothian*. Someone in the mess joked that we should stage another mutiny demanding we go to gaol.

Hookie, caustically, replied: 'You could effing well string the pigs from the yardarm and they still wouldn't put you ashore. Ole

156

Arthur George is going to join this invasion even if 'e 'as the 'ole effing ship in jankers. If the mutiny 'ad been back 'ome we'd all 'ave been inside long ago.'

It made the only sensible explanation we could accept, true or not. The comparative softness of our sentences were also underlined by the way no punishment whatsoever had been meted out to those seamen who had not walked ashore. They had played just as mutinous a part in the messdeck and on the fo'c'sle and yet they were being treated as if they had been angels. The whole business seemed crazy especially with Chiefs, P.O.s and killicks, who had none or little involvement, reduced in rank. Whatever justification there was officially it made no sense at all to us ratings.

Not even the belief that it was all, somehow, due to the pressures of the forthcoming invasion held much water after being put ashore to collect urgent stores in Hollandia. Arriving at the U.S. Navy supply depot it quickly became obvious that there had either been a serious hiccup in communications or the Americans were clearly not going to help us. The Supply Officer Lieutenant who came with us men under punishment bore a thick list of stores essential to the ship after such a long ocean crossing. The first U.S. Navy officer approached looked mystified, almost suspicious as to why the Royal Navy was demanding American supplies. He rapidly passed us on up the scale.

It was by the time we had called on the third, perhaps fourth, officer, a Commander, that it became transparent that no one knew a thing about *Lothian*, Force X or Admiral Talbot, or, more suspiciously, if they did were not willing to help. The American listened curiously to the 'Paybob's' repeated recitation and then said bluntly: 'You tell that Limey Admiral of yours that he don't get a nickel until Kinkaid gives the O.K.'

The working party busily eavesdropping chuckled heartily. We were firmly on the American's side in this since the last thing we wanted in the intense heat was to load stores. Our Supply Officer, more red-faced from embarrassment than from the sun, reluctantly led us back to our craft to return aboard where we happily recounted the events. The new Leading Hand of our mess, a Geordie, took it more seriously.

'That's it then, ain't it,' he said firmly. 'The Yanks don't want fuck all to do with us. They got the buzz all the way from Balboa.

157

Don't want nothing to do with an effing crowd of mutineers, do they?'

I felt there might be some other explanation but it did seem strange that, considering the ship must have radioed its coming plus request for stores, let alone any signals from Washington announcing our arrival, no one, apparently, knew a thing about us.

Whatever the true situation Arthur George wasted little time in making his and the *Lothian*'s presence known to Vice-Admiral Kinkaid, the 7th Fleet's Commander, aboard his flagship the U.S.S. *Tulsa*. We watched his barge skim across the broad harbour and disappear among the vast armada of landing ships especially interested since we believed his mission was to establish our exact role in the invasion. Equally curious we awaited his return. When he did step back aboard it was obvious from his grim expression that, whatever had been discussed, it had not been to his satisfaction.

Before the day was out the ship was alive with buzzes that Kinkaid had given us a sailor's farewell. The stories took various shapes but nearly all could be summed up simply as our rejection by the Americans. Reasons suggested ranged from the mutiny to a general objection to a British assault force presence. Another was that neither *Lothian* nor our L.S.I.s were considered suitable for landings in the Pacific war zone. We had to guess since nothing was officially divulged. Or ever was.*

It was typical of the constant state of internal warfare aboard *Lothian* that in spite of our deep concern about whether or not we would fulfil our mission around the world and join in battle with the enemy our thoughts were suddenly taken over by yet another slice of shipboard drama.

We were just finishing our meagre supper when a quartermaster dashed down to the messdeck with the news that we were to stage another court martial over the mutiny.

Only this time it was to be an officer on trial.

* Kinkaid's refusal to accept Force X as part of the Philippines invasion fleet is confirmed by former staff officers from *Lothian*. According to them he was friendly but was either under orders from above or felt the Force had arrived too late and was not properly equipped for the type of landings involved. He did, however, agree to the L.S.I.'s being used in a support role as store carriers and troopers far behind the front line.

It was, of course, the ex-Jimmy, Lieutenant-Commander Kenneth Buckel. Since being relieved of his executive position soon after the mutiny he had been, more or less, a passenger in the ship. Why such an out of the way spot as Hollandia and before the massed U.S. Navy should have been chosen to stage his court martial seemed peculiar although one explanation was that there were the statutory minimum two Royal Navy warships present in port with four-ring captains who could preside.*

This would be the first opportunity to hold a court martial since leaving Bora Bora although if we were to join an invasion it hardly seemed an auspicious way of setting about it. No, most believed it only confirmed the buzzes that we had been given the thumbs down since there was every sign that the decision to hold it had been taken at short notice – after Arthur George's return from seeing Kinkaid.

If we had had little affection for Lieutenant-Commander Buckel before the mutiny, and very few Jimmy's ever won much love, we now saw him more as a whipping boy. We believed it inevitable that the powers-that-be would seek a scapegoat and, as First Lieutenant, Buckel was bang in the firing line. Perhaps we were also typically as fickle as mateloes can be for instead of seeing him as an enemy determined to end the mutiny as we had done during our revolt in the messdeck we now saw him more as a fellow sufferer. In a similar contrary way the objections many had had towards him because he had come up through the hawsepipe and turned his back on the Lower Deck now switched to sympathy because he had been 'one of us'. One thing seemed certain – if we were approached to be witnesses at his trial few, if any, would give evidence against him. It also became common shipboard knowl-

* Court-martial procedure at the time stipulated that for serious offences the most senior officers present in their ships in the same port had to be chosen as members of the judging bench under a President who had to be a Captain. A minimum of five and maximum of nine had to sit. Normally the Captain of the ship involved acted as prosecutor but Captain Petrie was not chosen. According to Lieutenant-Commander Buckel a reason for this may have been Petrie's objection, stated to him, to the trial being held.

As official details of the Royal Navy court martials of this time are withheld from general public reading, I have obtained facts about his trial from Lieutenant-Commander Buckel himself. Too long to include as a footnote I have added it as Appendix II. It throws some fresh light on the mutiny itself as well as revealing some peculiarities of his trial.

edge that the *Lothian*'s officers shared the same view.

During the next day we puzzled over why Arthur George should have chosen (although technically it was the Captain's decision) to stage a court martial before the Americans when he must have been so much embarrassed at the mutiny taking place under their gaze. The answer to that came the next morning when *Lothian* raised anchor and we slowly steamed past the dense lines of U.S. ships until we were clear of them. Still wondering where we were heading we were surprised to find the ship going to anchor in a secluded bay out of sight of the invasion fleet.

The reason became obvious when the Union Flag was broken at the yardarm – the signal that a court martial was being held. Only this time no gun was also fired. That, we decided, was due more to avoiding attracting the attention of the Americans than of any Japanese skulking in the dense jungle that seemed only yards away from us.

We were being kept well clear of the after welldeck where the trial was to be held but we had a good view of any comings and goings alongside associated with the court martial. That produced our second surprise of the day. Stepping out of a launch and received with all the ceremony due to a President of a court martial came a Royal Navy Captain we had not seen before. But his reputation and that of his ship had gone on ahead.

Captain the Lord Ashbourne, R.N., commanded one of the Navy's crack and certainly fastest ships – the minelaying cruiser *Ariadne*. It was news to us she was also in Hollandia, but her boat's crew explained to us as they waited in the messdeck that the ship had been specially asked for by the Americans to play a vital role in the Philippine invasion. Because of her exceptionally high speed – over 45 knots – she was to carry an advance landing party of 400 U.S. Rangers (Commandos) ahead of the main invasion fleet. The Americans were already aboard and the *Ariadne* was expected to sail the next day. From what the crew told us Captain Lord Ashbourne was none too happy about being dragged off to preside over a trial only hours before starting such a demanding action.

When it was explained that we believed the Americans had turned us down for the invasion they were surprised. In their case, they said, the Americans could not do enough for them although they believed this to be due as much to their Captain as to the ship's special qualities. 'They love meeting a "real English milord" and he does it in proper style – all the wardroom linen's got his family arms on it,' they said proudly. We wondered why Arthur George with his strong sense of stately living had not thought of doing the same.

Before this conversation we had had our third surprise of the morning. Standing in one of the *Glenearn*'s boats as it came alongside were none other than the three mutiny ringleaders closely guarded by Royals. They gave us a brave cheer, which we heartily returned, before they were hurriedly brought aboard and quickly removed from our sight. There was no doubt they were attending the trial as witnesses – a fact which gave our lowerdeck lawyers plenty of food for argument. It was totally wrong, they protested, that anyone convicted on the evidence of someone should be expected to help in prosecuting that person.

Such finer points of law went over our heads. We were more concerned about what sentence would be passed for we had no doubt that whatever the evidence and whoever presented it our ex-Jimmy would be put on the rack. Just as we had done with the ringleaders' court martial we took bets on the outcome. As little money as we had, there was nothing else to spend it on.

But we were forced to wait far longer than we had imagined before we knew if we had won or lost. Throughout the morning, on through the afternoon, past the dog watches and almost up to the middle watch from midnight the court martial ground its weary way. Even then it was not ended. And all the time the intense heat and humidity turned the after welldeck into a Turkish bath. Whatever Lieutenant-Commander Buckel was suffering the physical torture was shared by everyone else as they sat and sweated in their full dress uniforms in temperatures touching the 100 mark.

The President, Lord Ashbourne, must have had extra reason to sweat it out as the precious few hours before he was due to set out on the invasion were eaten away and he still had to return the next morning. That he did in a crisp, fresh uniform but with creases of worry on his noble brow.

The Union Flag hung limp in the still, humid air as the court reassembled around 0830. The dank jungle smell added a stale prison-like odour to the final proceedings but by 1030 it was, finally, all over. In traditional Royal Navy fashion there was little need for the finding to be announced. Lieutenant-Commander

161

Buckel's sword, which had lain crosswise on the judging panel's table throughout the trial, now pointed directly at him.

Guilty.

His sentence? To be dismissed his ship.

It was no less than we had pessimistically expected. Indeed we felt he must have put up a very good fight to avoid worse retribution. Hookie expressed it almost as though it was some kind of victory. ''E wants to think 'imself lucky. I 'ad 'im on my chitty as getting dipped knowing 'ow they wanted their pound of flesh, blood an' all. Anyway 'e's an effing sight better off this crap barge than in it.'

I think many of us were genuinely envious of the Lieutenant-Commander. Wherever he ended up it would be better than this. But what was to happen to us next? We now seemed to be carried out of control on some great Pacific breaker about to throw us high and dry on some coral beach like castaway mariners.

17

Scuppered

On every side and from as far as sound could carry the impressive bustle of a mighty fleet raising anchor to sail into battle reached us aboard H.M.S. *Lothian*. The clanking of cables, the pounding of engines and the whooping of escorts' sirens created a dramatic overture to the warlike symphony to follow. Every player in this massive orchestra of destruction seemed to be performing their part – with two exceptions. H.M.S. *Lothian* and H.M.S. *Glenearn*.

The only sound of action aboard *Lothian* as the 7th Fleet prepared to leave harbour was the pipe: 'Men under punishment to muster.'

As we were lined up on the foredeck under the blazing afternoon sun and saw landing ship after landing ship steam slowly past us with their decks packed with armed and helmeted G.I.s I felt as shamefully insignificant as a triangle player who had only one note to strike and had fluffed even that. The effect on the P.O. in charge of us, a veteran of several Naval battles and landings, was far more bitter.

Addressing us with barely restrained fury he said: 'If those Yanks sail without us it'll be an effing disgrace on the whole Andrew . . . and you effing skivers will be to blame!'

From somewhere in the rear rank came the protest: 'There's more to blame than us.'

But the P.O.'s answer to that was simple. 'That man there will do one hour's extra drill.' Then he added savagely: 'And God help the rest of you lot from now on.'

He sounded passionate enough for us to believe we would be better off facing the Japanese. Perhaps, after all, we would. Maybe we were just being held back to form some kind of rearguard.

But we doubted it. Our expectations had been raised once already that day before being sent tumbling. As soon as the court martial was over we had raised anchor and steamed as fast as we could back towards the fleet. For a while we believed we were joining the first of the ships heading towards the open sea until, that is, we eased ourselves into our previous berth and dropped our hook close by the *Glenearn*. Normal harbour routine had been resumed and the only sign of extra activity had been an unusual amount of signals being flashed between ourselves and Kinkaid's flagship – mostly from us as best we could tell.

It added a little weight to the buzz that the U.S. Admiral had at last taken pity on us – born partly out of the fact that we had now been granted permission to draw on American stores ashore. But these had been a strictly limited amount – just enough to prevent us starving and for a few urgent repairs. But we were running short of water again and our oil fuel was certainly not enough to take us to the Philippines.

As we came to the end of our punishment drill we could see that even the supply tankers were raising steam preparatory to sailing after the fleet, most of which was now under way. Slowly the amount of open water around us grew ever wider until just the two White Ensign ships remained in our part of the Bay. Yorkie, looking around at our isolation, said: 'Reminds me of when I was a kid and me and my mate got left behind on't school ramble. Never thought I'd feel so bloody lost as I was then.'

I shared his sense of loneliness on realising we really were being left behind. Looking up at the bridge I saw Arthur George staring – glumly I imagined – after the departing invasion force. He turned and said something to his yeoman waiting with a signal pad. A few moments later our signal lamp began flashing out another message to the 7th Fleet flagship. It was brief but the reply that came back as Kinkaid headed out of harbour was even shorter. Rear-Admiral Talbot studied what his yeoman had written down and then turned very sharply away.

Yorkie, watching him as well, summed up the situation bluntly. 'What's betting 'e's just been given a right sailor's farewell.'

He was, perhaps, closer to the truth than he had joked. By

evening the ship was buzzing with the story passed down from the bunting tossers that our Flag Officer had been given one of the biggest brush-off signals ever sent. How much truth there was in it was never discovered but it seemed to fit our unhappy rejection by the Americans. The story circulating was that Arthur George had, magnanimously, signalled Kinkaid his best wishes for the success of the invasion. According to some bunting tossers, back had come the sharp reply: 'Thanks. Do not follow.'*

Yet a bare hour or two later we did. Only as we left Hollandia we altered course to the East whereas the invasion fleet had steamed North. Keeping station with us was the *Glenearn*. Her officers and ratings must, I felt sure, have felt more deeply disillusioned at not being allowed to take part with the Americans. She was one of the best L.S.I.s in the Royal Navy and commanded by one of its best and most experienced assault force Captains. Better designed for the tropics and much more spacious than the *Lothian* her complement had the eagerness and high morale we so lacked.

What could one say about our own very mixed feelings? We did suffer a sense of being let down on realising that we had a little pride left in belonging to the Royal Navy. But then there was our frustration born out of having suffered both from the faults of others and ourselves. We had endured two months and over 12,000 miles of steaming (in every sense of the word) only to find our mission a total waste of time and effort. To confuse our emotions further there was a growing uncertainty about where we were now heading.

Since the Americans did not want the *Lothian* we felt there were only two practical alternatives. One was to team up with the Australians, which was handiest, or to steam all the way to the nearest Royal Navy base although this would mean a long, circuitous voyage to Trincomalee, Ceylon. There was another line of thought, more pessimistic, that insisted we *were* a 'ship-in-disgrace' and, therefore, would be left to roam around the island like some kind of *Marie Celeste* until our sins were expurgated.

None of us took into account the possibility that the Admiralty might actually have plans of its own for keeping us in the South-West Pacific. Our thoughts went no higher than Arthur

* No confirmation can be obtained although former ratings in *Lothian* recall this incident clearly.

George. Wonderment about what he might be scheming also added to our confusion. He wasn't, we agreed, the sort of Admiral who would easily give up. As Hookie put it: 'I'll lay my next tot to a tin of tickler that 'e'll find a bit of war to fight even if 'e 'as to start a landing of 'is own.'

But as we left the coast of New Guinea and headed south into the Coral Sea we slowly and happily realised that we must be steaming towards Australia, which, like America, we saw not so much as a land of milk and honey as a country of steaks, beer and girls. At last confirmation came that our next port would be Cairns, Queensland. No one had ever been there but it assumed all the romantic lure of Hawaii or some other heavenly spot.

For a brief while we forgot the mutiny, our two-and-two, the Americans' rejection and even our basic discomforts. Then, with seeming inevitability our euphoria was doused cold. The day before reaching Cairns 'Clear Lower Deck' was piped and the whole ship's company ordered to fall-in on the after welldeck where so many dismal events had taken place. As we lined up a heavy tropical downpour descended and the dense black clouds cast an appropriate shadow of gloom over the tense scene to come.

What followed would have confused a layman with a more conventional sense of judicial proceedings and it even puzzled the majority of the 750 officers and men slowly getting soaked. We had been mustered for the formal reading out of punishment warrants. (In the months to come this was to prove such a common ritual that we came to know a lot of the Naval Discipline Act far better than the order of prayers at the church service). Only on this occasion the ratings being sentenced were not present – not even aboard.

The warrants were for the ringleaders who had returned to the *Glenearn* following the court martial of our ex-Jimmy. Although we did not know it at the time they were being paraded before the latter ship's company for a more orthodox 'weighing off'. Why it had been decided a similar reading of their warrants should take place aboard *Lothian* was at first a mystery. Only when the Captain was well into his delivery did it become potently clear. Looking more stern than we had ever seen him appear, and in a strained sounding voice he began reciting the appropriate section relating to mutiny and the penalties for committing such a serious crime.

The sound of the rain falling made it difficult, at first, to hear him clearly but as we adjusted our hearing and our concentration grew his words came across with greater impact. For a moment he paused as though to add extra drama to what came next. It added considerably to the chill beginning to creep over us from our wetting.

An icy shiver ran through me as he continued: '. . . every person subject to this act who shall join therein shall suffer death by hanging . . .'

Captain Petrie paused again, either from emotion or for deliberate effect. It could only have been for a second or two but it seemed far longer. Our silence was so intense that the sound of the ocean lapping against our sides as we steamed along had all the loud vibrancy of tumbrils beating.

Then, less passionately, he added: '. . . or such other punishment as is hereafter mentioned . . .'

An audible sigh of relief swept through our crowded ranks. We had, for a brief moment, genuinely believed the ringleaders were to be strung from the yardarm. But the final words suggested something far less horrific. Like other parts of the Naval Discipline Act hanging could simply be a reminder of more brutal days when the cat o'nine tails and flogging round the fleet was standard practice.

So it proved to be. We heard how the three men were to be imprisoned in the nearest Australian military gaol to serve their hard labour although we still wondered why their warrants had been read out in their absence. But a possible explanation emerged a few moments later when the Captain's place was taken over by Arthur George.

In spite of the heavy rain he had put on his full tropical regalia making an impressive, almost forbidding sight with the scrambled egg on his peaked cap and his golden Admiral's insignia glistening. As he stood at the rail above us looking slowly down at the ship's company it seemed to me he was using the reading of the warrants as a set piece for some stern homily to come. Then, in a voice which justified his 'Noisy' tag he launched into his speech.

'You have dragged the White Ensign in the mud – those of you who took part in the disgraceful mutiny. But I shall make sure you will make it spotlessly clean again. I intend to see that discipline and good order will be maintained and that before our commission is over my flagship will become a worthy part of our great service.

From now on I expect every one of you to do his utmost to make this ship one to be proud of.'

There was more but we were either too wet or too stunned by the surprise of his lecture to take much of it in.

I don't know whether he genuinely expected his homily to have such a worthy effect but I could see why it had been preceded by the awesome reading of the warrants. If he could not put us in fear of him we should certainly be put in the fear of God, and the Naval Discipline Act.

A few hours later we suffered a fright from a more fundamental risk to our lives. Just as we were about to sail through a narrow, potentially dangerous gap in the Great Barrier Reef our wayward radar broke down. It was a particularly dark, moonless night and being wartime the buoys that marked the passage were unlit. The reef had claimed many a ship in the past and our memories were fresh with the sight of several American vessels that had had their bottoms ripped out on reefs around the Solomons and New Guinea. Ending up at the bottom might be a fitting end to our inglorious mission but none of us fancied ourselves as shark bait.

Somehow we wriggled through, although, according to the Navigator's Yeoman, it had been a close thing with our echo-sounder several times showing our bottom perilously close to the hidden coral below. The sight of the Queensland coast as dawn broke was a doubly welcome relief. Our first view of Cairns, however, lowered our enthusiasm. It reminded me of a film I had seen of *Sanders of the River* and some remote jungle edge outpost barely managing to survive equatorial heat and lassitude. But no African harbour could have suffered such a sickly smell that drifted from the town and pervaded every corner of the ship until even our clothes stank from it.

'Molasses,' announced Postie. 'I smelled it afore when I was on the West Indies Station.'

Yet he looked surprisingly cheerful rubbing his hands with expectation. Perhaps having his badges dipped had at last unsettled him. Not at all. He gave us a brief lesson in sugar cane production. 'You gets molasses from it and then you gets sugar, treacle and . . .'. Here he paused to achieve full effect. '. . . or you gets rum – your real 100 proof.'

That only made some of us more frustrated by the thought we

had had our shore leave stopped but it made those who had avoided 'two-and-two' doubly joyful. Lord knows Navy grog was strong enough but the aficionados were always ready to try a rum more potent. Or any foul potion with a numbing effect. Shortly after the mutiny several of the stokers had experimented with a home brew made from yeast stolen from the galley. It contained wood alcohol – a great deal more concentrated than they thought. The fight that resulted must have been a good deal more violent than the seamen's revolt judging by the black eyes and bruises, not counting those who had been rendered unconscious by this self-induced Mickey Finn.

In our own messdeck some ratings under punishment, with their tot banned, had tried the more complicated process of trying to produce a substitute from, of all things, after-shave lotion. The NAAFI had bought a lot of it in New York but it was so scented that no rating dared risk applying it for fear of being called a 'brownhatter'. But they did discover it contained a small percentage of alcohol. Extracting it and trying to get rid of its foul taste posed a problem and the crude answer was to filter the after-shave through a loaf of stale bread and then mix the evil left-overs with Andrews Liver Salts. It was just as well this stirring enterprise soon ended. We needed the bread more than this explosive cocktail.

But rum, so pure and powerful and, apparently flowing as freely as spring water was an irresistible challenge. If the barkeepers of Cairns had known what an onslaught awaited them they would either have broached a good number of extra barrels or barricaded their premises. They needed to do neither. Fatally for their profits or wisely for their safety an advance warning of just how potent the local rum was arrived alongside the *Lothian* before shore leave was granted.

While we were unaware of it at the time a score of ratings from the *Empire Spearhead* had been landed as a berthing party to tie up their ship, which was entering Cairns behind us after disembarking its G.I.s in the islands. They could not have been ashore much more than an hour but it was sixty minutes too long.

The first we knew about them was when two rattletrap, open lorries wheezed to a halt beside our gangway. As broken down as they were they looked considerably more alive than the 'cargo' they carried. Piled high in their backs like an untidy jumble of hammocks was the lifeless berthing party. An Aussie policeman lazily climbed aboard and languidly told the bemused Officer of the Watch: 'Brought your Pommy sailors back – our gaol just ain't big enough to hold them. But they ain't likely to give you any trouble the state they're in.'

The O.O.W. hotly denied any ownership but it cut no ice with the policeman. 'You're the only Pommy ship around and that's good enough for me.'

With that he turns and begins to walk away but not before adding the scathing comment: 'Thought you Poms knew how to handle rum – these stiffs look like they've never drunk anything stronger than tea.'

Even by the thirstiest boozing standards of the Royal Navy we had never seen men drink themselves into such an unconscious state. Loading them off the lorries was like trying to hump sacks of coal. By the time we had got them aboard we were exhausted and the shelterdecks where the bodies were laid looked like the aftermath of a dive bombing onslaught. Half an hour later we had the tiresome task of heaving – there was no other word for it – the *Spearhead*'s berthing party back aboard her as she came alongside.

It was hardly any wonder they were accompanied by a shower of insults from the *Lothian*'s seamen. Our Jimmy, supervising their disposal, had made it clear that if that was the effect the local rum had on them then he certainly was not going to let it happen to his ratings.

During the three days we stayed in the port leave was limited to one run ashore per watch and drinking confined to certain bars where, at the least sign of drunkenness, ratings were quickly ordered back aboard by the shore patrols. It did not stop several ending up in cells nor rum being sneaked aboard but, at least, it made us men under punishment feel a bit less persecuted.

It was during one of the periods of extra duties that we were ordered to unlash and unload on to the quay the Admiral's Humber car which had remained securely tied down to the boat deck ever since leaving Balboa, where he had used it to make official visits and for sightseeing. He was, we assumed, about to do the same in Cairns but a short time later we saw his stewards carry ashore luggage for Arthur George, his Secretary and Flag Lieutenant. It only took a small incident such as this to send a buzz running wildly through the ship. Soon, anyone who could, was gazing down at the quay wondering whether we were about to see the last of our Flag Officer.

Perhaps there was some wishful thinking among us mutineers that he was going for good, for we blamed being a flagship for much of our trouble, but we gave a barely subdued cheer as he was driven away by his coxswain-chauffeur. Later, in the messdeck, we considered if his departure signalled the end of Force X. But, again, it was really more desperate hope than reality. Like General MacArthur, Arthur George was to return.

Less than a day later we found we had a new, unknown, quantity of a superior officer to contend with – one whose arrival signalled the start of a fresh era in our lives and that of the *Lothian* and yet saw us cast even deeper into the peculiar wartime vortex in which we had already begun to find ourselves.

18

Red Admiral

As the scruffy looking figure in dishevelled khaki shirt and shorts and a peaked cap that looked as though it had fallen under a bus mounted the gangway of *Lothian* the quartermasters and Officer of the Watch trying to shelter from the tropical sun gave him only cursory glances. Only when the figure had almost reached the top did they grasp this was no casual Aussie serviceman of whom a few drifted aboard in Cairns.

At closer quarters the faded gold bars on his epaulettes and the well worn oak leaves on his peak told them he rated the honours due to a Naval Commander. But too late. As he stepped on to the deck he snapped: 'Don't you pipe your Captain aboard anymore in this ship?'

A less satisfactory reception to a less welcome command could hardly have been received by Commander Geoffrey Branson. Coming at the end of a frantic, tiring journey from Milne Bay, New Guinea, where he had been Resident Naval Officer, it could hardly have improved his temper. So sudden had been his appointment to *Lothian* that there had been no time to have his khakis pressed. All his formal white dress was back home in Melbourne. Commander Branson, although English, was Royal Australian Navy.

Perhaps there had been other officers of equal rank more handily placed – even Royal Navy ones – but this one bore a second distinction. He was the brother-in-law of Arthur George.*

* Rear-Admiral Talbot married Commander Branson's sister when her brother was serving with the Royal Navy. He later transferred to the R.A.N. His

But that was as unknown to the Officer of the Watch and the quartermasters as was the fact the ship was to have a new Captain. Nothing had been announced about Captain Petrie leaving. We knew his health had deteriorated although he still seemed capable of commanding. The fact that in Cairns and for some days afterwards we did not see him meant nothing to most of us since a whole week might go by without him appearing outside the bridge of his cabin. Normally when a Captain was about to leave his ship the crew would be told and, frequently, he would clear lower deck to say goodbye. In Captain Petrie's case he simply vanished from us for good.

The speculation was intense. The general opinion was that he had left because of the mutiny. We dismissed the suggestion that he had done so due to ill health – a semi-official explanation – as a cover-up. We also believed the Captain, for whom we had a sneaking if sometimes indifferent regard, had not got on too well with Arthur George following our revolt. Perhaps we were wrong but the all too secret circumstances bred rumour.

Commander Branson's hurried takeover indicated the decision to change Captains had been a sudden one. We assumed Arthur George had requested any available officer of appropriate rank. We, however, knew nothing of the family relationship and simply wondered how our new captain would get on with the Admiral. We were not even sure Arthur George was returning.

At least for the next few days our new Captain had only his own authority to contend with as he took the *Lothian* to sea and, to our great joy, headed south to bigger, brighter Brisbane. As we lined the sides on entering the Moreton River Mick glanced up at Branson on the wing of the bridge and said drily: 'He's number four – one a month – reckon he'll last that long?'

The wonder was he lasted more than a few days. Nothing could go right for the *Lothian* and her Captains. Although Commander Branson was in no way responsible for the incident which almost ended her Naval career it was a miracle he wasn't made to take the ultimate blame. Arthur George was seriously embarrassed by the near disaster.

---

brother-in-law thought highly of him and, according to a relation, referred to the Commander as 'someone you would want to have alongside you if you had your back to the wall'.

The day it happened began happily enough even for men under punishment. We had just learnt that we were to remain in port for some three weeks in order that the urgent repairs so long delayed could be undertaken. First priority was being given to the water system which the patch-up job in Balboa had done little to cure. It meant the water tanks being completely stripped and relined – a task that might have been simpler if whoever had redesigned the ship had allowed a means of getting bulky items in and out of the engineroom.

To solve the problem the repair crew decided to cut a hole in the ship's side and move the debris and parts through this. As long as all concerned knew this was happening the risks were small. Unfortunately someone forgot to enter the fact in the engineroom log. When an engineer decided to adjust the ballasting of the ship by pumping water from one side to the other he knew nothing about the hole made in the side of another section of the engineroom.

The first we knew something had gone drastically wrong was when we were sent flying by the sudden sharp listing of the *Lothian*. Loose gear and men were flung together in the scuppers. Somehow I managed to cling to a guardrail I had been painting but I was horrorstruck to see that the only thing stopping the ship keeling right over were our hawsers. Now bar taut they were singing a wild song of suicide as they threatened to part.

A few seconds later the PA system was bellowing out calls for 'Every man to the port side'. If it had been 'Action Stations' the response could not have been swifter. In moments hundreds were crowded on the one side many leaning as far over the rails as they dare. I don't know how heavy some six or seven hundred men weigh but they had very little effect on our list. The hawsers cried out ominously. Then what had become melodrama turned rapidly to farce. Over the PA came the command: 'Commence jumping up and down.'

I suppose the theory was that by doing so we could rock the ship back to a more upright stance. In my alarmed view it only placed more strain on the hawsers one of which now cracked with a nerve shattering report causing the ship to list a little further over. Ignoring the order we stopped jumping for fear more would snap. Down below, as we found out later, the Moreton River was still pouring in through the hole in our side. Also out of our sight a desperate attempt was being made to lower our starboard side landing craft to relieve the list. It was a tedious enough job with the ship upright but at her sharp angle nearly impossible. A few made it but some had to be cut from their davits with axes.

Just as we were wondering, rather hoping, that this might be the *Lothian*'s final despairing fling she slowly began righting herself. The cause of her listing, the transfer of ballast, had been reversed to place as much weight as possible on the opposite side. And just in time. Our hawsers had all been stretched to a degree that made them unusable again. Arthur George's temper must have been strained nearly as greatly.

If we thought he had gone for good when he drove away from the ship in Cairns we were sadly mistaken. No doubt frustrated by the American rejection of his flagship he had decided to spend several days relaxing by driving to Brisbane. There he had chosen to enjoy the comforts of a hotel returning back aboard to hold a special luncheon.

It was far more important to him than just a social occasion. As it gradually became clear to everyone aboard he was still energetically seeking some active duty for Force X in the South-West Pacific. Since the Americans wanted little to do with us he now turned to the Australians, who had taken over the major task of clearing up the pockets of Japanese resistance left behind by the former's rapid leap-frogging advance. If there was one man more important than almost any other in agreeing our co-operation it was the Australian Army's General Sir Thomas Blamey, Ground Forces Commander South-West Pacific. It was he who was the guest of honour at luncheon in the Admiral's cabin along with several of his staff officers.

Arthur George's 'banquets', as we called them, were fairly stylish for a ship like *Lothian* in wartime – white jacketed stewards serving the kind of mouth-watering food we in the seamen's messdeck had long forgotten; good bone china, plated cutlery and wine in cut-glass decanters. For the General it was probably even more lavish and Arthur George, remembering the embarrassment caused by the mutiny when he was similarly entertaining important officers in Balboa, might have relaxed more easily knowing a repeat of that was extremely unlikely.

But this was the hoodoo ship *Lothian*.

The luncheon was well under way with wine and conversation flowing easily when the ship heeled hard over as though struck by a giant wave. Food, wine, plates, cutlery – everything slid from the table into the laps of everyone on the wrong side or crashed and broke on the deck. Staggering to their feet, clutching anything they could to stay upright the guests and staff officers made for the door and for safety.

After the General and his officers had departed abruptly and probably with grave doubts about the *Lothian*'s ability to stay afloat let alone go into action, the wrath of God descended on everyone involved with the near disaster. Considering that court martials had become part of our life we were surprised another did not follow this mishap.

Perhaps, we thought, this succession of disasters had finally taken its toll of Arthur George; that we could now hope for less severe retribution and a more peaceful time.

We should have known better.

Before we sailed from Brisbane another court martial had taken place.

It must be said that it was largely forced on the Admiral and there was certainly no way he could have ignored the offence that led to it. It was just unfortunate that he should suffer insomnia and that a certain engineer officer should have, at various times during our voyage, have fallen foul of him culminating in the hole-in-the-side mishap. Prior to that his main crime had been, so the stokers said, his difficulty in ensuring that Arthur George got his bath water hot enough. With so many souls aboard it was virtually impossible to keep water anything better than lukewarm. Down below we would have been happy to have had that – not our meagre ration of saltwater for washing.

Perhaps he was trying to drown his sorrows or had simply been treated to too much Aussie hospitality but this Engineer Lieutenant was in a fighting mood when he lurched back up the gangway in the early hours one night. The quartermaster on duty gave a vivid account to us the next morning. ' 'E was waving 'is arms about demanding to know where Arthur George was. "Where is the bugger?" he kept shouting. Then 'e goes on: "If I find 'im I'll punch 'im in the nose." '

The QM went on: 'The O.O.W. tries to calm 'im down and send

'im to 'is cabin. Then there's a voice like God coming down from 'Eaven. It effing well was, too – the Admiral's!'

What none of them had known was that Arthur George, unable to sleep had been pacing his deck directly above the gangway when the row broke out. He had heard every word.

'Send that officer to his cabin . . . under arrest. I'll deal with him in the morning.' Down from above came the stern pronouncement and the poor engineer had been marched off under Marine guard.

When he awoke the next morning he probably feared the worst although messdeck opinion was divided on the subject. The Royal Navy was pretty broadminded where returning from shore leave drunk was concerned – a night in the cells was usually the worst that happened. Since reaching Brisbane many of those lucky enough to get shore leave had staggered back barely able to get up the gangway but suffered no more than a hangover. We also recalled what had been a not dissimilar version of the engineer's crime with Arthur George showing remarkable restraint.

The offender on this occasion was our ginger-haired messdeck sweeper who carried on a special vendetta against the Admiral. He blamed him for our concrete deck covering and the cement dust that was the bane of the sweepers lives. He had started on his pet gripe one morning while we were crossing the Pacific and was working up a full head of steam: 'If that effing Admiral was 'ere now I'd shove this effing sweeper right up 'is arse,' he proclaimed loudly.

His threat came over unusually loud and clear as a sudden silence fell over the packed messes waiting to turn to. Ginger, unused to capturing much attention to his griping turned slowly round in wonderment. There, within broom handle's length, was Arthur George himself. And behind him the Captain and Jimmy. Since the mutiny the Admiral had taken to occasionally springing a surprise visit on different parts of the ship and he could not have chosen a more awkward moment for this one.

We watched his reaction as tensely as peasants on the slopes of Etna waiting for the volcano to erupt. Yet, apart from a deepening of his normally stern features, nothing happened. Perhaps the threat was so wild as only to amuse him or was he recalling the rough treatment we had given the last officer to lay down the law in the messdeck? Whatever the reason he had departed a few minutes later without a word. But as his little entourage disappeared up the ladder the Jimmy turned and told the Messdeck P.O.: 'Put that rating on my report.'

The fourteen days' 'No 11s' (punishment and stoppage of leave) Ginger got was, as he said himself, 'An effing cheap way of giving an Admiral a bollocking.' Since he was already doing punishment for the mutiny it added up to almost nothing extra.

But officers, even the RNR and RNVR engineer officers whom the regular executive branch often regarded as little better than garage mechanics (more for their lack of good accents and polish than any lack of skill) and nicknamed 'plumbers', could hardly expect to get away with insulting Arthur George as lightly. It may not have had anything to do with the latter's decision to force a court martial but it could not have put him in any happier frame of mind to learn the morning after the crime that the Americans had landed on Leyte – without any help from him or Force X.

The only gun we ever fired in anger was our court martial signal and once again it could be heard when the engineer was brought to trial. That was almost all we knew, but a few days later a peculiar story began circulating that suggested Arthur George had not had things all his own way. It appeared that for his counsel the engineer, acting quickly, had called on the services of the only officer aboard who had, in civvy street, been a barrister. A day later the Admiral had ordered the same legal expert to be the prosecutor! He had not been amused when the latter insisted it would be a breach of professional etiquette for him to switch roles. What hurt more was the fact that the defendant's 'friend' (as counsel is known in these circumstances) had insisted on the Admiral being called as a witness and had then proceeded to cross-examine him sternly.

The court's decision, however, was almost inevitable. The engineer was found guilty and dismissed the ship. Was it just coincidence, we asked ourselves, that his counsel, a Lieutenant RNVR Communications Officer, was drafted from the *Lothian* almost straight afterwards?

Such departures, usually more ignominious than not, only aroused our envy and increased our frustrations at being in a port flowing with good grub, beer and women (in that strict order) and not allowed shore leave. Every day we saw hundreds of the rest of the complement heading for the seductions of Brisbane while we lined up for punishment drills and extra duties. Almost sadistically those seamen who had miraculously avoided being weighed off for the mutiny would return full of leering stories about the 'Sheilas' who were apparently queueing up to satisfy sex-starved mateloes. As if that weren't enough they revealed that Brisbane had a thriving red-light district where, according to these insatiable customers, brothels were legal. Their descriptions of the erotic practices indulged there made the Kama Sutra seem like a Girl Guides' handbook.

Yet it was soon obvious that they got more for their money than sexual treats. Rose Cottage, our V.D. Mess, which had been noticeably empty for most of the time since leaving New York, now began filling up until it became the most crowded mess in the ship. When we moved ashore for a few days while the ship was dry-docked to have her bottom scraped of its jungle of tropical ocean growth and to be fumigated in a mostly vain attempt to get rid of our army of rats the V.D. Mess filled most of a wooden hut dormitory.

What the Royal Australian Navy said when not only these men but several score of others 'confined to barracks' arrived added a whole new chapter to the thick volume of nautical swearwords. The several dozen others who got charged with being absent without leave or were arrested by the local police for drunkenness, fighting and even theft moved the Aussie Jaunty to raise his hands in despair and ask the Almighty why he should punish him in this way. Turning to us he added: 'It aint as if we didn't get enough Pommy convicts in the old days – now we get you load of gaol scrapings.'

He suffered us for just days. But for Captain Branson, trying to mould us back into something approaching a trustworthy, well trained crew, we represented a headache that could last for months. One of the very first tasks he had on board was the reading out of warrants for those who had committed serious crimes. He must have raised his bushy eyebrows when he saw that in only the first three months or so of our commission the warrant numbers had already touched the seventies and looked well set to create some kind of Naval record. It was one we were to achieve with room to spare.

Far more outgoing than our previous Captain he was, however, determined to face the challenge – as I was soon in a position to learn at first hand. As we steamed out of Brisbane I found myself detailed off to be his 'runner' (messenger and general handyman). Although it was considered a 'soft number' I did not fancy having the problems it would create. On the one hand was the Captain expecting me to be a messdeck listening post for him while on the other were my messmates relying on me to pass on all the titbits I could glean in the course of my new duties. The answer, I decided, was to act as dumb as I could.

But deaf I certainly was not. Not a word that could be overheard through the open ports of the Captain's cabin evaded my ears as I waited to run his messages. Somewhere I had read the phrase 'the exigencies of war' and this I decided, as I shed any remaining sense of decency I had, definitely justified my eavesdropping. My only regret was that whenever Arthur George wanted a serious talk with the Captain it took place in the former's cabin guarded by a Marine sentry. Even so I learnt a lot about the conduct of naval warfare at more rarefied levels. Or the lack of it as it proved to be in the case of H.M.S. *Lothian* and Force X.

One of the first comments I heard Captain Branson make, just after leaving the Moreton Bay as we headed back to the islands was a reply to the Jimmy's query about the possibility of enemy action.

In his deep voice he retorted drily: 'From what I can tell so far our biggest problem will be getting close enough to the war to find any enemy to fight. First we have to overcome the Americans!'

19

Castaways

Nobody loves us
Nobody cares
Why doesn't someone
Answer our prayers?

Yankees don't want us
Nobody does
We're on a pox ship
Too far from Guz.

We sat on our stages slapping paint on the ship's sides in time with
this ditty composed by one of the more poetic A.B.s and trucu-
lently not caring if it was irritating any P.O.s or officers on deck.
But they may well have been sympathetic. From Captain to
canteen assistant the *Lothian*'s company was fed up with the weeks
we had spent steaming uselessly around the South-West Pacific in
a vain search for a slice of action, however tiny.

In the ten weeks since leaving Brisbane we had called at as many
ports in New Guinea, Solomons, New Caledonia and Northern
Australia. The stops had been brief – just long enough for us to
find out no one wanted us. Arthur George would speed off in his
barge to call on some American or Australian Commander and
then return soon after looking more depressed than when he had
set out. At other times he would send some staff officer flying off in
any handy Dakota or Catalina to hunt further afield. Always they,
too, would return empty handed.

This blatant rejection by the American Navy and the apparent disinterest by the Aussies in making some use of us, although they had no real call to use a Headquarters Landing Ship in our area of confinement, was seriously reducing our already low state of morale. It wasn't doing much good for the ship herself. The jungle of tropical marine vegetation flourishing on her bottom was slowly dragging down her speed. One day as the Navigator left the Captain's cabin with yet another order to prepare to steam elsewhere I overheard him say to the officer with him: 'If we keep going round in these ever decreasing circles we'll end up vanishing up our own orifice old chap.'

Down in the messdecks we expressed a similar thought more crudely.

The Admiral was clearly losing his patience and, I suspected, some of his zeal as the weeks dragged uselessly by. He had taken to pacing up and down the deck with his brother-in-law, the Captain, and venting his frustration fairly openly – loud enough for me, ostensibly polishing the Captain's brasswork, to overhear. He was, it seemed, in a cleft stick.

The Admiralty appeared reluctant to withdraw his flagship while the 7th Fleet were still making some use, if largely in a behind-the-lines role as troop and store ferries, of the L.S.I.s of Force X. There was, as we had also heard rumoured around the messdecks, some possible new task for the ship although this lay several months away. It was also important, I gathered, that some kind of Royal Navy presence be maintained with the U.S. Navy in the area preparatory to the sending of a big British fleet to the Pacific.* All of this was, apparently, taxing Arthur George's

* The large British force was the British Pacific Fleet agreed to between Churchill and Roosevelt but strongly objected to by Admiral King, U.S.N. C-in-C. The latter's disapproval and blunt statement that the Royal Navy would have to fend for itself in the Pacific had seriously worried Admiral Bruce Fraser, the BPF C-in-C, in his preparations to organise the massive back-up operation the fleet must have if it was to be stored, ammunitioned and fuelled in such a remote and vast area. It was vital to him to know what the reaction of the U.S. Navy commanders on the spot was likely to be as their co-operation would be needed to a great extent.

The experience of the *Lothian* and Force X could not have made him very confident but the probability was that he thought they could serve as a kind of listening post. In the event we were never allowed close enough to the main U.S. commanders to obtain anything very helpful. As events transpired the BPF, with ingenuity and forbearance to the limit particularly as his attitude towards the Americans, never very warm, had worsened a lot.

It would have suited him if the 7th Fleet had wiped their hands clean of us but as long as we remained well out of the way thousands of miles from the main action now in the Philippines and while the Admiralty insisted on having a flagship for the Force, the rest of which it rarely met, it seemed content to let us stay attached. Were the Americans even aware of us any more? we sometimes asked ourselves. But the answer to that was right there among us.

For a reason we could never properly fathom the three U.S.N. signal and cypher officers with their half a dozen 'sparkers' and cypher ratings we had picked up in New York had stayed aboard. Their presence seemed totally unnecessary since any radio traffic between ourselves and the Americans, never great, had become almost non-existent. These U.S. Navymen, however, were transmitting and receiving a good deal that was strictly for their own interests.

They had insisted on their own private radio office. Royal Navy personnel were not allowed to enter, nor permitted to see any of the signals handled in it. All the American signals were in their own cypher – not divulged to us – with the cypher machine kept strictly guarded against our possibly prying eyes. Once when it broke down the Americans preferred waiting some time for a U.S.N. mechanic rather than take up our offer of using one of our own machines.

It was hardly surprising, therefore, that such tight secrecy should lead us seamen, but especially the Communication ratings, to believe the Americans were simply aboard to spy on us and report our movements and actions to 7th Fleet Command. But, then, we had a distinctly anti-American bias. Much of this was a natural consequence of our rejection by the U.S. Navy. No one liked being treated as inferiors by a Navy with a far less prestigious and historic reputation even if we did not think highly of the R.N. ourselves.

A far more personal and telling reason for our dislike of the

---

the immense support of its huge Fleet Train of store ships, did find welcome co-operation from Admiral Nimitz, C-in-C of the U.S. 3rd Fleet with which the BPF operated.

Americans resulted from the very long delays in receiving mail from home. It was nearly four months before most of us got one of the flimsy, single-sheet letters to the Forces allowed in wartime. Our great distance from Britain was a major cause – made worse by the fact the letters had to come via the United States. We were convinced that because we were not an American ship the mail sorters in the U.S.A gave us a low priority. The fact that we were now rarely long enough in any one place for the letters to catch up with us added to our frustration.

The mail did not always bring the pleasure that one might have expected. Instead of feeling less cut off we sometimes felt more isolated. In spite of all our efforts to get round the censors (our own officers) by vague references to palm trees and hot weather; flying fish and sharks as a clue to our rough location none of our friends and relations had a notion of where we might be. Nor could we make them aware that all was far from well with us. Any mention of the mutiny or other troubles was strictly banned and ratings who dared to get the message across got promptly hauled up before the Jimmy.

It was no wonder that writers at home got a totally wrong impression. Cockie exploded with fury when his mum wrote from London's East End: 'Think yourself lucky you're missing the doodlebugs and having such a lovely time with all that warm weather. We could do with seeing them exciting places you're visiting.'

We had just stood down from a sweltering session of oiling the wire stays and hawsers – before turning to again for our punishment muster. And no one in their right mind would have described Empress Augusta Bay, Bougainville, as an 'exciting place'.

But 'Mum' was right in suggesting she was suffering far more hostile action than her son. There were pockets of Japanese resistance on the far side of this island but well away from being any danger to us. We had called here in the hope the Australian Army would find us useful in their cleaning up operation but they had made it clear they could cope adequately on their own. Bougainville had, however, proved the one and only place where we saw a landing craft put hurriedly into the water in anything approaching anger.

H.M.S. *Lothian* had almost beached herself, in fact. As we

steamed slowly into the Bay, relying on an ancient German chart, we ran smack into a coral reef that had appeared in the intervening decades. The impact sent a shudder throughout the ship and Captain Branson, leaning well over the wing of the bridge to try and spot any reefs, only just managed to save himself being thrown overboard. But not his cap with its golden scrambled egg.

With great promptitude he bellowed: 'Lower No 1 Landing Craft.'

With rather less speed since they had got out of practice with their emergency drill the Royals got their L.C.A. away. Their next move, as all the watchers aboard believed, might be to take a hawser and try and swing the ship clear. But the next order from the bridge was: 'Find my bloody cap.'

Turning to the stupefied officer behind him Captain Branson said bluntly: 'I'm not going to lose that cap – it's the only decent one I've got'.

We were all relieved when he not only got it back but we managed, with little more than denting our bows and any nautical pride, to get clear of the reef and go to anchor. Had the Japanese been closer we would have made a sitting duck of a target.

Our grounding proved to have a more symbolic than physically damaging effect. It seemed to signify we should, for the time being, bring our gypsy like roaming of the islands to a halt. For twenty-four days we lay in the bay as though we were some unemployed freighter for whom her owner was finding a weather safe lay-up berth free of harbour dues.

Nothing displayed a better example of the tedious frustrations of unemployment than the *Lothian*'s 750 strong complement. As day after boring day crept by we behaved more like the street corner jobless of the 1930s depression. We seamen went about the mostly unnecessary deck duties like factory hands out to defeat a time and motion study expert and with little else to force upon us our P.O.s and the Jimmy were disinclined to hurry us along. Our off-duty hours, especially for those of us under punishment, became an endurance test and our irritation grew as prickly as the ship's bottom growing more like a marine nature reserve every day.

Whether it was due to such enforced idleness, the intense heat and humidity or simply to most ratings' baser instincts, but it was obvious to me that sex was becoming even more abnormally dominant in the messdeck. In our remote Pacific lay-by it could definitely not have been normal. From time to time we spotted a native Melanesian woman passing in an outrigger canoe but anyone who raised their sights above bare-breasted eye level quickly had any urge quelled by faces that I believed not even the randiest mateloe could fancy. They were never given a chance to disprove me.

That thoughts were being forced in the only other sexual direction possible aboard gradually became clear to me whenever I went for a saltwater shower. Perhaps I did look more innocent than most and my accent – like my cheeks – was softer than many but there had to be a reason why I was now getting predatory glances from several hairy chested seamen. The same occurred whenever I stripped to get into my hammock. Before long I began acting more like a convent schoolgirl shyly undressing for bed as though exposing her flesh was a cardinal sin.

I was innocent enough with a knowledge of homosexuality that would not bring blushes to a novice nun. Naïve, too. I accepted references to that Naval phallic symbol the 'Golden Rivet' and to 'arse bandits' and 'brownhatters' as no more than typical earthy messdeck terminology – just as I regarded the singing of a ditty about the fondness of stokers for Scapa Flow sheep as customary bawdiness.

'Queers' were a perversion that I vaguely believed emanated mainly from public schools – not in the rough, tough atmosphere of a Naval messdeck. Yet I could not avoid noticing that the ratings showing unnerving amorousness were mainly the hairiest, most muscular seamen around. I tried shrugging off my anxiety as being no more than the effect of being confined for so long in the same male company but it was Mick, as fundamentally forthright a Christian as only an Ulster Catholic can be who convinced me I had every cause to be aware.

He had just met me on deck after I had taken my usual stroll for some badly needed fresh air before turning in and for a rare chance of being alone for a few minutes. 'You'd best watch it,' he warned me earnestly. 'The fo'c'sle's no place for you on your own.'

Alarmed I sought the cause of his concern. Eyeing me like a Father forced to reveal the facts of life to a puberty stricken daughter he explained forcibly: 'There's things happening up there at night you wouldn't even find in the Bible. I tell you –

Sodom and Gomorrah has got nothing on this ship.'

From thence forward I always sought safe company whenever I visited the fo'c'sle by dark. And there was no one safer, in this respect, than the 'ancient mariner' Postie. It was he who filled in the gaps of my education where 'brownhatting' was concerned and its place as one of the Royal Navy's older traditions.

After hearing me tentatively ask whether he thought it was a problem aboard he answered: 'There's always bin a smell of it in any ship I've ever bin on a long commission to stinking 'oles like this. Corse it wuz more common when there wuz them old wooden walls and a Jack wouldn't see a tart for months on end but it don't seem so popular nowadays. Mind you in this excuse for a warship with effing Brylcreem Boys and Christ knows 'oo else aboard it's a wonder they don't 'ave one of the messdecks rigged up as an effing brothel.'

There was possibly no need. The murky talk in the mess suggested that some of our many nooks and crannies in the forepart of the ship were serving the purpose adequately. The unfortunate R.A.F. men became an inevitable part of such conversations for the seamen rarely ceased to slander them. Their part in shipboard life had become increasingly useless and they were, a few minor duties and exercises apart, the passengers we had always accused them of being.

At times I wondered why the officers or P.O.s made no apparent move to curb the growing taste for what mateloes in their curious phraseology also called 'Navy Cake'. I began to believe Postie's assertion that it was too long a Naval tradition for anyone to try and stamp on it. Yet, if that was so, then it must have been regarded more as a Lower Deck trait. Definitely not approved of in senior officers.

The buzz that raised the peculiar moral issue of the rights and wrongs of homosexuality according to rank had taken a long time reaching our ears. That was hardly surprising. Everyone concerned from Arthur George downwards must have taken all possible steps to prevent news leaking out of the highly embarrassing circumstances. The incident that led to the Admiral being forced to take official action had also occurred in one of the L.S.I.s out of sight of us. Now the news of it had reached us along a long line stretching through the Force in its various scattered locations.

Leaving out the inevitable gory additions the news boiled down to the fact that a Captain of an L.S.I. had been dismissed his ship because of 'attempted buggery'.

One account said there had been a court martial while another said there had just been a court of inquiry with the Captain told to leave quietly without fuss. That the First Lieutenant had taken command was not in doubt.*

What surprised me as much was the general messdeck reaction. The crude jokes apart there was some unexpected moral indignation.

What appeared to be inevitable if not wholly acceptable among ratings was thought obscene for Commanders or above. Cockie interpreted the reaction rather differently. 'I'm not saying them arse bandits around 'ere is any better but at least they ain't got any other effing pleasures like them pigs 'as got. What does an effing Captain want to go buggering about for when 'e's got all that effing booze to drown 'is sorrows in?'

The subject of officers and the drink they could readily and in generous quantities obtain in the 'pigsty' had, despite the fact that it was a situation that applied in every one of H.M. ships and had done so ever since there was a Royal Navy, become a sore grievance among many of us. The daily tot, powerful though it was and sometimes illegally supplemented from rum sold or bartered by many of the R.A.F. men and Royal Corps of Signallers who did not like it, was never enough, especially in the intense heat where it was quickly sweated out. Men under punishment or under twenty never got that. The tiny ration of drinking water, which always had traces of oil in it, even when mixed into a fizzier cocktail with Andrew's Liver Salts, was hardly any substitute.

But the really irritating feature for us was the way the officers would blithely tipple and skylark in the wardroom on gin at 1p a glass apparently totally unconcerned there were thirsty mateloes with tongues hanging out within earshot. Every night in harbour the 'pigs' seemed to be entertaining themselves and visiting Aussies with raucously lively parties in which they leapfrogged furniture and indulged in other rough and tumble games before tottering to their cabins to sleep it off. One of the very same officers

* Due to the ban on public inspection of court-martial records it is impossible to verify or disprove the alleged offence. It is certainly confirmed by one senior officer on the Force X Flag staff. Without documentary evidence, however, it would be wrong to state names.

might be the one some unlucky rating was marched before on 'defaulters' the next day after being caught with a can of beer bummed off some Aussie soldier at their base camp ashore.

Our hostility over this was possibly no more than symptomatic of our general state of frustration at what we believed were almost deliberate attempts to grind us down. There were two examples in particular which we felt were callous if not intended as such. One concerned the 'General Muster' that took place annually in H.M. ships and seemed nothing more than a hangover from Nelson's day when manning was a more slap happy affair. Every man aboard was lined up and had to double forward individually to have his name, official number and rating checked against his 'parchment' (official record). On this occasion it was the Admiral himself who held the muster. But he had also chosen to conclude it with a stylish deck buffet for the officers. As we doubled away around the other side of the Captain's cabin we found stewards laying out the kind of mouth-watering spread we had forgotten existed.

It did not make it easier to swallow the dehydrated veg and hash we had for our meal. Nor did we find it easy to swallow what happened when Arthur George decided to stage a lavish picnic for his staff officers and himself on a nearby islet. Having to hump the heavy hampers of tasty food into his barge was bad enough for our digestion. When we found out what was in a large sack we were ordered to take extra care with we almost mutinied again. Carefully encased in thick ice was a big ball of solid icecream specially made for the occasion.

Had we not been so annoyed we might have been calm enough to read into the organising of the picnic, and other clear signs of Arthur George's more relaxed attitude, a definite indication that he had come to terms with his and Force X's hopeless position and was trying to enjoy it as best he could.

20

Naked Stains

Like a sword that lies rusting in a damp attic *Lothian* and other ships in Force X were rapidly deteriorating from disuse in the decaying tropical humidity of the islands. No more so, however, than many of the men. The futility of it all had got as much beneath our skins as the prickly heat and ringworm was attacking their surface. If there was any point to remaining we were left in total ignorance, perhaps because no one knew what to do with us.

Surely, we told ourselves, someone, be it our Admiral, their Lordships back in London or even the Americans must bring the farce to a quick end. How much longer could we stay at anchor in Empress Augusta Bay before we grounded on our own 'gash'? Even the Aussie troops had begun to crack scathing jokes about our immobility. Returning from the grim task of trying to winkle the Japanese out of their jungle hideouts they would make pointed comparisons between 'Pommy sailors and kippers – two-faced and gutless'.

If Arthur George was in any doubt about the growing despair in his flagship it was as nothing compared with the slump of morale and discipline elsewhere in Force X. When *Empire Arquebus* and *Empire Mace* joined the *Lothian* in enforced idleness, the 7th Fleet no longer finding any use for them even as supply and troop ships between the islands, Arthur George took the opportunity for his first visit to either ship for many weeks. The rust-stained *Arquebus* had barely anchored before he set out in his barge complete with his large entourage of staff officers. An Admiral's inspection at the best of times and for the smartest of warships can be a nerve-racking affair. At short notice and for a vessel that had been serving as a rough and tumble ferry for months among the islands it proved traumatic.

It did not help matters that at the very time the Admiral set out the ship's supply officer had all the stores possible brought up on to the foredeck to be checked – a definitely unorthodox method of stocktaking. It seemed, we learned later from the ship's seamen, that his accounts had got hopelessly out of step and that he felt this quirky method was the only safe way of accurately finding out what was left aboard.

The mountainous jumble of boxes of canned goods, sacks of dried vegetables and cartons of lavatory paper plus goodness knows what else met Arthur George squarely in the eye as he came alongside. The dressing down he gave the poor supply officer set the tone for the rest of his inspection. ' 'E went through the ship like an effing torpedo gone mad,' an *Arquebus* quartermaster said later. But he had, it appeared, found more than enough to justify his fury. Ordering Lower Deck to be cleared at the end of his inspection he told the assembled ship's company angrily: 'This is the dirtiest, most disgraceful warship I have ever seen. It brings shame on the whole Royal Navy.'

Three days later a similarly thorough examination of the *Mace* brought down further retribution on her complement. Yet what must have undoubtedly disturbed the Admiral more than most signs of slackness he found was the state in which he had discovered the normally smart, trustworthy Royals.

News, especially bad news, travels fast between warships of the same squadron lying at anchor together and it was not long before we learnt via our own Marines that their counterpart 'flotillas' in the two *Empire*'s had been severely reprimanded. Their condition and organisation was so poor, it was said, that both their C.O.s had been reduced on the spot from Captains to Lieutenants.*

---

* The brief war diaries of the various Royal Marine flotillas attached to Force X confirm the poor state of affairs and the dismissals of the commanders.

The entry for December 9 for the *Arquebus* (Flotilla 536) states: 'Cleanliness of flotilla below average. Messdeck filthy and congested. There is no efficient administrative organisation.'

That for December 12 for the *Mace* (Flotilla 541) states: 'Below average appearance. In many cases rifles showed signs of neglect. Kits below average. Craft (landing craft) work poor.'

Both statements concluded with the fact that both Acting Captains in command were relieved of their position and reduced in rank to Lieutenant.

The significance of all this was not lost on us in the messdeck. As Yorkie expressed it in Tykish bluntness: 'If them Royals can't keep up bullshit there's no use expecting us Jacks to keep ourselves champered up (clean and bright)'.

Perhaps, as we agreed with him, we were simply seeking justification for our own sloppiness. The cramped conditions and lack of facilities or enough water to help us smarten ourselves was nearly excuse enough but we had also lost any desire to be other than in an almost constantly slovenly state. Most of the efforts by the P.O.s and officers to force us to look clean and neat had largely been defeated by an unavoidable and overwhelming problem that affected all aboard, rank regardless. It was certainly one that the Admiral, weighing up the problems of continuing to seek action for Force X, could hardly avoid taking into account.

Any stranger visiting the *Lothian* might well have believed the Royal Navy had devised a strange new method of personal camouflage. There was not a man aboard who was not painted over a good part of his body with bright purple lotion. A fair number also sported touches of glaring orange. In theory these vivid tinctures were supposed to ease the prickly heat rashes, ringworm and footrot from which we now suffered torments due to the lack of fresh water to clean the dirt and sweat that was further irritated by our badly washed clothes. In practice they did little more than provide temporary easement from the urge to scratch ourselves like a tribe of apes.

The overwhelming effect of this, the generally unhealthy conditions, intense heat and poor food was to fill the few beds in our cramped hospital and constantly lengthen the queue for daily treatment at the sick bay. Although it was better than risking death and injury from enemy action we would almost have welcomed that in order to take our minds off our debilitating bodily irritations. Captain Branson, for one, saw the urgent need to keep our minds occupied elsewhere while trying, at the same time, to improve our fitness.

I had turned up for duty at his cabin one morning looking even more like an Indian brave painted up to set out on the war path. Eyeing me up and down from beneath his bushy eyebrows he snorted: 'It's high time, Glenton, you stopped looking like some New Guinea tribesman. We've got to do something drastic about these rashes.'

I listened, unbelievingly, as he briefly propounded what he considered was the cause and the cure for our ills. 'It's those filthy clothes that don't get properly washed. What's clearly needed is for all ratings to get a good washdown in fresh water as often as possible. From now on I intend to clear Lower Deck whenever there's rain and have you all exercised without any clothes on.'

When I repeated his amazing proposal to my messmates they believed I was joking. 'Bollock naked! 'E can't be serious!' Or: 'What! Jump around naked with all them arse bandits around!' And so on.

Yet, as we should have guessed, Captain Branson was in deadly earnest. He had already startled us by his unorthodox efforts at keeping himself fit. One of the strangest sights in the *Lothian*, as it would have been in any warship, was to see in the early light of dawn our Captain dancing around his deck as he went several rounds with one of the killicks, a New Zealander recently joined, who had a reputation as a good boxer.

I used to watch in fascination – more so because both men were exposing tattoos of a highly colourful kind on parts of their anatomy which the Captain, at least, normally kept hidden from public view. But even this weird scene could not compare with the ones that shortly took place as he carried out his extremist keep fit scheme.

Earlier, the radar watch, had received orders to inform the bridge immediately it picked up echoes of imminent heavy rain clouds, which used to break over the islands mountains and briefly shed their load in a dousing downpour. The first time it did so the general command was piped over the PA system: 'All hands muster on the foredeck – rig of the day naked.'

If we looked stupid enough without clothes the effect was made more peculiar by our purple paint which coated private as well as public parts. As we were ordered to go through the physical exercise routine the War Dance image became even more obvious. Even if we had been fit, however, the effect of jumping up and down on the spot without supporting shorts would have been more uncomfortable than we could bear. Yet even that was better than doing press ups on the burning steel deck.

Cockie, trying desperately not to let vital parts of his body get in contact with the deck, gasped to me: 'They ain't satisfied with putting bromide in the porridge – now they 'as to effing well burn our balls orf.'

We couldn't wait for the black clouds above to shed their monsoon downfall on us. As the rain, unexpectedly icy, drenched us we leapt around voluntarily our joy mixed with an uncontrollable reaction to the cold. As far as it went the experiment succeeded in that it cleaned our bodies properly for the first time in months (we had been issued with soap to wash ourselves down on deck) and it eased our irritating rashes for a while. Unfortunately the scheme did not take into account the problems inherent in trying to turn a ship into a part-time nudist camp.

A rolling, pitching ship at sea demands clothing as protection against being thrown against the many, potentially damaging steel objects or from having skin rubbed clean on rusty decks and bulkheads. Even in harbour there was still the burning danger from the tropical sun. After three or four times the Captain's bright idea came to its inevitable end. I was at my post beside his open cabin door when the Chief Surgeon arrived with his daily sick list, that appeared to fill several sheets, and very forcibly begged his Commander to call off the scheme. The number of men reporting to his sickbay with severe scratches, cuts, bruises and sunburn was making life unbearable for himself and his staff. It was all they could do to cope with the ailments that led to the experiment and they were still plentiful.

Reluctantly Captain Branson agreed although he was still determined to raise our standard of health. Steaming between the islands one day we suddenly found the ship heaving to in several hundred fathoms of water. Over the PA came the order: 'All hands to bathe.' In theory all Naval ratings are supposed to be able to swim but there were a good number aboard who could only just paddle let alone dive into a seemingly bottomless deep. The sight of a boat being lowered as a rescue craft did not cheer them up either – it was manned by Royals with loaded rifles in case of sharks. Even when issued with lifejackets many had to be almost thrown into the sea and whatever good the saltwater did for the rashes it severely unbalanced them mentally.

For the majority of us this was a 'Branson Special' we welcomed. At the very least it eased the nearly unbearable monotony of our lives and in its deeper implications it bore out our growing belief that authority had finally decided the Force X charade was nearly over and we should be allowed more fun. That opinion took greater grip as 1945 arrived with a clear indication that we could expect, as far as Arthur George was concerned, a happier new year.

'Clear Lower Deck – all hands muster on the quarterdeck.' We heard the pipe over our messdeck speakers and reluctantly struggled to our feet to obey it. We had heard it too often for it to raise more than a customary groan. 'Some poor bastard's going to be weighed off' was a typical reaction. By now the number of warrants for serious offences were touching a century. No longer for mutiny they had become individual offences such as insolence, sleeping on watch, absent from place of duty and so forth. A steady stream of men had gone to cells aboard or been shipped away to the Australian Army gaol in New Guinea.

But as we assembled in the after welldeck that served as the quarterdeck we sensed that this could be an unusually less serious occasion. Certainly no offenders were on parade under the Jaunty's guard and we waited with increasing curiosity. At last there was the command to 'Attention' and into view on the deck above us hove Arthur George in his formal Admiral's regalia. Could he . . . was it possible . . . Yes, he was actually looking cheerful.

In his deep, penetrating voice he began referring to our unhappy past, the mutiny, the generally bad state of indiscipline and all our other vices, yet in a more academic than bitter way. Then, raising his tones higher, he added: 'The last time I addressed you I told you that you had dragged the White Ensign through the mud and that I would give you time to wash it clean. I now believe you have gone a good way to doing that. I think the time has arrived when this ship can be regarded again as being a fit part of a great Service. I rely on you all to carry on maintaining the high standards demanded of the Royal Navy.'

With that he turned and walked smartly away leaving us more puzzled than pleased. We returned to the messdeck to try and make more sense out of his words. The clear opinion was that we certainly had made no deliberate effort to 'wash the Ensign clean'; that, in some respects, we were less a credit to a 'great Service' than ever before.

'So what,' as Mick asked suspiciously, 'is Arthur George up to?'

Almost instinctively we turned to Hookie but even he seemed at a loss. At last he said: 'You can't tell with Admirals and them other 'igh ranking pigs. They say one thing and mean another. But I'll say this – 'e 'ad an effing good reason for saying it whatever it was.'

Next the mess turned its attention on me. Hadn't I overheard anything as Captain's Runner? I had not – nothing concrete that was. All I could recall of vaguely connected importance were a few words recently offered me by Captain Branson. He rarely, despite my fears, asked me about messdeck affairs and opinions, but on this occasion he had enquired whether I thought the men were settling down better than before. I knew very well they were not and said so as inoffensively as I could. The 'Old Man' pondered my reply a while and then answered: 'Well, we must do something to raise their spirits.'

Hearing this Cockie burst out: 'That's it, ain't it! All that bull about cleaning the Ensign's just a way of kidding us into thinking we're a crowd of effing pusser's men. It's like my Pa used to give me a belting and then, when 'e'd cooled orf 'e would 'and me a tanner and tell me to be a "good little kid".'

I felt there was a lot of sense in what the East Ender had said, but I could not avoid the irony of the situation in which so many seamen under punishment for mutiny were being given a verbal pat on the head and told they were good little boys.

We had barely finished our messdeck conversation, however, when it became clear that Arthur George must have felt some more emphatic sign of his approval of us was needed. As we men undergoing 'two-and-two' lined up for punishment duties the Jimmy arrived with a totally unexpected announcement. It had been decided, he stated formally, that the final three months of our sentence was to be suspended and that as long as we behaved ourselves we would never have to serve it. It was New Year's Eve and the best present we could hope for.

That evening the messdeck was cheerful for the first time in months although, when I thought closely about it, it was difficult to see exactly what we were so happy about. True, we could now get shore leave but there was nowhere worth going. We could also enjoy the afternoon stand-easies without mustering for defaulters but I had to admit that the latter had become more routine than punishment during our long lie in port with little work to do. There was little to choose between us and the non-defaulters as far as the intense boredom was concerned.

Then, Arthur George appeared to want to remedy that too. Suddenly we upped the hook and sailed the comparatively short distance to Tulagi, the tiny island capital of the British Solomons, north of Guadalcanal. There were still signs of the recent Japanese occupation and the place was little more than a shanty village but, at least, it was prettier than Empress Augusta Bay. Our sole purpose in going there seemed, on the surface, simply to allow us some relaxation and recreation swimming, playing soccer or stretching our sea legs. That was what we were encouraged to believe.

But was there an ulterior motive we asked ourselves a few days later. Just before sailing from Bougainville a buzz had gone through the ship that yet another court martial was planned. Only this time not on board *Lothian*. Nor, it was rumoured, was the defendant some rating or junior officer. It was to be aboard one of the L.S.I.s and, if the allegation was correct, it was to be a Captain – the second to be tried.

Returning very briefly to Bougainville a few days after, the buzz grew stronger with the added suggestion that the main reason for our surprise 'R and R' diversion was to help keep the trial secret for fear of its possible bad effect on discipline. But it proved impossible to verify the buzz and we speculated that it was as a consequence of the Admiral's inspection of the *Arquebus* but it was no more than guesswork.*

Some court martial, for sure, had taken place but we kept getting reports of officers being tried. Earlier the news had reached us via the *Lamont* that her senior engineer officer had been dismissed the ship. Nothing to do with her technical problems, apparently and it was obvious that whoever had taken over could not cure all of those. On being reunited with us after her delay in Balboa the first signal Arthur George had sent was: 'Stop making smoke!'

With such a decline in morale we felt our early return to civilisation must be at hand but this took a bad knock when we found ourselves steaming to one of the 7th Fleet's main bases,

---

* Again the lack of written evidence due to the time ban on public disclosure of court-martial proceedings makes full verification impossible. But I have been able to obtain confirmation from one of the officers who took part that the Captain was tried. Further confirmation has been obtained from a member of the *Arquebus* crew. But neither can accurately recall the exact result of the trial.

Manus. Was the Royal Navy, at long last, to be allowed a slice of the action? But the only connection between this equatorial island north of New Guinea and us was the fact it was part of the Admiralty Group. When we steamed into its vast natural harbour we were the only White Ensign among scores of Stars and Stripes.

The early departure of Arthur George's barge towards the U.S.N. flagship may have been a sign of his continued efforts to win favour but as the hot, humid days crept by it became more and more clear that we were suffering just another tedious lay-up. During our eleven-day stay the Admiral seemed more interested in inspecting shore installations (one that whetted our interest was a complete Coca Cola factory hidden in huts in the jungle) and in taking pleasure jaunts.*

Nearly every day he visited one of the outlying atolls for picnicking and swimming. But one outing intrigued us far more than any. Watching his barge return one afternoon I wondered why he and some of his staff were clustered well forrard. As the craft came alongside, however, the reason was obvious – the barge's after cockpit was overflowing with plump fish. That they found their way to his table and to the wardroom rather than to us surprised us far less than the way they had been caught. They had been blown up with sticks of dynamite.

That was the closest we ever got to any kind of explosive action.

---

* We were unaware at the time that Manus was to become the main base for the British Pacific Fleet already being assembled in the Indian Ocean and elsewhere. It was vital for Admiral Fraser, the C-in-C, and his staff to learn exactly what facilities they could expect to find there since the Fleet would have to rely on some American help even though there would be the large Fleet Train with its many supply vessels. Neither did we know what part was now planned for H.M.S. *Lothian* in that 'Train'. Admiral Talbot's visit, as confirmed by former staff officers, was to report on the base and that he had given up (or been told by the Admiralty to do so) any hope of further 7th Fleet involvement.

He might have reported back that Manus was one of the hottest, most humid and unhealthy places any Fleet could choose. Rear-Admiral D. B. Fisher, the future Flag Officer Fleet Train, certainly thought so. He described conditions there as 'nothing less than awful'.

21

X Equals Nothing

The Bismarck Sea looked as peaceful as a boating lake but about *Lothian* there was sudden alarm. Loose objects went flying as she listed hard over and turned a full 180 degrees from her intended course. Increasing speed she steamed as fast as she could from some unknown danger that was only suspected.

A few minutes earlier we had seen on our radar screen a collection of echoes far away and invisible to the lookouts on the bridge. It could and probably was a squadron of American warships but Captain Branson was taking no chances. As unlikely as enemy attackers were so far South at this stage of the war he obviously felt *Lothian* with just her twin four-inch guns no equal to anything but an armed trawler.

For two hours we steamed away from the possible risk before cautiously resuming our previous direction. Going below after ending our action stations we exchanged caustic comments on what we saw as a typical example of our ship's total inability to go into battle. Even if we were relieved, fighting the Japanese was the last thing we sought at this stage. There was now every sign that her mission and that of the rest of Force X was at last being brought to an end.

After lying idly in Manus we now steamed towards New Guinea although the buzz was strong that we would continue on to Sydney to link up with the British Pacific Fleet, which, we had heard, was being formed. Perhaps it would make better use of us although we failed to see how we or the L.S.I.s would be any good for landings. The Americans had made that abundantly clear.

199

As much as we disliked their offhand treatment we felt compelled to accept they had good reasons for finding fault with the style of our ships and some of our equipment and methods. As good as these would have been in European battle zones they had serious flaws in the type of assault important in the Pacific and techniques employed by the Americans.

The much greater distances, intense heat and lack of handy repair and storing bases were just part of it. We might have overcome that but not one aspect the U.S. Navy had pointed out as a distinct drawback – our type of landing craft. As soon as they had seen our L.C.A.s, smaller than the craft they used, they had declared them unsuitable. In their long, hard-gained experience ours would not last five minutes on the razor sharp coral and in the dangerous surf that beat down on many island beaches.

Our own Royals, stoutly defending their reputation had protested but had been abruptly told: 'If the Japs don't sink them cockleshells the goddamn Pacific will.'

Not that the Yanks appreciated the Marines' technique, either. They had insisted the latter learn the U.S. Navy way. From what we had gleaned from the crews in the L.S.I.s of the Force the relearning of landing methods had proved a serious drawback and a reason why only a small use had been made of them for training U.S. troops in rear areas.*

Aboard *Lothian* we had come up against another drawback. In spite of our highly sophisticated communications system, superior to anything the Americans used, it was simply not designed, nor were the very large complement of 'sparkers' and coders trained, to cope with American style systems.

Much of the time during our long voyage to the islands had been spent re-training our staff. But, on arrival, they had been given very little chance to apply their new knowledge in practice. That,

* The 'Command History' of the 7th Amphibious Force, U.S. Navy, in virtually the only reference to Force X states: 'The design and material conditions of the British L.S.I.s made them unsuitable for use in assault operations and they were assigned to the Amphibious Training Group for duty [in fact they were little used – Author]. These ships carried the British type L.C.A. and it was not practicable to alter them to accommodate the U.S. type L.C.V.P.'

War Diaries of the Marine Flotillas in the Force confirm the problems of using their landing craft and refer to several losses during exercises on island beaches. Captain W. C. Curtis, R.M., of *Lamont*, stated: 'U.S. authorities informed us our craft were unsuitable.'

by comparison, was a good deal more than the use to which our sophisticated Operations Room and its big staff had been put – nil. Some senior U.S.N. officer had been brought aboard proudly to be shown its stylish layout and the expertise of its crew only for him to look bemused for a different reason.

Turning to the officer in charge he had asked wonderingly: 'Hey, what have you got all those British Air Force and Army men for – you're operating with the U.S. Air Force and G.I.s, don't forget.'

There was really no answer to that. We ratings had been puzzled ourselves as to how the R.A.F. and Pongos could cope with the American air crews and ground troops style of doing things if we ever went into action. Even the former had grave doubts themselves.

All this tended to pale against the general background of American doubt and indifference towards us. Who could blame them? we sometimes admitted. If we lacked any confidence in our own abilities and ships due to the mutiny and to such obvious drawbacks as the *Lamont*, for example, showed, that of the 'Yanks' must have been near zero. It hardly needed the well-known antagonism of Fleet Admiral King to have made the whole mission useless.

Yet it was Arthur George's increasingly relaxed attitude that convinced us more than most that we could expect an end to it all. Believing anything he did must have a hidden motive we wondered for a while if he had some mischief up his gold braided sleeve. After all our troubles any generosity was unnerving. But Postie, from his many years of Naval experience, placed a particular interpretation on it.

Sitting under the stars on the foredeck one evening he told us: 'You H.O.s wouldn't know but I've seen Flag Officers get matey afore when their time's up. Take it from me Arfur George is slinging 'is 'ook. The larst Flags I wuz under did jest the same. An' the one afore 'im. The pusser bullshit got less an' they wuz all smiles and friendly chat. You see they don't want to leave an un'appy ship be'ind them – wouldn't look so good with the next Flags to take over. An' Jack's a real soft bugger – the last Admiral like 'is last ship is always the best one.'

There Postie lost our confidence. Not in a hundred commissions could anyone of us see the *Lothian* as anything but a nightmare. As for Arthur George? Well, we couldn't see the ship ever being used for a Flag Officer again so the matter was probably academic. Only a short time earlier I had heard the Admiral refer scathingly to Captain Branson about the ship's total unsuitability for himself and his staff. There had also been a more muffled mention of something she was expected to do with the British Pacific Fleet, something important. But my curiosity was out-weighed by disbelief that a similar role was planned.

Any such thoughts vanished as we learnt that we were, in truth, bound for Sydney – a port lively and brash enough to make any mateloe happy with anticipation. More so the ex-mutineers with their punishment ended and facing their first good shore leave since leaving America. Getting drunk and finding the first avail-able 'Sheila' would be the main priorities, I felt sure. Not so. The talk around the messdeck centred firmly around something more fundamental to living – food. After months of dehydrated veg and mince meat, stodgy sweets and soup crawling with weevils and cockroaches I suppose it was not that surprising.

Oggie would sit for a long time, a dreamy look in his eyes, talking about how he 'would murder' enough steaks, chops and slices of beef to feed the whole British public. For Mick it was gargantuan plates of bacon and eggs and even Cockie put sexual prowess aside long enough to drool about iceberg size dollops of icecream. Yorkie was a little more wistful his Yorkshire dales never far from his mind. 'When I've stuffed belly full ah'm going to roll in't grass like a gimmer full o'ticks,' he announced joyfully.

There were some less happy. For those their only exercise would be daily doubling under guard in some Australian military prison. *Lothian*'s crime rate had continued to escalate. We were now over the century mark for warrants and prison sentences had become too common for comment. We had even ceased to wonder any more that an offence as comparatively insignificant as being absent from a place of duty or one man refusing a superior's command was being treated as worse than the mutiny by many of us.

Many convict ships have steamed between Sydney Heads in time past but some could hardly have had more convicted aboard than we had as we steamed through. It was a burning hot early February day as we lined the sides in our heavy uniforms but we revelled in the baking sunshine. Even the wail of the New

Zealander's bagpipes sounded like heavenly music in our ears and Sydney's famous 'coathanger' bridge looked like the Pearly Gates.

On the wing of the bridge even the Admiral looked happy as we sailed slowly passed other, smarter warships and received their bugle calls and pipes in recognition of his 'two red balls' flying from the masthead. Hookie laughed and told us: 'Make the most of it lads – its the last effing time anyone salutes this load of old scrap.'

We were pretty sure of that now. The evening before the news had been announced that Arthur George was to leave. Nothing had been added about the end of Force X but we assumed that had to be inevitable.

Neither was there anything about our future role but that concerned us less at this joyful moment than the fact we were tying up in the heart of the old sailors' quarter, Wooloomooloo, with more temptations than we had dared dream about. Strangely enough as we finished berthing and went below to smarten up I sensed an air of almost desperate nervousness. It seemed as though most were scared that it was all a mirage about to vanish or even that they no longer knew how to tackle such unbounded delights.

It took a huge meal, gallons of beer and the undivided attention of a wanton whirlwind of whores to restore confidence for many but before the first shore leave was over normality had returned. By the next morning even *Lothian* had exceeded its boastful reputation for defaulters. Perhaps it was as well that our money ran out more quickly than our opportunity for shore leave. Within a brief time we became unhappily aware that one of our hated old burdens, storing ship, was once more becoming a dominant factor in our lives.

Normal supplies were one thing but the mountains of crates, boxes of official documents and all the signs of something abnormal in the way of stores were becoming all too unhealthily apparent. This, we seamen told ourselves, was where we had come in on the quayside at Greenock. Visions of Arthur George's arrival with his voluminous staff and their equipment returned like the sour taste of stale beer the morning after.

Surely, we tried reassuring ourselves, he or some replacement Admiral for Force X was not expected? He had moved with his staff to Sydney's downtown, into the Bank of the New South Wales Building, where his flag had been seen flying. A party of the lads seeking something more exotic in the way of aphrodisiacs had visited one of the city's oyster bars. There, to their embarrassment, they had found the Admiral and several of his staff already tucking into the shellfish.

They had segregated themselves at the opposite end of the bar but as one A.B. told us soulfully: 'Fat chance of getting 'orny with 'im and all those pigs around!'

I had begun to have doubts about the end of the mission when I read a signal Captain Branson (just promoted from Commander) had just sent. It was addressed to 'Flag Officer Force X'. When I passed the news on it brought moans from the rest of the mess. But we were confused. Shortly after our arrival in port our R.A.F. and Royal Corps of Signal detachment had packed their kitbags and departed the ship. If they went with little regret on our part it was more due to the fact that they left us with more space and less cleaning up to do. They, certainly, were not sorry to go. This time they gave us a loud raspberry as their coaches drove off to some pleasanter haven.

This general joy was shared equally by our officers. Never very happy about having an Admiral and his staff around they now relaxed considerably. There was more space for them, too, and they seemed to be expecting that pleasanter situation to continue. But we were all brought abruptly down to earth before we had been in Sydney much longer.

A brief statement in the Daily Orders revealed that *Lothian* was soon to become a flagship again. Only this time not in an assault role. We were, it said, to be 'Flagship R.A.F.T.'

Reading the initials Oggie commented: 'We might just as well be an effing raft – we're all bloody castaways.'

We were not much wiser when the translation was made. 'Who in Hell's name was "Rear-Admiral Fleet Train" and what were we supposed to be – an effing puffing billy?'

Whatever was being said back home no one had bothered to reveal to us the creation of the mightiest fleet of supply ships ever put together by the Royal Navy – to serve the British Pacific Fleet and overcome the enormous distances it would be from anything but remote island bases.

Lothian's part was to serve as the command ship for nearly 100 freighters, tankers and other support vessels that would be stationed in the Philippines and in the harbour we had learnt to hate –

Manus. When we heard that our spirits went down quicker than a tot of rum. Mick moaned: 'More prickly heat, more starvation, more effing misery.' It was one of the only times I had heard him swear.

Captain Branson did not seem any less upset. He paced up and down his deck with the Jimmy anxiously discussing how they were going to cope with the new Admiral's staff. From what I could tell it was going to be much larger than even Arthur George had with him. Some junior officers would have to double up in cabins – there was a possibility some might even have to sleep on deck. It was time they suffered more like we had below decks I thought happily – but only for a brief while.

New ratings, part of the Admiral's 10-strong staff, began flocking aboard. In addition, we took aboard scores of men intended to act as stevedores in the handling of cargo on the supply ships. Once more the messdecks bulged at the seams. The biggest surprise was still to come. We were painting the sides when a convoy of cars drove up alongside. Out stepped one of the strangest collections of Royal Navy Captains any of us had seen.

There were seven and only one was of executive rank, the Chief of Staff. The rest were specialists, some bearing between their gold rings distinguishing colours that were only seen in very rarefied Naval headquarters. Apart from an Engineer Captain, Paymaster Captain and Surgeon Captain there were ones from the Shipwright's, Education and Electrical branches. All looked in their fifties, even older and seemed bewildered at having to go to sea. As they looked up at *Lothian* doubt was clearly obvious on their wrinkled faces.

When someone standing watching with me muttered, 'That lot look like they should be in an 'orspital ship – not an effing headquarters ship,' it was fairly close to the truth. The Captains were to suffer greatly in the months to come as each tried to cope with their enormous tasks of supervising their particular aspects of the Fleet Train in working conditions that, had this been an industrial operation in peacetime, would have had a factory inspector promptly close it down. Knowing the difficulties of Admiral Talbot with his smaller staff we seamen simply could not credit that anyone, even the Admiralty, could be crazy enough to employ the ship on such a taxingly important duty.

If Rear-Admiral Douglas Fisher, our new Flag Officer, thought as much, he was too gentlemanly to let his views be known at the time. In almost every way he had a personality quite different to Arthur George. No 'Noisy' nickname for him. He spoke quietly yet with authority although he never interfered with the running of the ship. While he must have been fully aware of our evil reputation he never showed any sign that he thought the worse of us. His trust and obvious fairness must have been a reason why we seamen who had mutinied just five months earlier were to put up with conditions that, incredibly, would get worse than we had already experienced. But perhaps more important, we were at last carrying out a wartime task, however secondary, about which we need not feel ashamed.

The major credit, however, had to go to the Aussies. The enormous kindness and generosity they poured over us quickly rid us of our phobia that nobody wanted us. There was barely a man aboard who had not found an 'up-homers' with some Sydney family only too glad to offer them meals, a bed for the night and entertainment. The affection went much deeper. When we sadly and reluctantly sailed after our fifteen-day stay the quay was lined mainly with young girls – several of them already engaged to men aboard.

There was nothing so impetuous about our movements as we set about letting the ship go. We had to be bullied into it. At least, we consoled ourselves, there was a minimum of bullshit about our departure. No bagpiper to serenade us to sea. Hopefully it was a sign of a more understanding management to come.

But should we have been bound back to the islands at all?

In the days that followed we learnt that *Lothian* had only been chosen as Fleet Train flagship as an emergency stop-gap measure or, as we put it: 'a cock-up by the nuthouse'. The warship chosen for the part the large depot ship *Montclare*, nearly three times our size, had, for reasons undivulged, been delayed.* Since we were

* According to Admiralty signals and memos on file in the Public Record Office there had been ample time to prepare a headquarters ship for the Fleet Train. As early as the Spring of 1944 a party of senior officers had gone to Australia to make advance preparations for the proposed British Pacific Fleet. Assembling of ships had begun as soon as the Quebec Conference of September, 1944, agreed to its sending. *Montclare* had been chosen early although it is believed her preparation created problems. By the time she did arrive the war against Japan was nearly over.

206

already in the area and, technically at least, a headquarters ship the choice as substitute had unhappily fallen on us. Our obvious disadvantages and the criticisms we knew both Admiral Talbot and Captain Branson had made about our unsuitability had been pushed aside.

We prayed that the specially adapted *Montclare* would arrive quickly. God, having saved us from hanging or imprisonment, must have decided we needed to suffer more immediate inflictions much longer. Nearly another five months lay ahead before we could expect salvation.

22

Sea of Troubles

'In these conditions which can only be described as appalling 110 officers and 650 men lived and worked in a space suitable for two thirds their number and it is not surprising that the great majority suffered in varying degrees from skin trouble. This varied between prickly heat at the best to a multitude of boils and consequent invaliding at the worst.'

> Rear-Admiral D. B. Fisher, Flag Officer Fleet
> Train referring to his flagship H.M.S. *Lothian*.
> *Forgotten Fleet* (author John Winton).

'All ratings showed signs of strain. A lot went to sick bay with dizziness and general weariness . . . With 750 men aboard it is impossible for communications or any other ratings to attain adequate fresh air, exercise or washing facilities when off watch. All told I consider they have done well.'

> Captain Geoffrey Branson in confidential message
> to Rear-Admiral Fisher.

The White Ensign drooping over the *Lothian* in the boiling, windless atmosphere of Leyte was sparklingly clean in every sense but at a cost to her Lower Deck. Right now it hung at half mast. In the early light of dawn five of our stokers stitched in canvas shrouds with lead weights at their feet had slid from boards over the ship's side to lie many fathoms deep in unmarked graves.

They had died not directly from the illnesses from which most of us suffered but certainly as a consequence of the unhealthy shipboard conditions. That and an unfortunate circumstance.

With the messdecks almost unlivable and definitely dangerously suffocating to live in we had been given permission to sleep on deck and issued with light, foldaway camp beds begged from the Americans. Some ratings, however, preferred to sling their hammocks wherever a handy guardrail or some other convenient fastening place could be found along the crowded upper deck. The stokers, living aft, inhabited the poop. For some weeks several had lashed one end of their hammock lines around the smoke floats kept there in case we should ever have to lay a smoke screen. But the constant wearing away of the ropes had loosened the top of one of these dangerous appliances.

Without warning one night the top came adrift. The dense, suffocating fumes impossible to breathe in, covered the poop in an impenetrable cloud. When it had cleared the five men lay dead.

The burial party of seamen that, Captain, Jimmy and a couple of Engineer Officers apart, was all that mustered at their final departure heard the 'Sin Bosun' (chaplain) read out the opening words of the brief service: 'We therefore commit their bodies to the deep, to be turned into corruption, looking for the resurrection of the body, when the sea shall give up her dead, and the life of the world to come, through our Lord Jesus Christ; who at his coming shall change our vile bodies, that they be like his glorious body . . .'

Cockie, mustering just enough reverence to withhold any comment until later, could not resist saying as we marched away afterwards: 'Christ can't come soon enough for us lot – 'e can change my vile body for a start.'

Vile looking we certainly were with our purple painted ringworm, footrot and prickly heat even worse than during our previous, if more useless, months in the islands. The heat stroke and other serious complaints were as bad or worse. I had just returned from a few days in a Dutch hospital ship with neighbouring beds filled with men from the *Lothian*. The officers' ward contained others of our complement.

But the crisp clean sheets, the air-conditioning and the sight of the pretty, amazingly clean nurses had done a lot to cheer me up. It also gave me plenty of time in which to think clearly about all that had happened since leaving Scotland. Even so it did not make much sense. I found it hard to understand why, having mutinied over conditions that were bad but not as grim as our current ones, we seamen were not showing similar rebelliousness. The amount of individual disobedience had continued to grow with men on jankers in abundance and the cells almost always full but there had been no combined revolt.

There were several possible explanations. One was that having tried once we did not want to risk the certain great severity of punishment that must follow a second attempt. Another was that we were simply ground down by the awful conditions – often physically unfit to fight back. A third was that we were spared no time to do anything more than carry out our extra workload, which now included doubling up as stevedores unloading the Fleet Train cargo ships. Being more closely involved in the war was an added reason, but not one which I thought overcame some of the suffering. The feeling that the Pacific campaign was 'not our war' was still strong.

One thing which we appreciated, although it was a secondary satisfaction, was that everyone aboard shared in the misery in one way or another – from Admiral downwards. The 'pigs-and-us' attitude had become less marked and I knew from overhearing the Admiral's chats with the Captain that he understood how bad messdeck life really was and sympathised. It also came across in the way all unnecessary formalities had been shed – no Divisions or Evening Quarters. We had also been issued with sensible khaki tops and shorts that were more comfortable and more easily dhobied.

One of my regular duties as Captain's Runner was a good example of how everyone had to share the cramped conditions. At 5.30 a.m. Wakey Wakey I carried out a task that must have been unique. It was to wake up the six specialist Staff Captains – but not in their pokey cabins. To get much needed fresh air they all slept on campbeds around Captain Branson's deck. One by one I would shake their beds and yell that it was time to get up. Almost always they were slow to arise and at their averagely elderly age I was not surprised.

The answer was to tell the waiting seamen anxious to wash down deck to turn on their hoses and let the water run under the campbeds. Moaning greatly the Captains would totter to their feet and, grasping their little bundles of pillows and sheets, dash off in their pyjamas and bare feet for the safety of their cabins. It was one of our rare moments of pleasure in the Lower Deck.

Lying in my hospital ship bed I reflected that we seamen might have been given a more human understanding of our superiors before the mutiny if something similar had happened. And that, I decided, was what had been missing in those very early days of our commission – a lack of understanding on both sides. Perhaps it was right that we young O.D.s should have been tightly disciplined and exercised to make us ready for our first battle blooding but too much had been expected of green H.O.s fresh out of training establishments, especially when we formed such a big part of the seamen's messdeck.

On our part we had expected our commanders to show more consideration forgetful that after a long, hard war normal standards of fairplay and decency often go overboard. On the other hand we did have some very green officers directly responsible for us. A lot of the blame had to be attached to them and others more senior who had let a violent situation develop despite clear signs. Too much work and responsibility had fallen on the Jimmy to give him time and opportunity and *he* had been made the fall guy.

Yet one did not have to look any further for a major cause than the *Lothian* herself. Clearly she should never have been chosen for such a long demanding mission in tropical waters. No proper ventilation, a water system that quickly collapsed, inadequate amenities for the over-large complement and in need of repairs. Furthermore there had been no normal working-up period which was absolutely essential for a newly converted warship manned by so many inexperienced ratings. Even had the other aspects been better, I thought, *Lothian* would have taxed most complements to their bitter limit.

Of course there were other bad ships in the Royal Navy and thousands of mateloes had suffered similar hardships in this war so why had not we borne them as bravely? Why had – still was to a large degree – our morale been so low? If an extra reason on top of all the others was needed I felt it had to lie in the fact of our totally wasted Force X mission. Even before the mutiny the Lower Deck had sensed there was something ridiculous about such a motley collection of converted freighters being despatched right around the globe ostensibly to aid the Americans when we knew they felt quite capable of handling the Pacific War on their own – with massive fleets of warships to do so.

The U.S. Navy's total rejection of *Lothian* and its indifference to the rest of the Force could not have been clearer proof of the idiocy of it all and in looking for the biggest idiots of them all I had no difficulty placing the blame on the 'nuthouse'. Not only had the Admiralty rushed the Force to sea with ridiculous panic, choosing ships obviously unsuitable and, in the process, preventing us having proper foreign-going leave, it appeared to have shrugged its shoulders of any responsibility once it had become part of the U.S. 7th Fleet. Even when the latter ignored us their Lordships appeared indifferent, leaving *Lothian* to wander the islands like an orphan child.

Not that they appeared unduly concerned about us now we were back in the fold. The wrath of us who had brought the ship out from Britain was raised when men joining us in Sydney direct from the United Kingdom had announced how well they had been treated before being drafted. Some had been given as much as twenty-one days foreign-going leave – an unheard of act of war-time munificence – with the promise of a special BPF bonus pay. With the European war nearly over the Navy, they said, was anxious to placate ratings who felt they were having their active service unfairly extended by being sent so far to continue hostilities. We had been told nothing about this or been given or promised any such consolations.*

It once more raised the old spectre that we were being treated as a 'ship-in-disgrace' or as Hookie said: 'Once you got mutiny on your tally you get every shitty duty around and gets shoved to the back of the queue when there's any 'andouts.'

I put it down more to the kind of indifference we had come to take for granted. The pleasant attention I was receiving in the hospital ship highlighted what I now saw as an overall cause of much of our disgruntledness. War bred indifference to a high

* On June 29, 1944, the Board of Admiralty had already met to discuss ways of coping with possible Lower Deck trouble over being sent to the Pacific. In a memo Vice-Admiral Algernon V. Willis, the Second Sea Lord, recommended ways of doing so. They included 'extra long foreign leave'; 'bonus payment' and a guarantee that men 'would not have to go to the end of the queue for civilian jobs on being demobbed'.

degree that would, I felt sure, be unknown in the peacetime Andrew. With so many being killed and maimed who in authority could care about a comparatively tiny number of men undergoing suffering they felt could easily be avoided by someone just being a bit more considerate? Even the kind nursing staff around me were intent on restoring our ability to go on suffering the hardships.

But I had to admit some of them were surprised at how debilitated and malnourished their *Lothian* patients had become. My own weight had sunk to under eight stone while others were in worse condition and likely to bear their ailments far longer. Several had T.B. Such was my loathing to be returned to the '*Loathsome*' that I almost envied the fact these unfortunates could stay in hospital.

Yet when I got back aboard I found the messdeck happier than I had known it for a long time. It had just been announced that we were leaving Leyte to return to Manus to hand over to the *Montclare* now steaming north from Australia. After that we optimistically believed our days in the islands would be brought to a welcome end. If we were delighted Admiral Fisher and Captain Branson were no less so. There was relief mixed with pleasure on their faces as they discussed methods of making the switchover. Even our covey of Captains looked joyful. They could not wait to pack their bags – behaving more like schoolboys eagerly anticipating the 'summer hols'.

But had the Japanese decided to pull the plug out on us before we could all escape? A short time before we were due to sail away, after the tropical darkness had fallen, an alarmed Officer of the Watch sounded off Action Stations. He had, he swore, seen a mysterious swimmer in the water alongside and, apparently, intent on sticking something on our hull. If true it could only have been one of the enemy whose limpet mines had already taken several Allied ships to the bottom in Leyte Gulf.

There was a technique for removing mines although I suspected it would have resulted in us being blown up anyway. A cable would be lowered over the bows and with scores of hands pulling be dragged along each side of the ship underwater hopefully removing any unwanted object. The principle was dubious enough and in *Lothian* totally impossible. There was no way we could get the cable over the landing craft hanging from our sides and in the panic no one had lowered them. When they eventually did, so much time had elapsed that any danger was probably over. Captain Branson, who had been visiting another ship, returned to find our fears had turned into a hysterical skylark with ratings splashing around in the sea having pretended to fall overboard as they manoeuvred the cable along.

Still in one piece we sailed for Manus. To our great relief the *Montclare* was lying at anchor there and, wasting no time, we tied up alongside. One might have thought we really were in danger of going to the bottom judging by the frantic way in which the Admiral and his staff of over 100 switched ships. We worked just as swiftly to transfer their mountain of stores and luggage – glad to see them go. In under three hours and despite the boiling heat an operation that might normally have taken over a day was completed.*

Exhausted but eagerly anticipating we could now sail south to renew the friendships we had made in Sydney and restore our health we settled back happily under masts that neither bore an Admiral red balls or even a 'Union' court martial flag. Fools that we were. Five weeks later we still had not departed. It had been decided that we must sweat on as an accommodation ship with the seamen detailed, once again, as stevedores.

Somewhere I had read the phrase 'gaol fever'. Now I saw just what it meant. Like convicts who could not wait a brief time before their sentences ended but were driven to 'go over the wall' ratings became more bloody minded and disobedient than ever. That some should do so was not surprising for a high proportion of the men we had taken aboard in Australia to help unload ships were straight out of military prison. Our crime rate shot up and daily defaulters looked almost like the Divisions we had previously had to endure.

It looked to me at one stage as though there would be no seamen left to handle normal duties since many others spent their time queueing at the Sick Bay or were in hospital ships. My own bouts of dizziness and fatigue returned. Seeing me look particularly faint one day Captain Branson announced consolingly: 'You won't have to put up with this much longer – I've requested our urgent return to Sydney.'

---

* Admiral Fisher, after the war, told how he and his staff transferred to *Montclare* 'with alacrity'.

There was no need for him to spell out why. It was clear he felt the sickness and indiscipline had gone too far. His appeal must have been persuasive enough for, at last, we sailed.* The day before, the Americans ashore and in their warships had celebrated the Fourth of July with turkey and other delights we never enjoyed. But to us the Fifth was a far more glorious day and our inevitable servings of hash, dehydrated veg and figgy duff just as grand a feast as we departed Manus for good.

Except for a score of men.

They were to stay incarcerated in the South-West Pacific for much longer. On July 6 and, again, in the rainstorm that always seemed to accompany the ritual of reading out of punishment warrants (nearing 150) we anchored in the harbour of Lae. The scene would have done justice to Captain Bligh and our Captain seemed to want to add extra drama as he stood at the rail above us while we cleared Lower Deck to hear the twenty men sentenced. After the warrants had been read he gazed slowly down on the sodden, miserable looking wretches his face full of scorn. Shouting above the hammering of the rain on the decks he told them: 'You are being sent to one of the worst prisons in the world. It has no bars or walls but don't try and escape.'

There was a pause as he seemed to be seeking a more melodramatic effect. Then he concluded: 'If the wild animals don't eat you the Japs will.'

Even we innocent felt appalled. God knows how the convicted felt. Our sympathy went with them as, a few minutes later, they were put aboard a landing craft and taken ashore. But one A.B., the one who had earlier been sent to Lae for ninety days for being asleep on watch and had just returned, could not stop laughing. 'The old man's 'aving them on. That place is more like an effing 'oliday camp – not a gaol! I 'ad a smashing time there. As long as we be'aved the Aussie guards didn't give a fuck – let us go swimming and lie on the beach all effing day.'

---

* Captain Branson had already, according to a signal on file, made his views firmly known about the misuse of *Lothian*. He reported: 'She [*Lothian*] was designed as an operational and not administrative HQ Ship. She is not designed to carry in comfort a large staff for a long period . . . very desirable she go for refit . . . ship's bottom very dirty through lying in tropical harbours for six months.' He concluded: '. . . been in commission since August 1944, without performing any of the major functions for which she was designed.'

215

Then he really rubbed it in for us ex-mutineers. 'The buggers knew what they were doing when they kept you lot working ship instead of shoving you off to prison.'

He was right. We had done nearly twelve months' hard labour that would have been considered bad enough in chain gang days, or so we thought. But that was now all over – like the farce of Force X and our Fleet Train endurance trial. Now we had just one thought – drowning the harrowing memories of it all in the bars and up-homers of Sydney. But not, if most of us could help it, as part of *Lothian*'s complement. The many ratings applying to go on training courses in Australia or scheming to get compassionate leave underlined our desperation to put the ship as far behind us as possible.

Captain Branson was no exception. He had by *Lothian*'s standards served a remarkably long time as commander – nine months – but too long it seemed. Before we berthed at Wooloomooloo he revealed to me we would be parting company. He had applied to be put ashore. I expressed some bland comment but I was really thinking: 'Goodbye No 4 – come in No 5.'

There were to be many ratings who would have no choice but to leave. As we tied up, coaches arrived to take away those in need of urgent hospital treatment. Later, we learnt, that over fifty had been found to have suspected T.B. This, if nothing else among the seemingly endless list of examples of *Lothian*'s total unsuitability for tropical warfare, should bring her pathetic career to an end. Yet, as we should have learnt long since, it would take more than common sense and more than the usual demands of war to achieve that.

It did. It took the Atom Bomb.

A month later the horror of Hiroshima proved our salvation.

23

Saved by the Bomb

It was exactly twelve months since we had sailed from Greenock, us fresh faced, innocent and eager-to-prove-ourselves-in-war young seamen yet it seemed more like two years or more. We were tougher, more worldly-wise and somewhat more efficient but we were also more embittered and disillusioned. Few had any respect left for the Service and hardly any much taste for continuing the war. In this we were not entirely on our own. After six long years of campaigning the older hands had had enough and the gruesome *Lothian* had been enough to make them, let alone us, despair for release.

But it was also part of the broader malaise among the Fleet where the Pacific campaign was concerned. Chatting with ratings from the armada of Royal Navy warships in port we found them dissatisfied with having to extend their active service by fighting the Japanese for some indefinite period and so far from home especially since all considered the Americans capable of doing so on their own. Their discontent had got no further than typical messdeck grumbling yet it was, apparently, enough to increase the worries already held by the 'nuthouse' over Lower Deck unhappiness about this extension of their war.

The greater amount of Admiralty signals urging more and more pep-talks to stir up Lower Deck passion for taking the battle closer to Japan was one part of it that came to my notice as I went about my duties as Captain's Runner. Another were the leaflets issued to us containing similar propaganda. Neither method had much effect although the latter had a practical use we seamen appreciated.

They made a handy substitute for Navy issue toilet paper, which was both thin and in short supply and using it as such gave us a malicious satisfaction.

Our anxiety for the only pieces of paper we really wanted – draft chits – grew as a certain strong rumour circulated the ship to our dismay. It began the first week in August 1945, as we left our handy berth at Wooloomooloo to enter the more isolated Naval Dockyard at Cockatoo Island, Sydney. The repairs and other work being started suggested the Navy was still intent on finding the ship some other long-term duty in the Pacific in spite of our basic unsuitability. It also linked with headline stories in the Australian press suggesting the Allies were planning a massive invasion of the Japanese mainland – something far bigger even than that at Normandy or Leyte. The buzz quickly became elaborated to suggest the *Lothian* was to head one of the task forces.*

No confirmation or denials came from above which seemed only partly due to tight wartime secrecy. I felt the Captain and his senior officers were nervous about what our reaction would be. And rightly so. One mutiny was enough and although the odds against us trying it again were high the prospect of a 4,500 mile voyage or longer with a reluctant, notoriously ill-behaved crew spelled trouble. It did not help that many of the ratings (and a good few officers) had still not been battle tested and any invasion of the Japanese homeland would surely prove to be a very bloody affair. Yet such was our concern about the potential misery of the voyage itself that we spared little thought for the action that lay at the end of it.

It was true that having survived what we considered was the worst the Royal Navy could throw at us we had no desire to risk being killed or maimed by the Japanese although we may have viewed the possible loss of the *Lothian* by enemy action with more delight. Even so we prayed for some other way of getting rid of her and for an end to our saga.

There seemed to be no immediate prospect of that and the

* A signal from the Admiralty to the Captain of the *Lothian* just before she returned to Sydney in July, 1945, stated that she along with H.M.S. *Glenearn* and *Spearhead*, would be needed for a major assault force 'early in 1946'. No doubt this was for the anticipated invasion of Japan.

seamen's messdeck at Wakey Wakey on August 6 displayed its usual dismal scene of hungover mateloes rueing the last few glasses of Australian beer the night before; the rabble of cursing ratings stumbled over one another as they lashed up their hammocks and the men-under-punishment grimly turning to for extra drill and duties before breakfast – all to the hacking noise of men coughing away the effect of the humid stench of too many bodies in a badly ventilated steel box.

Then, suddenly, above the row came the unusually excited, loud cry of one of our quartermasters as he thundered down the ladder. Barely able to get the words out quickly enough he yelled: 'Pin your ears back lads I got some effing great news . . . the Yanks 'ave just given the Japs an effing big 'ammering . . . right in their own backyard . . . some effing secret weapon . . . killed thousands according to the Aussie radio.'

Our sudden silence was due more to our surprise at having our early morning moment of morbid adjustment to a cruel world suddenly interrupted like this. A long, violent war had made us, like most, almost immune to news of sensational action – even to reports of secret weapons. But this was something bigger, more violent and potentially more victorious than anything before insisted the Q.M.

'The Yanks dropped something they calls an Atom Bomb – blows 'ole cities to bits it said on the radio. What's more they says the Japs will 'ave to surrender if they don't want the 'ole country effing well blown sky'igh.'

This time we did take full notice. The cursing, the coughing and the headaches vanished magically. If what we had been told proved true, we told one another, all our troubles were over. The war, too, but especially our particular problems.

When, later, we heard and read more about the appalling slaughter at Hiroshima, followed by that at Nagasaki, we were as awestruck as anyone but for us the great mushrooms of death that rose above those decimated cities was hardly more tangible than the cloud of depression that rose from our shoulders. We realised then that nothing short of the end of the war could have stopped the Admiralty persisting in using the *Lothian* for her original purpose in spite of strong objections from Flag Officers and almost anyone who had had dealings with her. If something as horrific as the Atom Bomb was acceptable to the powers-that-be then the often needless suffering of a few hundred Navymen had to count for almost nothing.

The sad saga was almost over but it would take more than the world's worst weapon of destruction to wipe out our memories of a commission we would prefer to forget. We tried hard enough with plenty of assistance from the bars, Sheilas and up-homers of Sydney but even the most drunken seamen could not find total oblivion from the experience. And there was always some pusser type to remind us seamen of our disgrace.

We were gathered on the foredeck ostensibly stowing gear but more interested in discussing our chances of being sent home when the G.I. interrupted us. 'What have you lot got to crow about?' he demanded. 'You load of skivers don't deserve being sent home – not when there's plenty of decent, honest men who really did some fighting. All you lot did was have a mutiny and bring shame on the whole Service.'

Yet shame was the last thing anyone of us felt. Whatever wrong was committed the 'Andrew' had brought it upon itself and, anyway, we had paid the price. But there were a few with regrets. Old Postie, who had been brought back from retirement to serve throughout the war, was one. I had asked him if he wasn't looking forward to leaving the Navy soon. 'Yes and no,' he answered carefully. 'This ship's bin the last straw but I can't say I fancy ending my service 'aving bin dipped and with a mutiny on my chitty – not arfter thirty-five years a Jack.'

He looked around him wistfully: 'It would 'ave bin nice to 'ave steamed into Guz with a battle flag at the mast'ead and the Royals band playing us 'ome wiv an 'eroes welcome. All the nut'ouse will do with this rat-trap is give us a raspberry and sneak us into a berth as far from decent ships as they can find. Not that she don't deserve it,' he ended sadly.

I sympathised. A mutiny and a record number of punishment warrants was hardly something to place on a Naval roll of honour. But he was an exception. Most of us would have been happy, then, to have stepped on to home shore from a gash barge.

It was appropriate that when VJ Day came the 'Loathsome' should be lying idly in drydock unable to perform the function for which she had been intended and which she had never fulfilled. Typical, too, that at the very moment peace was declared I should be 120-feet up inspecting a radar aerial at the top of our main mast.

Saved by the Bomb

As Hookie retorted when I eventually got down to find the Main
Brace already Spliced and all the rum gone: 'What's your gripe?
We've all been up the pole since we joined this effing ship.'

Postscript

One mutiny, two Admirals, six Captains, nearly 200 warrants, innumerable cases of illness, 67,000 miles after commissioning, H.M.S. *Lothian* completed her brief Royal Navy service never having once performed the task for which she had been intended.

For the whole of one year she had earned, for many aboard, the unenviable reputation of possibly being the most discontented, unhappiest ship under the White Ensign. Yet, paradoxically, during her last six months before she paid off in Devonport in March, 1946, she became a safe, welcome haven of relief for hundreds of Servicemen and civilians.

After leaving Sydney after the war end, ironically with many of the improvements which she had so desperately needed, she sailed on missions of mercy rescuing P.O.W.s and civilians captured by the Japanese in the Philippines, Shanghai and Singapore. In messdecks now empty of many ratings, like myself, who had left the ship in Australia, crowded emaciated Britons and many Indians including whole families. The sick bay which had vainly tried coping with our tropical ailments became a maternity ward when one Indian mother gave birth aboard.

The gratitude of these ex-captives contrasted sharply with our own, sometimes violent discontent. Had we also suffered the harsh treatment they had been subjected to under the Japanese no doubt we would also have been grateful. Yet, in a way, we saw ourselves, many seamen that is, as prisoners of another, more perplexing kind – of our own side. We were willing, even keen, to be fighting men but against the Japanese – not the 'Andrew'.

222

The attitude of the Admiralty, which we seamen deeply believed had ranged from hopelessly haphazard to inhumanly indifferent, was obvious where *Lothian* and her miserable past was concerned. As soon as possible after reaching Devonport she was ordered to the Mersey to end her Royal Navy career. Just two years after first being commissioned there at a reported £1 million and with considerable delay work began on reconverting her back to a freighter. She returned to the Ellerman Line on May 6, 1947.

All that now remains of her is the ship's bell – hanging among happier souvenirs of the Kiwi bunting tosser who was Arthur George's reluctant bagpiper. He acquired it when the ship went for scrap in 1961 – more to mark an unforgettable milestone in his Naval life than for its purely sentimental value. In direct contrast the Admiralty (now M.O.D. Navy) were as anxious to bury any trace of the ship many fathoms deep in its files as it was to celebrate the Navy's more glorious World War II episodes. Few official documents concerning her remain and most of those are undoubtedly the records of her court martials securely barred against public eyes.

It showed, and still does, a similar desire to sink Force X without trace (other than a few lines of brief confirmation it existed). Its disbandment was, in the main, as hasty as the disposal of its flagship. Of the six L.S.I.s three, the *Empire Battleaxe*, *Empire Mace* and *Empire Arquebus*, were ordered back to Britain not long after the Force, per se, was formally ended in March 1945. In that month Rear-Admiral Talbot and several of his senior staff embarked in the *Arquebus*, which he had so thoroughly castigated during his inspection in Bougainville, to sail back to the U.K. from Sydney. Whether he chose her to ensure her standards were raised or for some other reason is not known but during the long voyage back across the Pacific he made sure, as one of the quartermasters later told me, that 'our feet didn't touch the deck'.

Neither had Arthur George, apparently, lost any of his inimitable taste for musical ceremonial. According to the same seaman the Admiral had been much taken by the performance of a young Marine during a ship's concert in which he had forcefully rendered 'Goodbye Hawaii'. When the *Arquebus* was about to leave its refuelling stop, Tahiti, the Admiral decided the French Governor, who was to make a courtesy visit to the ship, should be similarly serenaded on being piped aboard. Only this time he ordered the name in the tune to be changed to 'Tahiti'. It was a strange variation on bosun's calls or a Marine band and made more farcical by unfortunate errors in judging who was the Governor.

Every time an official black Citroën drew up alongside the poor Marine was ordered to start singing. Only it seemed every possible Government official was determined to get ahead of the Governor. By the time he actually arrived the Marine was almost too hoarse to perform.

The ship's company were relieved when Arthur George suddenly decided to leave the *Arquebus* in Panama along with his Admiral's formality and fly back to Britain via Washington in order to take up a new command (believed awaiting him in the Burma war zone). But, like the ship, his war was virtually over.

The *Arquebus*, like *Battleaxe* and *Mace* plus the *Empire Spearhead*, which had stayed behind in the Pacific a little longer, were very soon decommissioned becoming merchant ships from 1945 and 1946 under a variety of national flags. *Clan Lamont* also sailed back to Britain before the war ended after a brief time as an accommodation ship in Manus being reconverted to a cargo vessel in 1945 as well. *Glenearn*, the only efficient ship in the Force, finished her Pacific duties in the less glamorous role of trooper between Australia and the islands for the BPF. Sadly an explosion in petrol supplies she was carrying resulted in the deaths of several officers and men and injuries to a score of others. On her return to the U.K. she was handed back to her civilian owners. All six ships have long since been scrapped.

The immediate post-war years also saw the end of their Naval careers for most of the officers. The Wavy Navy ones were demobbed; the R.N.R. mostly returned to the Merchant Service and even the great majority of R.N. regulars left either resigning voluntarily; axed by peacetime cuts or returning once more to the retirement from which they had been recalled at the start of hostilities.

Rear-Admiral Talbot, on returning to London from the Pacific, found he was reassigned to leading another task force – part of the mammoth one of forty-three divisions that was planned for the anticipated landings on Honshu, the Japanese mainland. But the dropping of the Atom Bomb abruptly terminated the necessity for what would have been a massive slaughter on both sides.

For a short period he chaired an Admiralty committee studying improved ways of life-saving at sea before being appointed Head of the British Military Mission in Greece. For nearly two years he was based in Athens, taking with him part of his 'family', including his Secretary, who had been with him since before the war, and his coxswain-chauffeur. By the end of 1947, however, Arthur George retired – promoted Vice Admiral and awarded the C.B. (Commander of the Bath). It was the Admiralty's usual style of a parting gift.

Born on the broad Yorkshire acres of Earl Fitzwilliam's estate at Wentworth, near Rotherham, where his father had been Agent, the Admiral had always held a passion for the land and farming. With the same determination he had shown in *Lothian* he set about starting up his own agricultural enterprise in Broadstone, Dorset. Former ratings who had served under him in the Pacific and who had so often griped about being 'pigs in shit' might not have been surprised to find him now parading among his battery of sties as a newly fledged pig farmer.

But Arthur George had as little success with rearing his Landrace porkers as he had trying to make better seamen out of us mutineers. Over abundant competition and the peculiar swine ailments ended this venture. He moved into a small flat in Bournemouth and, on October 15, 1960, died of a brain tumour. His burial was back on the estate where he had been born, Wentworth, in the Fitzwilliam family cemetery. He was survived by his widow Doris and a married daughter Diana, who had been in the W.R.N.S.

The Admiral was aged sixty-eight – exactly the same age as Captain Christopher Henry Petrie, when the latter died of a sudden heart attack brought on by arteriosclerosis on May 1, 1957. He had retired to live in Westminster with his last days in the Royal Navy serving as Naval Attaché in Warsaw immediately after the war. His replacement, Captain Geoffrey Charles Fremantle Branson, died in 1977 in Australia.

Among the surviving Force X officers the one who suffered the consequences of the mutiny most, Lieutenant-Commander Kenneth Buckel, returned to Britain after leaving the *Lothian* in Brisbane, getting passage in a U.S. Navy troopship to the States – placed on half pay. Shortly afterwards he transferred to the Royal Indian Navy as Director of Personnel Services. A brief period back with the Royal Navy ended in his retirement to a civilian post. Now he lives in France, the memory of the mutiny and what he deeply considers his unjust treatment still fresh in his thoughts. He was, he told me, assured by a Naval legal expert who examined the court martial records that they could be overturned on appeal. He sometimes wishes he should have done so but, at the time, he was anxious to forget the whole sorry affair. With his wife he now helps needy ex-servicemen and their widows.

That attitude is obvious, for other reasons, among several ex-Force X Staff and *Lothian* officers. It is a period of their Naval careers for which they take no pride for themselves or their Service. Universally, though, they place the main blame on American indifference or antagonism and on miscalculations by the Admiralty.

Two of them extend their criticism to include Churchill himself. They believe it was his ardent desire to see Britain closely involved in the Pacific as well as European and South East Asia campaigns that drove the Admiralty on to sending the Force despite obvious difficulties. There is no clear evidence of this. All are perplexed by Admiral King's request for the Landing Ships since it clashed with his known determination to try and keep the Pacific war to the U.S. Navy. The only explanation most can find is that he was acting under duress and orders from Roosevelt anxious to satisfy Churchill. An opinion held by one or two is that he had given in to pressure from other U.S. Admirals who believed that since they had supported the Royal Navy so strongly in Europe it should respond by assisting in the Pacific.

But the direct cause for the succession of troubles in *Lothian* is laid fair and square on the ship herself. Condemnation of her for service in the tropics and, particularly, as a flagship over a long period is unanimous. She was converted to be a headquarters ship for short assault operations – a task she would have coped with admirably and with her sophisticated communications equipment was the best L.S.I.(H) in the whole fleet – but should have been used as such.

While it was far from evident at the time the officers now agree that messdeck conditions were extremely bad. Yet few accept this as an important reason for the mutiny although in my opinion and that of most former ratings it was. There is a tendency among the ex-Upper Deck to find the cause among less consequential factors. Several blame drink – both the rum and that smuggled aboard –

yet I am sure that this only added extra determination (and mainly among the ringleaders) to men clearly set on revolting having come to the end of their tether. Most officers also excuse the total rebellion of the seamen in its stages before the seventeen were finally left on the Balboa quayside as a case of young, naïve seamen being led by the nose. That we needed leading was true but only the obvious hopelessness of our situation forced most to give in.

Characteristically officers whose responsibility it was to look out for and help prevent the causes of the mutiny do not accept they could have done so. Yet there is no doubt had proper supervision been made and steps taken to ease, in some way, the seamen's burdens the mutiny might never have occurred. Little else could have been expected when so many executive officers were green Wavy Navy junior officers, many joining their first ship. But in making the First Lieutenant take most of the blame it does seem he was being made a scapegoat for something circumstances put out of his control. He was clearly overburdened with duties that should have been shared with a Commander or some other senior officer and the target from both the ratings and from above.

What responsibility the Captain and Flag Staff should accept depends mainly on who among officers and men one asks. Although, in theory, the former had to accept ultimate blame for anything going wrong in his ship it is clear he was not fully aware of just how likely the revolt was. The Jimmy had, he says, informed him there was trouble brewing but he was undoubtedly, like all the officers from Admiral downwards, taken by surprise. We seamen at the time and now, long after, do not blame him for the causes.

We were more likely to relieve our frustration on the man at the top, Arthur George. Because he was that much closer to the Admiralty and had a forceful personality we found him an easier target. His very presence aboard with a large staff that added to our strain gave us cause. Technically the Flag Staff were just passengers but their presence was definitely felt, especially on such a long, arduous voyage, and it was difficult to see how an Admiral of such an ebullient kind would take a back seat. There were times when we saw far more of him than the Captain – on the bridge and elsewhere – looking every inch a man determined to create a fighting force out of us.

It was because we saw and felt his presence so much that we believed he should have known more about our hardships and, therefore, taken personal action to resolve them. In the view of officers close to him, however, Admiral Talbot could not usurp the Captain's role in this regard. Needless to say we seamen would not have credited this. As just or as unjust as our attitudes were it seems to me, on reflection, that in view of the special circumstances of *Lothian* and Force X's mission it called for a particular type of Flag Officer with a different personality and Service background. In fairness it was difficult for one like Arthur George, just fresh from leading a major assault, and with a capital ship wartime background, to adjust to such a plebeian and small squadron as ours. By contrast Rear-Admiral Fisher, in his calmer, more phlegmatic way, received our support.

Yet it would have taken all his efforts to both prevent our mutiny and satisfy the frustrations of such an ill prepared and, often, basically unwilling, complement of seamen as we were. Mostly fresh from training with some military gaol sweepings plus ex-soldiers wishing they had never transferred and with very few experienced seniors we were ripe for discontent. The very fact we mutinied only a month after sailing from Greenock showed how quickly we cracked. We toughened up later but fear of worse reprisals made us mainly accept the bad ordeal to come.

The question really is: Were we any or much worse than many a ship's company? After five years' war there must have been quite a number of warships with similar misfits. So why did we mutiny and not them? The answer has to be a combination of circumstances – the awful conditions aboard; the over-intensive work in blazing temperatures; frustrations over lack of long and shore leave; over discipline; poor supervision; bad food; lack of water; malcontents among the ratings; lack of belief in our mission; ill-preparedness to go into action; over-hasty decision-making by the Admiralty and so on.

All in all it makes a rich recipe for mutiny. Although it looks obvious in hindsight it was not so, apparently, for those responsible at the time. One can only assume that by the end of summer 1944, it was being taken for granted that seamen would put up with anything, however desperate. Or had the Admiralty simply stopped caring? Perhaps it was both but we in *Lothian* proved there was a breaking point. Nothing, not even the disgrace of preventing a warship going into action or threat of imprisonment let alone being shot or hanged had stopped us. What we had done was worse than at Invergordon, where the mutiny had received enormous publicity although unarmed, less hostile and, in our eyes, over something far less harrowing – a cut in pay.

Yet, until now with the writing of this personalised account, the *Lothian* mutiny has gone unknown to the general public. The fact it took place so far away when so much else of vital importance to the war was happening was a reason at the time. But why nothing since? The Admiralty, now Ministry of Defence (Navy) can claim the major credit for this. Obviously ashamed of the whole affair, both the revolt and the Force X farce, it has done its best to keep it secret. Any remaining files have either been destroyed or lost deep in the archives – apart from a few scattered references that have found their way into the Public Record Office. Only intensive searching and a good deal of luck was needed to extract them under index titles that give only a vague (if that) hint.

The only reference to '*Lothian*' as such as actually been mis-printed on the Admiralty file cover as '*Lowthian*'. Since the name of the ship is accurately stated a number of times inside, the possibility of this being a deliberate error must remain. A more obvious ploy has been used to hide details of the mutiny. In Rear-Admiral Talbot's only 'Letter of Proceedings' to the Admir-alty from Force X, covering the time from his appointment as Flag Officer and dated September 11, 1944, the report comes to an abrupt end exactly at lunchtime on September 1 – the time the mutiny began.

The only reference to it on file in the P.R.O. I came across by chance in the War Diaries of the Royal Marine Flotillas for the Force. As previously mentioned *Lothian*'s R.M. Captain refers briefly to a 'mass insurrection'. All attempts to get direct answers to questions about it put to the Ministry of Defence (Navy) have been thwarted by statements that no information is any longer available. There are, of course, plenty of facts in the court-martial reports but because of the fifty-year ban on release of these to the public they cannot be checked. Just why the Navy should prevent publication seems strange since it has for very many years from before the last war allowed the public to attend these trials.

Fortunately I have been able to contact and interview many ex-officers and men, including several of those with close knowl-edge of events in *Lothian* and Force X, and obtain much vital information. Only that which I have been able to double-check between two or more persons is contained in this account. Some equally surprising stories have been omitted for lack of supporting evidence either verbal or in documents. At other times I have relied on personal recollection or notes written at the time. The quoted conversations are clearly based on an inexact memory of what was actually said but in every case the 'chats' took place if in not so many words. To avoid offensive boredom I have reduced the volume of swear words, substituting more often than not 'effing' as an acceptable euphemism.

Could such a mutiny occur again? Perhaps. Nelson's men would have found our problems acceptable while we would consider today's standards de-luxe. It is what ratings are used to and given another war and much more brutal times they might rebel at losing their comforts and easy discipline. But if we mutineers achieved anything it was to give the Royal Navy a lesson it will not easily forget. Today's Captains go to sea with a confidential reference book containing details of what happened in *Lothian* at Balboa and recommendations on how to avoid such a mutiny.

Appendix I

Admiralty Orders to Flag Officer Force X

August 2, 1944 [the day before the Force sailed]. Top Secret.

I am to inform you that Force X is being placed at the disposal of the Commander-in-Chief, U.S. Fleet, for services in the South-West Pacific and you are to carry out any orders issued by him or any other authority designated by him.

2   In the event of your receiving an order which in your opinion unnecessarily risks H.M. ships under your command to which you consider the attention of your immediately senior officer should be drawn, you should take such action either by signal or otherwise as you would take under K.R. and A.I., Article 8,* were you under the command of a British Flag Officer, and you should, in addition, make an immediate report of the incident for the information of the Admiralty.

3   In the unlikely event, however, of your receiving instructions which in your view will give rise to a grave and exceptional situation and should the procedures in paragraph 2 have failed to secure withdrawal or modification of these instructions, you have the right to appeal directly to the Admiralty provided that by so doing an opportunity is not lost nor any part of the Allied Fleet endangered. You will, however, first inform the Flag Officer under whom you are working that you intend so to appeal and you will give him your reasons.

4   You will forward to the Admiralty regular reports of your proceedings.

* Article 8 concerns a similar situation arising within the Royal Navy itself.

5   A copy of this letter has been sent to Commander U.S. Naval Forces in Europe.

By Command of Their Lordships.

The Orders were signed by a J. D. Higham, an administrative official of the Admiralty.

Appendix II

Lieutenant-Commander Buckel Court Martial

Six charges were levelled against this R.N. officer who had risen
from the Lower Deck to Executive rank. They were:

1 He did not use his utmost endeavours to quell mutiny.
2 He did not at once arrest ringleaders when Master At Arms
had given him their names.
3 He did not take steps to find out where the ringleaders were.
4 He did not obey the Rear-Admiral's orders.
5 He removed the Marines at the wrong time.
6 He suggested to the ringleaders they go to his cabin to
discuss their grievances.

The vital 'Circumstantial Letter' containing the charges was
only delivered to the Lieutenant-Commander just over 24 hours
before the time the court martial began. This was virtually the
minimum time permitted under regulations but, normally, accused are allowed far longer in which to study it and compile a
defence. Furthermore, states the ex-officer, he was asked to return
the Letter a few hours before the trial began so it could be altered.
To show willing, he says, he did so although he knew he was
entitled to object.

A further difficulty forced on him was that he was suddenly
asked to give up the officer he had chosen as his 'Friend' (defending lawyer). There were only two officers aboard with legal
training and one was already committed to be a court official.
Another was essential for the job of Deputy Judge Advocate and
Admiral Talbot was having great difficulty finding anyone to

233

perform it. He requested that Lieutenant-Commander Buckel give up his representative, Paymaster Commander C. B. Hinde.

With no one else as well skilled to choose from, the accused could well have refused but appreciating it could place the Paymaster Commander in an invidious position he agreed. But it meant there was very little time to prepare a defence with the substitute 'Friend', Paymaster Lieutenant W. N. Ash. They had to sit throughout the night before appearing at the trial sleepless.

With the Admiral's Chief of Staff, Captain A. C. Duckworth, D.S.O., R.N., acting as Prosecutor the court martial opened in what was all but a steam bath beneath the awning over the after welldeck. One by one he called sixteen witnesses, most of them mutineers, to confirm statements already taken from them. In the couple of days prior to the trial the ringleaders had been visited in their cells aboard *Glenearn* to obtain their signed evidence.

Most of it was similar allegations of verbal abuse by the accused. He had, they claimed, called the ship's company 'yellow bellies'; had said they had 'shagged all sense' out of themselves in New York and had sworn 'fucking arseholes' at a ringleader. On top of this they blamed him for threatening a rating with violence.

Much of what they affirmed, according to Lieutenant-Commander Buckel, had little or nothing to do with the charges and he felt his counsel dealt very effectively with it. His hopes also rose as other accusations were, he believed, successfully answered. But much hung on the accusation that he had asked the ringleaders to discuss their complaints in his cabin. Had he done so it would have helped the prosecution prove he had 'treated' with mutineers, a definite offence.

The three ringleaders insisted he had although, claims Buckel, they contradicted one another about who had said what and how. When it came to his turn to give evidence he emphatically denied ever having asked them to come to his cabin. That, he explained, had been done by the Petty Officer present with him as a ruse to get the three arrested.

Just as firmly he denied blame for other incidents forming the charges. He had made every endeavour to stop the mutiny (as we on the messdeck could have confirmed had we been asked); he had been unable to arrest ringleaders when given their names because it had proved impossible in the violent circumstances; he had taken all possible steps to find out who they were (his several visits to the messdeck proved that); he had not deliberately disobeyed the Rear-Admiral's orders but had used his discretion to avoid the bloodshed that was highly likely; it was the Marines who had appeared at the wrong time – not he who had made them do so and had they not tried to enter the messdeck the mutiny might have ended there and then.

There had been a potential ace in his pack of refuting evidence that he had hoped would confirm how he had tried to prevent a mutiny before it even took place. He had, he told the Court, discussed with his senior Chief Petty Officers the question of growing signs of discontent among the seamen and as a result of their fears about the danger of it erupting had immediately informed the Captain. But when the latter was asked to confirm this he denied remembering the incident. It took Lieutenant-Commander Buckel by surprise particularly as Captain Petrie had shown every sign of being on his side. Not only had he told Admiral Talbot that he did not think the court martial should be held but had also, states Buckel, advised him to use 'persecution by Talbot' as part of his defence.

Later the Captain was to show strong support for his former No 1 but not until the trial had sweated itself into a semi-stupor by the time midnight had been nearly reached and it was adjourned until the next morning. Several pounds lighter and literally ill from the tension and heat Lieutenant-Commander Buckel spent another sleepless night unsure which way the verdict would go.

The next day feeling 'more dead than alive' he waited with agonised impatience for the summing up and verdict. When he was at last led formally back he noticed one person present who, previously, had only been there in most people's minds. Standing to one side staring intently was Arthur George.

Under his firm gaze the Deputy Judge Advocate announced the court martial's decision. But there was no need. According to Naval tradition the defendant's sword had now been placed to indicate which way the finding had gone. It pointed directly at Lieutenant-Commander Buckel.

Guilty.

But not of all the charges. Only those of not having tried to find the ringleaders immediately and of the latter's accusation that he had invited them to discuss their complaints in his cabin.

As he was still trying to cope with the shock Captain Petrie rose and asked permission to address the court on his ex-Jimmy's behalf. It was an entirely voluntary gesture and came to most there as a surprise. According to Lieutenant-Commander Buckel's papers he said: 'During the time Lieutenant-Commander Buckel was Executive Officer his conduct was entirely to my satisfaction. He was conscientious, hard working and very loyal. He never spared himself in any way and, in fact, I approached the Principal Medical Officer because I thought he would break down by working too hard. It was against my wishes he was relieved of his appointment and, in fact, I subsequently approached the Admiral with a view to having him reinstated.'

No First Lieutenant could have hoped for a better recommendation. Spoken in front of the Admiral it carried great impact. Most eyes turned towards Arthur George but he remained impassive. Whether the plea had any influence on the verdict is not clear but Buckel was dismissed his ship. It was bad enough and, in his firm view, totally unjust. All he could do was console himself that he had not been demoted.

Yet his official record would bear this black mark throughout his remaining career. If past experience in other cases was any guide it effectively spelled the end of any chances of promotion. Considering he had striven so hard and proved one of comparatively few to rise from the Lower Deck, which he had joined as a Boy Seaman, it was particularly disillusioning. The war was not over long before he left the Service – still the same rank and still convinced he had been unjustly treated. Over forty years later his feelings remain the same.

Glossary of Naval Terms

A.B.   Able Bodied seaman.
Andrew   Royal Navy.
Asdic   Sonar for submarine detection.
Badgemen   Ratings with good conduct stripes.
Barrack stanchion   Man who rarely goes to sea.
Brownhatter   Homosexual.
Brylcreem Boys   R.A.F.
Bubbly   Rum.
Buffer   Senior petty officer (usually Chief P.O.) seaman.
Bunting tosser   Signalman.
Buzz   Shipboard rumour.
Captain's runner   Captain's messenger.
Champer   Clean and polish.
Chock-a-block   Fed up.
Cook of the mess   Hand detailed to fetch meals.
Crusher   Ship's policeman.
Defaulter   Man accused of crime.
Dipped   Reduced in rank.
Divisions   Morning parade. Also 'part of ship' into which crew are
    split.
Dog watches   First 'dog': 4–6 p.m. Last 'dog': 6–8 p.m.
E.R.A.   Engineroom Artificer.
Evening quarters   Evening muster.
Fanny   Food container.
Figgy duff   Type of suet pudding.
First for the chop   First to be punished.
Gash   Shipboard waste.
G.I.   Gunnery Instructor usually C.P.O. and drill martinet.
Golden Rivet   Mythical and obscene object supposedly in every keel.

Gulpers   Gulp of a tot of rum.
Guz   Nickname for Devonport Naval barracks.
Harry Flakers   Tired out.
Heads   Lavatory.
H.O.   Hostilities only rating.
Hoggin   Sea.
Hook   Anchor.
Hookie   Leading seaman.
Housewife   Sewing and darning kit.
Jankers   Imprisonment or other punishment.
Jaspers   Weevils.
Jaunty   Senior ship's policeman usually a C.P.O.
Jimmy the one   First Lieutenant and Executive Officer.
Kai   Cocoa.
Keep yardarm clear   Avoid being blamed for crime or mistakes.
Killick   Leading Seaman.
K.R.s and A.I.s   King's Regulations and Admiralty Instructions.
Liberty   Shore leave.
Lobscouse   A type of hash, often with mincemeat.
L.S.H.(L)   Landing Ship Headquarters (large).
L.S.I.(L)   Landing Ship Infantry (large).
Mateloe   The Royal Navy spelling
Navy cake   Homosexuality.
Nettles   The lines between hammock and ring and securing rope.
Nos 1/2, etc   Types of uniforms ranging from best to working gear etc.
Nuthouse   Admiralty.
Nutty   Chocolate.
O.D.   Ordinary seaman.
Officer's friend   Counsel appointed to help officer facing court martial.
Oppo   Any friend.
Paybob   Paymaster officer.
Pig   Officer.
Pigsty   Wardroom (officers' mess).
Plumber   Nickname for engineer officer.
Poker   Nickname for stoker, more often for Chief Stoker.
Pongo   Soldier.
Pusser   Smart – according to best standards. Often used derogatorily.
Pusser's blankets   Indicating someone born into a Naval family; i.e.
   'born between pusser's blankets'.
Rabbits   Smuggled items or other illicit goods.
Rattle   Cells.
Rig of the day   Uniform as stated in daily orders.
Rose cottage   V.D. mess.
Royals   Royal Marines.
Sin Bosun   Padre.

Slops   Stores where kit and other items for men are issued.
Sparker   Radio operator.
Stone frigate   Shore establishment.
Suck a fish's tit   Caustic reply to anyone telling a tall story.
Swallowing the hook   Act of leaving the Service.
Three badger   A rating with three good conduct stripes.
Through the hawsepipe   Promotion of an officer from the Lower
   Deck.
Tickler   Cigarette made from Navy issue tobacco or the tobacco itself.
Tiffies   Ratings such as stewards, sickbay attendants. Also Engine-
   room artificers.
Two blocks   Fed up.
Up-homers   Visiting a private family offering hospitality ashore.
Wardroom   Officers' mess.
Wavy Navy   Royal Naval Volunteer Reserve whose officers had wavy
   rings.
Weighed off   Act of being punished for some offence.